Great Ideas in Management

W. Jack Duncan

Great Ideas in Management

Lessons from the Founders and Foundations of Managerial Practice

Jossey-Bass Publishers

San Francisco • London • 1989

GREAT IDEAS IN MANAGEMENT
Lessons from the Founders and Foundations of Managerial Practice
by W. Jack Duncan

Copyright © 1989 by: Jossey-Bass Inc., Publishers
350 Sansome Street
San Francisco, California 94104
&
Jossey-Bass Limited
28 Banner Street
London EC1Y 8QE

Library of Congress Cataloging-in-Publication Data

Duncan, W. Jack
Great ideas in management.

(Jossey-Bass management series)
Bibliography: p.
Includes index.
1. Management—History. I. Title. II. Series.
HD30.5.D86   1989   658'.009   88-42787
ISBN 1-55542-122-9

Manufactured in the United States of America

The paper in this book meets the guidelines for permanence and durability of the Committee on Production Guidelines for Book Longevity of the Council on Library Resources.

JACKET DESIGN BY WILLI BAUM

FIRST EDITION

Code 8850

The Jossey-Bass
Management Series

Consulting Editors
Organizations and Management

Warren Bennis
University of Southern California

Richard O. Mason
Southern Methodist University

Ian I. Mitroff
University of Southern California

Contents

Preface

This is a book about management—specifically, about great
ideas in management. It is also about origins and outcomes—
how the guiding ideas of today's large corporations and small
businesses came into being. In a way, this is a history book, but
not in the traditional sense. The emphasis here is not on times,
eras, or even heroes. Instead, this book focuses on what Burke
(1978) calls "triggers"—ideas, events, and sometimes people
that set into motion a new management process.

How can writers of twenty years ago, much less of more
than a century ago, speak to today's organizational problems?
Current political, business, and social environments are so different from those of the past. Do such radical differences make
history irrelevant? I think not; perhaps events may become irrelevant but not ideas (Kantrow, 1986). That is why this is a book
not about management history but about management ideas—
ideas that are as relevant today as when they were first formulated in the steel mills of Pennsylvania, the factories of Detroit,
or the quarries of France.

Sometimes the managers who so beautifully orchestrate
the operations of large organizations find it difficult to verbalize
underlying concepts. Often these managers do not have the
words, terms, or vocabulary necessary for such a discussion of
ideas. The purposes of this book are to provide that vocabulary
and to present prospective managers with a sense of how management ideas of the past became part of the repertoire of tools
and techniques used by today's executives.

It was an executive in a *Fortune* 500 corporation who first suggested to me the need for a book that would help managers appreciate the origin of management ideas. On the fast track, he was an engineer with a law degree who had almost no time to study management, much less management history. He got his ideas on management from best-selling books of the type sold at airport newsstands.

No wonder he was surprised to hear about Chester Barnard's acceptance theory of authority. He thought *he* instead of Barnard had originated the idea that managers can be effective only if followers accept the legitimacy of the leader's right to command. He was even more surprised to learn that the classical concept of unity of command accurately predicted the problems he experienced in implementing what he thought was a "relatively simple matrix structure." The history of management thought confirms that there is no such thing as a relatively simple matrix structure.

One afternoon as he prepared to return to the hustle of New York City he asked, "Why don't you write a book for managers on the essential concepts of management history that are relevant today? Not something for your colleagues but something that will help those of us in the trenches!" "Forget it," I replied, "I fancy myself a specialist on planning, organizing, controlling—a teacher, researcher, and consultant, not a historian." "That's my point," he replied, "this type of book should not be written by a historian but by someone who applies concepts rather than tracks them." That was the end of that, I thought. To his credit, he asked me at least once a year when the book was coming out. My reply was always, "Never!"

Since that time I have reconsidered and discovered for myself what the Durants (1968, p. 102) meant when they wrote history is not just a "warning reminder of our follies and crimes but an encouraging remembrance of generative souls." I hope the readers of this book will make the same discovery. Most of all, I hope their curiosity will be aroused, as mine was, so that nothing short of going to the library and researching the ideas contained in the classics will suffice.

The intended readers, then, are the managers of today

and of the future who will be responsible for administering complex organizations in business, government, education, and health care. The goal of this book is to build their confidence in dealing with the uncertainty of the future by increasing their knowledge of the past.

Overview of the Contents

The book is divided into five major parts and thirteen chapters. Part One sets the stage for what is covered in the book. In Chapter One the need for the book is addressed, and the rationale for selecting certain ideas and actors is presented; apologies are made for those that were, by necessity, omitted. Chapter Two illustrates the importance of the "trigger." Before Frederick Taylor began his work, European industrialists had discovered the benefits to be gained from specialization. It was the idea of division of labor that spawned the factory, the setting where most early management took place. Chapter Three explores the issue of efficiency. The need for efficiency became the focus of early scientific management writers.

Part Two looks at the art and science of management. Chapter Three begins with an illustration of how early management evolved from the need to apply science to the study of work. The application of science to industry was an essential prerequisite for establishing the legitimacy of management as a field and as an occupation. The evolution of this quest for legitimacy is traced to modern times, where management has become secure enough to advocate that traditional scientific applications be replaced by innovative and less conventional methods of analysis. Chapter Four examines what has been historically the most scientific of all aspects of management—the "heart of executive activity," decision making. Without arguing against the use of science, this chapter reviews evolving developments in decision theory, which have focused more on how managers actually make decisions than on how they ought to choose among alternatives. The thrust, in other words, has become descriptive rather than prescriptive.

Chapter Six departs from the evolutionary pattern of earlier chapters. This is done for two reasons. First, the discussion of descriptive analysis needs to be extended to management behavior in general, since the issue of how managers actually manage has implications for numerous areas of management thought. At the same time, with the exception of Fayol's analysis, descriptive analysis does not have the long tradition typical of other issues. For these reasons, the orientation of the chapter must be more contemporary and less historical.

Part Three examines the purposes and goals of management. Chapter Seven on goal setting and task management reinforces the view that before one can manage, a clear sense of purpose and goals must be formulated. Chapter Eight, like Chapter Six, is more contemporary than historical or evolutionary. The ultimate responsibility of management can be easily traced through the pages of the management classics, but the most persistent debates are more modern than historical.

Part Four deals with the evolution of the human factor in management thought. Chapter Nine traces management's view of the human being, from Taylor's ox analogy to Mayo's mental health view, shared by other writers of the human relations school. It returns full circle to the current mechanistic view of human behavior adopted by operant conditioners and behavior modifiers. Chapter Ten reviews the complex issue of leadership. Contrary to what many believe, the foundations of a relatively sophisticated theory of leadership existed in management history.

Finally, Part Five deals with the problems of coordination and change. Authority and influence, the supreme coordinating powers, are discussed in Chapter Eleven. The richness of history is clearly illustrated in this chapter in the ideas of Weber, Follett, and Urwick. The evolution of the concept of authority is traced through Barnard's acceptance theory and to more contemporary concepts that have been used in current organizational design and development. Chapter Twelve provides a final overview of the evolution of management and organizational thought, from the absolute orientation of early classical views and that of human relations to the relative, situational, or contingency views of contemporary organization theory and practice.

Chapter Thirteen presents a summary of the lessons offered throughout the book. The classics illustrate a number of lessons that all managers, students, and teachers of managers should remember and employ in their work. First, coordination and cooperation occur only when they are consciously developed. Second, human dignity is an essential element of organizational success. Third, the classics remind us that efficiency is a worthy goal but that the demands of efficiency in the form of order, structure, and rules will, in the absence of conscious management action, reduce the organization's ability to adapt to change. Fourth, successful management requires a sense of purpose, and those organizations whose futures are left to fate will not prosper or even survive. Fifth, human beings "do not have the wits to maximize," so they must make decisions with less-than-perfect knowledge. Sixth, history tells us that management has a social responsibility and that managers must serve as role models for responsible behavior. Seventh, management is both a science and an art, and the insights of both should be freely applied to problems of organizations. Eighth, specialization has provided great personal and social benefit, but it can also rob the individual of meaningful work. Ninth, management techniques are important, but implementation is an art that depends on political skills. Finally, we must always remember that management principles and concepts should be carefully adapted to the demands and realities of the situation.

The lessons of the classics should be understood by all managers. The value of the heritage of management is that knowing what the early writers had to say is the most efficient way to begin learning how to manage.

Acknowledgments

Many people share in the writing of a book. Your family provides support and willing sacrifice, while students and consulting clients bear the burden of listening to what the most recently read classical writer had to say about the problem under consideration. Colleagues encourage you, bosses support you, friends continue to like you. I have always been fortunate to receive support from those around me. I hesitate to mention any by name for fear of an embarrassing omission. However, in spite of that risk, there are a few people who must be acknowledged. M. Gene Newport, dean of the School of Business and Graduate School of Management at the University of Alabama at Birmingham, provided untiring support for yet another project. Support was also provided by Dean William Bridgers and Associate Dean Stuart Capper of the School of Public Health at UAB. Paulo Cesar Motta, head of the Department of Administration at the Pontificia Universidade Catolica do Rio de Janeiro, where I served as a visiting senior Fulbright scholar while I wrote much of the first draft of this book, saw to my every need during my sojourn in Brazil. A special note of thanks is due to Dalton M. McFarland, university professor emeritus at the University of Alabama at Birmingham, who now lives in Michigan but remained in Birmingham long enough to provide sage advice on issues relating to management history, theory, and research. Alfred A. Botton of C&P Telephone Company and the American University and Daniel A. Wren of the University of Oklahoma served as demanding yet encouraging reviewers. Their helpful suggestions greatly improved the final version of this book.

I dedicate this book to Judy Duncan and Lyn Duncan, my wife and daughter, who cheerfully (well, at least willingly) followed me to Boston, Brazil, and back to Birmingham while this book was in process.

Birmingham, Alabama   W. Jack Duncan
September 1988

The Author

W. Jack Duncan is professor and University Scholar in Management in the Graduate School of Management at the University of Alabama, Birmingham. He is also professor of health care organization and policy in the School of Public Health. He received his B.S. (1965) degree from Samford University and his M.B.A. (1966) and Ph.D. (1969) degrees in management from Louisiana State University. He is past president of the Southern Management Association and the Southwest Division of the Academy of Management. He also served as a member-at-large of the board of governors of the Academy of Management. In 1978 he was elected a fellow of the Academy.

Duncan has served as a visiting professor at Northeastern University in Boston, the International Business Institute in Switzerland, and at the Universidad Peruana Cayetano Heredia in Lima, Peru. He was also a visiting senior Fulbright scholar at the Pontificia Universidade Catolica do Rio de Janeiro, Brazil. Duncan is the author of *Decision Making and Social Issues* (1972), *Essentials of Management* (1978), *Organizational Behavior* (1982), and *Management: Progressive Responsibility in Administration* (1983). He has published articles in the *Academy of Management Journal*, *Academy of Management Review*, *Management Science*, and numerous other journals in the field of management.

Duncan is a frequent consultant to business and health care organizations. He is a founding principal of Southern Organizational Consultants.

Great Ideas in Management

CHAPTER 1

Introduction

From Classical Ideas
to Practical Action

Henry Ford believed that history is "more or less bunk" and that the only history that matters is what we make today. The philosopher George Santayana thought otherwise and argued that those who do not remember the past are condemned to re-peat it. As a practical matter, James Burke (1978) says it best when he asserts, "Why should we look to the past in order to prepare for the future? Because there is nowhere else to look" (p. 287).

It has always been assumed that history is not top-priority reading for managers. Their lives are too busy and things happen too fast for them to spend time reflecting on the advice of writ-ers of fifty years or a century ago. The purpose of this book is to prove that assumption wrong. Understanding the rich legacy of management will not ensure that mistakes of the past will not be repeated. Like Adolph Coors Company, others will dis-regard at times the importance of external factors, especially competition, until serious harm is done. Dictatorial and mis-guided leaders will again emerge as they did in Montgomery Ward and send major corporations in ill-fated directions from which they may never return (Hartley, 1986). All this could happen in spite of the vast stores of historical information avail-able to managers today.

The Ford Motor Company remains an economic miracle, and some of the innovations introduced by Henry Ford and his company changed America and the world forever. A disregard for history, however, does not account for this success. Ford was at times close to financial ruin, and the Edsel continues to be one of the lasting marketing jokes of all time (Lacey, 1986). Burke's advice is sound. We should look to history because it is all we have from which to learn about the future. The perceptive manager cannot afford to ignore good advice, regardless of its source. Management history is full of valuable lessons for those who attend to what it can teach.

Managers and Management Thought

Everything has a beginning and, so far as we know, everything has an end. None of us alive today will witness the end of management as a social institution. In fact, management has never been more popular. Managers such as Lee Iacocca are folk heroes, and books written by managers actually make the best-seller list. We are all interested in management because we recognize that decisions made by managers affect our lives and those of people around us.

Books by managers are not new. Only our interest in them is novel. In the not too distant past, thoughtful and instructive books were written by managers such as Chester Barnard, then president of the New Jersey Bell Telephone Company; Henry Dennison, president of the Dennison Manufacturing Company; Henri Fayol, president of the Commentary-Fourchambault Company in France; and others. Their books never made the best-seller list and have, for the most part, been seriously read and studied by only a few management historians. This is unfortunate, because their advice and insights are practical, to the point, and useful to managers who regularly make decisions in large corporations and small businesses. The wisdom of these writers deserves wider circulation than it can be given by professors in management classes. It needs to be applied at the "cutting edge" of organizational life. It needs to be understood and acted on by managers today.

The 1980s are a good time to reflect on the evolution of management thought because in 1986 we observed the Centennial of Management as designated by the Academy of Management. The beginning point of management, according to the Academy, was the 1886 meeting of the American Society of Mechanical Engineers. Of course, no one seriously suggests that management is only a hundred years old. People have practiced management for thousands of years. In a 1987 speech broadcast by closed circuit to selected business firms and universities around the nation, Peter Drucker stated that the best managers in history were those responsible for building the pyramids of Egypt. They had little time to complete the projects and limited transportation and scientific resources, yet they built one of the great wonders of the world. Unfortunately, the Egyptians told us little about their techniques and shared almost none of their know-how. Therein lies the difference between knowing how to do management and contributing to the development of a field of knowledge that others can learn and practice.

The emergence of a *systematic* field of management is what we can trace to the 1886 meeting of the American Society of Mechanical Engineers. At this meeting Henry Towne, cofounder and president of the Yale and Towne Manufacturing Company, read a paper titled "The Engineer as Economist." In it he called for the recognition of the "management of works" as a practical art similar to engineering. Essential to this recognition was the development of literature and the formulation of normative principles.

Towne's paper was not profound. Presentations at academic societies rarely are. Its effects, however, were revolutionary. His plea that engineers should be concerned with more than technical efficiency even to the point of considering costs, revenues, and profits was new. No major change took place in the society or its charter, but the presentation was attended by one whose ideas altered the entire direction of American industry. This was Frederick Taylor, the "father of scientific management." Taylor's introduction gets us ahead of the story, however—we will discuss his contributions in Chapter Four. For now, some justification is needed for the approach to be taken in the remainder of the book.

Ideas and Actors

This book is organized around a relatively few of the most frequently discussed and debated ideas in management. All these ideas are alive today and are just as important and controversial as they were when first presented. They have been selected from a search of the classic books on management and chosen from literally hundreds of important ideas and concepts that were candidates for inclusion. The selected issues, each given a separate chapter, are specialization, efficiency, management's search for legitimacy through the application of scientific methods, decision making, the nature of managerial work, goal setting and task management, managerial responsibility, rewards and motivation, leadership, authority and influence, and organizational design.

Every chapter analyzes, in some detail, the thoughts of several writers who have devoted attention to the specific issue under examination. Rather than merely cite the many comments that all the classical writers have made about an issue, I have chosen to provide details on the ideas of only a few. In addition, each issue is traced to modern times to illustrate, with actual companies and organizations, that the topic remains important today.

The array of writers assembled in this book is an interesting mix, reflecting a mysterious characteristic of management literature. For example, until the Hawthorne studies, most of the contributors of significant books in the field of management were people who either ran business firms or acted as consultants to those who did run companies. Frederick Taylor, Frank Gilbreth, Henry Gantt, Henri Fayol, Lyndall Urwick, James Mooney, Chester Barnard, Mary Parker Follett, and Henry Dennison were all actively engaged in the day-to-day management of businesses or served as consultants. With the exception of Hugo Munsterberg and Lillian Gilbreth, most of the writers during the first thirty years of management's development were never college professors.

Professors entered the picture with the events surrounding the Hawthorne studies. The work of G. E. Mayo, F. J. Roethlisberger, Herbert A. Simon, Rensis Likert, Fred Fiedler, Paul Lawrence and Jay Lorsch, and others illustrates how completely the development during the last six decades has been dominated by academics.

A balance of the writings of both practicing managers and academics has been provided in this book because it is important to see how similar at points and how different at others the ideas of the two groups have been. Fortunately, the contributions of both groups are significant, and collectively they account for the profound modern institution known as management. There is no reason to attempt to evaluate the relative importance of the ideas of academics and practicing managers, because they are all important and add to our knowledge of organizations and people at work.

There are many other writers whose ideas could have been analyzed, and given enough space their thoughts would have been included. A goal of this book is to focus on representatives from the major streams of thought that make up modern management theory and practice. Ideas are discussed that find their origin in the period of scientific management but are as modern as today's headlines. Specific representatives from each period have been selected because of the significance of their thoughts on the topics selected for discussion. The logic of my selections will become more apparent as the issues are introduced and discussed.

Plan of the Book

A chapter-by-chapter overview was presented briefly in the Preface. At this point I will simply say that the chapters to follow attempt to select a few recurring themes in the short but glorious history of management and illustrate their importance for the practice of management today. Part One begins with the reasons for the emergence of management as a recognized discipline, while Part Two looks at the requirements for the legitimacy of this developing discipline and what its practitioners actually do. Part Three examines the goals, purpose, and responsibilities of management, and Part Four focuses on the human factor. Part Five concludes the book with an analysis of organizational cooperation and change.

When writers are first discussed a brief biographical sketch is provided. The information in the biographies comes from such sources as the *Golden Book of Management, Current Biography, Men and Women of Science,* and so on. Specific citations for biographical information are not provided because it is assumed the reader will be more interested in the ideas than the people.

PART ONE

Exploring the Seeds
of Modern Management Thought

When does a field of study begin? When will it end? As we begin to examine recurring themes of management, we have to decide where to start. Some believe we have to go back to Moses and the sage advice of his father-in-law, Jethro, on how to delegate authority. We might just as well go back another thousand years.

We certainly could begin in the fourteenth century with Machiavelli's consultations in *The Prince*. No doubt we could learn much from Moses, perhaps Jethro, and maybe even old "Nick." To take management back that far, however, would be an illusion, a myth, a fairy tale. Of course there were managers and organizations, and some people understood management processes and leadership. But there was no discipline of management. Sage advice, important as it may be, does not constitute a field of study.

The seeds of management thought were not planted when people started "doing management"; they were sowed, quite literally, into the soil of human history when people started trying to make sense out of what was being done. Management as a discipline began when people started systematizing it, codifying it, and developing prescriptions for how to manage better. Eventually theories that could be taught and learned emerged. That was the beginning of management.

We begin, after a proper introduction in Chapter One, with

the work of Charles Babbage and Andrew Ure, at a point where
the "roots" began to grow. Babbage and Ure anticipated the development of systematic management. That is where the story,
the search, the quest must begin. It begins in the dreary, smoky
factories of England and Scotland. It will take us to the high-
technology firms of Silicon Valley, along Route 128 in Boston, and to North Carolina's Research Triangle. The journey
will require us to travel fast and far—through the steel mills of
the industrial Northeast, to parts of France, Germany, and England, and, briefly, to Japan.

   The trip is long but the path is exciting. Those who per-
sist will better understand where the legacy of today's managers
began, how little of management is really new, and where all
these management ideas are likely to take us. I am not among
those who believe there is nothing new under the sun. However,
it will become obvious that much of what is advertised as new
and revolutionary is little more than a logical extension of ideas
developed in another place and time. Much of what is true is
not new, and much of what is said to be new is not true. We
must be cautious. We must be objective in our evaluations of
usefulness.

   Why people did not codify management earlier we will
never know. Why it takes writers of "pop" management to present ideas that executives will read is even more mysterious.
Many executives are not aware of the sage advice of classical
writers because they have little contact with academia. That is
unfortunate. We are all worse off for it. The ideas of the classic
writers have been there, for those who sought them, for more
than a century. Without a guide, however, the exploration ends
before it begins. This book is intended as such a guide, and it is
designed to stimulate reader interest in continuing the journey.

   Part One contains three chapters. The first is an introduction and an apology. The important writers are many but the
space is limited. The introduction offers an explanation of the
choices of people and ideas included in the book.

   Chapter Two talks about specialization and how it led to
factories. The factory and the specialized tasks performed in it

required coordination. That is where the need for management and managers enters our picture of history.

Chapter Three is about efficiency—the gospel, the "good news" that management made possible. It was the possibility of efficiency, more than anything else, that created the conditions necessary for the emergence of scientific management.

CHAPTER 2

Progress Through Specialization

From Making Pins to Robots

Tracing the roots of modern management requires, like so many other things, a focus on England and Scotland. It was, after all, in Great Britain that the Industrial Revolution began in the mid-eighteenth century. Great Britain at that time was an exciting place, yet the excitement, attitudes, and machines took almost a hundred years to reach the shores of the New World. There were, to be sure, only a few attempts during the Industrial Revolution to commit management ideas to paper with the ultimate effect of developing principles, so we can hardly argue that management was an important aspect of the Industrial Revolution. The necessary conditions for the eventual evolution of management thought were, however, firmly established during this time.

Steam power created the potential for the Industrial Revolution, but mass markets made it necessary. Nowhere was this more evident than in mid-nineteenth-century America. Immediately following the Civil War, the United States became "railroadized," with a sixfold increase in miles of track in the last half of the nineteenth century. The population increased and headed west and demanded more and more products and machines. A mass market developed, transportation facilities were in place, and workers had discovered strength in numbers, thereby accelerating union activism and militancy.

It was clear to perceptive industrialists that merely adding more laborers would not solve production problems (Duncan, 1971). With stronger unions it might not even be possible. It would certainly be expensive. Productivity on a large scale was a necessity, and that required larger factories. Factories, however, required investments of capital, specialized machines, and machine operators. That is where management entered the picture.

Management is the coordination of human and nonhuman resources toward the accomplishment of organizational goals. When machines and human beings began moving to progressively greater levels of specialization, management was necessary to coordinate diverse tasks and operations. Two individuals, Charles Babbage and Andrew Ure, were instrumental in advocating two important ideas that, along with mass markets, made factories inevitable and the emergence of management as a discipline inescapable.

Division of Labor and the Economics of Specialization

Charles Babbage was born in 1792, the son of a wealthy English banker. If his father had not been rich, he would have likely died in childhood, because he was ill much of his life. The weaknesses of his body accounted for the strength of his mind. He was curious, inventive, and more intelligent than most children of his day. It may have been his illness that made him cranky and impatient. It was not uncommon for him to blow horns outside his home to drive away organ grinders who disturbed his work. One person said of Babbage that "he spoke as if he hated mankind in general, Englishmen in particular, and the English government and organ grinders most of all" (Moseley, 1964).

Babbage was always interested in how things work, an interest that led him to study mathematics at Cambridge. His mathematical talents aided him in inventing the famous "analytical engine"—the forerunner of the digital computer (Froehlich, 1985). His broader interests in science led him to travel around Europe for over ten years observing and studying factories before returning to Cambridge and settling down in a mathematics professorship in 1828 (Moseley, 1964).

One of Babbage's most lasting contributions was the publication of his book *On the Economy of Machinery and Manufactures* ([1832] 1982). Ten years of visiting factories clearly influenced the content of the book and the enormous range of topics he discussed. A sample of the contents reveals discussions of the importance of tools, plant location, unions, and the use of calculating machines operated by punched cards. It is, however, Babbage's discussion of specialization, or the division of labor, that aids us in understanding the nature and importance of the factory.

Babbage was not the first to discuss the virtues of division of labor. More than half a century earlier Adam Smith ([1776] 1937) had published his famous *Wealth of Nations*, the first three chapters of which dealt with the importance of the division of labor, complete with an example of its use in making pins. Babbage's debt to Smith is obvious, although he was able to extend and improve on the original ideas.

One of the most important distinctions presented by Babbage had to do with the division of physical and mental labor. If specialization is good for factory workers, asked Babbage, why not for mathematicians as well? In our society specialization is easy to appreciate and understand. We are used to doctors who only work on ears or bones, lawyers who concentrate solely on real estate, and accountants who deal exclusively with taxes. That was not the case in eighteenth-century England. Specialization was not so obvious to the farmer or the worker in a cottage industry. Before factories and assembly lines, people were generalists who plowed the land, planted the seeds, fertilized, and harvested the products of their labor.

Babbage was quick to recognize the potential of specialization. In fact, he stated that the division of labor is the most important principle for all the people who perform work. Like Adam Smith, he was careful to list the virtues of specialization, the more important being:

1. It reduces the time needed for learning a job. The time required to master a job depends on its difficulty and on the number of distinct processes it requires. The more difficult the task and the more processes it involves, the greater the potential benefits of specialization.

2. It reduces the waste of material during the learning stage. When people learn to do a new job, they inevitably do things wrong. Waste results. Waste is reduced when people confine their attention to one task that they can then learn faster.

3. It eliminates the time consumed in changing from one task or job to another. Someone who specializes in carpentry does not lose time stopping to do plumbing or electrical work.

4. It allows for attainment of high skill levels. Theoretically, quality is improved through the division of labor because repetition leads to speed and excellence.

5. It encourages labor-reducing innovation. Like Smith, Babbage believed that the specialist who becomes an expert in performing a single task is more likely to invent or create a tool or process to improve his or her work.

6. It allows a more careful matching of people and tasks. If a person is hired to do everything, he or she must be capable of doing the heaviest or most demanding subtask in the complete job. With specialization, skills and physical abilities can be more easily matched to the subtask.

Babbage thought that, as a rule, the higher the skill required by a job and the less time the skill is actually employed, the greater the advantage of specialization. The worker performing a single task can do it exclusively and learn faster. The worker who must perform a variety of tasks will be slower at developing the skills needed to perform a specific demanding task. Without the division of labor, learning requires time, waste increases, and inefficiencies result.

As we might guess, Babbage was not satisfied with the mere specialization of physical labor or occupations. Should mathematicians perform the "lowest processes of arithmetic"? Of course not! That is precisely why he developed the analytical engine—to relieve talented people of the chore of routine calculations.

Babbage was a dreamer but not altogether unrealistic. He knew that there must be mass markets for the "product" of the specialist's labor and that capital would be required in greater amounts if specialization were to be practiced on a grand scale. The requirement of capital brings us to an important Scotsman.

Substituting Capital for Labor

Andrew Ure was born in Glasgow, Scotland, in 1778, just two years after Adam Smith published the *Wealth of Nations*. Ure earned a degree in medicine and embarked on a career as a scientific writer and chemist. What led to his interest in factories no one knows. It might have been the popular scientific lectures, the first of their kind, that he prepared and delivered to the working men of Glasgow. Factories were what his audiences understood best, and perhaps his search for meaningful examples enlightened the teacher as much as the pupils. How he became interested is not important; that he became interested is the critical point.

Ure was particularly concerned about the progress of British textiles. He made careful studies of factory districts and actually tried to "eat, sleep, think, and feel" like the factory worker. He talked to workers, observed them, and finally wrote about them in a book titled *The Philosophy of Manufactures* (1835). Ure's book has been called many things, including the "railings of a frustrated mechanic" and a "defense of manufacturing and manufactures." It is both and more. It is one of the most important books ever written about the factory system of England.

Ure's book begins with tremendous amounts of demographic and public health data, no doubt attributable to the demands of his scientific nature and the fact that he was a physician. He established the average age of the British industrial worker, broke employment figures down into male and female workers, reviewed their health status, repeated their complaints, and reported on their habits away from work.

The important aspects of Ure's philosophy were formed

as he attempted to refute a report by a Mr. Sadler, who accused
Britain's industrialists and their factories of being too harsh on
workers, abusing children, and generally allowing a variety of
poor working conditions. Not so, argued Ure. The real culprit
was the lack of automation. Data showed that the best work
was done entirely by machines, thus relieving humans of heavy
and boring tasks. Workers in automated factories with steam engines were more satisfied, according to Ure, because they were
relieved of heavy work and could acquire more than a subsis-
tence level of existence.

The Sadler report blamed machines for worker misery
and child abuse. Ure blamed the conditions on the way factories
were operated. Children in textile factories were ruled by spin-
ners and the men who operated "slubbing" machines. These
slubbers supervised children and were paid on the basis of how
much work the children accomplished. Any mistake or failure
to work hard led to a beating. Most of the cruelty "complained
of in the factories [took] place between the slubber and his
pieceners" (Ure, 1835, p. 179). It had nothing whatsoever to do
with machines.

The most basic principle of the factory system, as Ure
viewed it, was to "substitute mechanical science for hand skill"
(p. 20). In other words, substitute machines for manual labor.
Machines reduced tiring work, cut boredom, and promised a
higher standard of living. *The Philosophy of Manufactures* was
nothing more than an exposition of the general principles on
which productive industry should be conducted by self-acting
machines. The mechanic in Ure is easy to infer from his writings. Where Babbage had called for specialization, Ure seconded
the call and extended it with a plea for machines as well.

English Factories and the American System of Manufacture

Even at this time, the fascination with machines was making its way to the New World. In this new and exciting place,
the government encouraged western settlement with cheap land.
Many of the men headed west and left large numbers of relatively unskilled women to run the farms or to move to the city in

search of work. The entrepreneurs in the textile and other manufacturing industries took Ure's advice seriously and opted for machines. Low-skilled workers could tend the machines even if they could not operate them. At the same time, military men in Europe had discovered the value of interchangeable parts for muskets and handguns. When the idea of interchangeable parts and automated factories were combined, a new phenomenon known as the *American system of manufacture* resulted (Rosenberg, 1969).

The significance of the American system of manufacture was far reaching. Machines worked fast and people of relatively low skills could operate them. At the same time, inventors devised schemes for using interchangeable parts in a variety of needed goods, from sewing machines to bicycles. Eventually, and most significantly, the automobile would be produced in large numbers because of advances in this concept of manufacture. Manufactured goods could at last be produced in the quantities demanded by a growing market with increased transportation capabilities. Mass production and mass consumption go hand in hand, even though we cannot always determine which is cause and which is effect. Once the process is started, the management problem becomes one of how to efficiently respond to the opportunities and needs that mass consumption and production create.

Mass Production and Economies of Scale

The substitution of machines for manual labor and the resulting specialization signaled a death toll for the mom-and-pop manufacturing business. When products were needed in large numbers, such volume could not be supplied by small manufacturing firms. The conditions for the large-scale factory were created. The size of manufacturing facilities in modern times illustrates just how far economies of scale can be taken. For example, at peak employment in the early 1970s, the General Electric Company's Major Appliance Group in Louisville, Kentucky, employed over 20,000 workers. Today single factories employing 5,000 workers are commonplace.

The trend toward mass production and the accompanying economies of scale began in the American automobile industry. Oldsmobile was the first to introduce the "nonmoving" assembly line. After a fire had destroyed its Detroit plant in 1900, Oldsmobile contracted with local machine shops to make component parts and deliver them to the new factory, where they were carried from one worker to another to be assembled. Using this technique, output was increased from slightly over 400 cars in 1901 to 5,000 in 1903. The Oldsmobile sold for about $650 and became the first popular car in America. Oldsmobile, however, was never able to accomplish the goal of making an automobile for a mass market. The genius of that accomplishment belonged to Henry Ford.

Ford's objective was to build a car that people from all occupations could afford. He achieved this goal in 1913 with the installation of the first moving assembly line. Just five years before, Henry Leland of the Cadillac Automobile Company had impressed the world with the practicality of perfectly interchangeable parts by conducting a simple experiment. Prior to Leland's vision, parts had been made for specific automobiles and had to be matched with considerable accuracy. This consumed large amounts of time. In 1908, Leland sent three Cadillacs to England, where they were disassembled and their parts mixed with other parts from dealers' warehouses. The parts were then reassembled into three workable Cadillacs. What military men had discovered about muskets, automobile makers now discovered about cars: Great speed and economies can be achieved through the use of interchangeable parts.

In 1913, Henry Ford combined the previous ideas of Oldsmobile and Leland into his famous moving assembly line. The frame of the automobile moved through the plant on a conveyer belt while workers on each side of the line placed parts on the frame. In 1908, before installation of the moving assembly line, a Model T had cost about $850. This was more expensive than the Oldsmobile and beyond the reach of most industrial workers. After installation of the line, a Model T could be built in less than two hours and sold for about $400. The concept was so successful that for more than fifteen years, between

1913 and the late 1920s, half the cars sold in the United States were Fords (Bryant and Dethloff, 1983).

The concept of the assembly line accomplished several things and set the stage for several others. First, the assembly line combined both the desire for specialization championed by Babbage and the substitution of machines for manual labor envisioned by Ure. The result was a production process that consisted of a series of relatively simple tasks organized in a continuous flow along a long, moving line. Each piece of equipment and all required materials, at least in theory, arrived at the right place at precisely the right time.

The theory of the assembly line was to break each job down into a sequential series of simple tasks. The point where work was actually done demanded little thought. Good work habits, it was hoped, would lead to more and higher-quality products. The artisan and apprentice and their careful but relatively expensive way of doing work virtually disappeared. Georges Friedman (1961) illustrated the degree to which division of labor was extended by showing how the relatively simple task of making a man's waistcoat was broken down into sixty-five different units of work.

The savings were incredible. Lacey (1986) states that the output at Ford in 1911–1912 was over 78,400 cars, produced by 6,867 employees. The following year both production and the number of workers more than doubled. In 1914, the first operational year of the moving assembly line, production almost doubled again but the number of employees actually dropped by about 1,500.

The moving assembly line was perfected in time to become a major element in the Allied victory in World War II. Ford Motor Company applied its mass-production techniques to airplanes, and industrialists such as Henry Kaiser were able to apply innovative prefabricating techniques to construction of Liberty ships, the all-important supply carriers. During peak operations an entire ship could be welded together in only eight and a half hours (Bailey, 1977).

Mass production and economies of scale were the answers to the problem of supplying mass markets composed of relatively affluent shoppers. The assembly line, in fact, so revolutionized our lives that Burke (1978) lists it along with seven other innovations (the atomic bomb, the telephone, the computer, television, plastic, airplanes, and guided rockets) as things that "may be most influential in structuring our own futures and in causing a further increase in the rate of change to which we may have to adapt" (p. i). By the 1970s, changes brought about by the moving assembly line were under way that would have surprised even Babbage and Ure. The most significant of these changes was the industrial robot.

Robotics and the Limits of Specialization

Economies of scale, moving assembly lines, and increased mechanization created new possibilities. The more predictable and programmable that work became and the more interchangeable the parts used in manufacturing, the more easily work could be performed by machines. The prospect of automation offered solutions to several of the primary problems faced by businesses in the mid-twentieth century. Automated factories, for example, could be located in lower-cost areas since large supplies of human resources were not required. Also, industrialists observed an interesting phenomenon: Often workers were more willing to accept the start-up of a completely automated factory making new products in a new location than they were the conversion of old facilities making an old product into a more automated plant where workers were displaced (Diebold, 1952).

The development of an industrial society depended on capital as the critical resource. The most competitive automobile plants were those backed by the capital necessary to stay at the edge of industrial technology, and not many people had such storehouses of funds.

Great stores of capital remain important today, but another resource has become equally critical to industrial success. Naisbitt (1984) illustrates that information has now displaced capital as the scarce resource of modern times. This is no less true in manufacturing than in space exploration. Capital is necessary but information is essential.

Computers are effective in processing information rapidly. When the information-processing capabilities of computers was directed toward the control of artificial limbs in precise and predictable ways, the industrial robot was born. With the birth of the robot, people began to look forward to the day when machines, especially robots, would perform all the routine, boring, and repetitive work (Maccoby, 1981).

What manager would not like to have an employee who could insert over 7,000 components into a printed circuit board in less than an hour, tighten 16,000 screws a day and never get bored, and paint, weld, and operate in the midst of toxic fumes and never take a day off for sick leave? You are right if you say, "No human can work like that." However, robots can, and those manufactured by companies such as Hitachi and Matsushita Electric, the company that also makes Panasonic and Quasar products, can do even more. For example, a Hitachi robot called the "visual-tactile sensing robot" has multiple arms, has seven cameras for eyes, and can independently assemble home appliances such as vacuum cleaners. The company's motto is "We believe robots free the minds to create by freeing bodies from toil."

Serious interest in the use of industrial robots started in this country in the late 1960s, but most of the applications have taken place in the last decade. Industrial robots are predictable extensions of the automated machine—automatic but capable of much more flexibility. The difference between a robot and an automated press, for example, is that the robot is capable of relatively free motions much like the human arm or hand. That is why robots are sometimes called programmed manipulators or programmed automaters. Most industrial robots are in Japan but the United States is gaining in overall usage. Almost all robots used today are employed in manufacturing operations such as appliance assembly and automobile production. In the early 1980s the majority of industrial robots were used for materials handling; spot and arc welding came next in usage. Painting and finishing operations also made extensive use of robots. In fact, robots have been useful in relieving human beings from dangerous and boring work of all kinds. It is estimated that by 1990 robots will continue to be widely used for materials handling, welding, and painting. The major increase will be in areas such as assembling finished goods.

One of the most impressive integrative applications of computers, robots, and human beings is at the Orion, Michigan, plant of General Motors. This megafactory encompasses almost eighty acres and relies on over thirty miles of conveyer belts. At any time one can find 2,500 Cadillacs or Oldsmobiles on the line. More than 3,000 employees work side by side with almost 160 robots. The robots do most of the welding and painting. As the underbody moves down the line over a period of two and one-half days, it accumulates 15,000 parts in the process of becoming a Cadillac or Oldsmobile. At full operation the plant is expected to send about 75 cars an hour on their way to an eager public (Hamel, 1984). All this is made even more efficient by the use of *just-in-time inventory control systems,* which ensure that just enough raw materials and supplies are available to keep production running without incurring large and unnecessary inventory carrying costs.

The Orion plant is one of General Motors's most significant investments and is a monument to the company's commitment to modern manufacturing techniques. Perhaps the most ambitious move in the company's history, however, is its building of the $3.5 billion Saturn plant in Spring Hill, Tennessee. The plant will incorporate some of the most modern manufacturing concepts in use today (Wheelwright and Hayes, 1985). It is designed specifically to make the Saturn, a subcompact car that will compete with less expensive foreign models.

At the Saturn plant long assembly lines are eliminated in favor of modular assembly techniques in which stand-alone, prefabricated modules, such as front ends, are assembled and tested by production teams before being installed on the car. Where assembly lines exist they are short and are flanked by feeder lines. The factory will employ a 100 percent just-in-time inventory control system that will ensure even more efficiencies and increase the competitiveness of this American automaker (*General Motors Public Interest Report*, 1985).

The growing popularity of industrial robots is primarily a matter of economics. In 1964, Robot Systems, Inc. estimated that the average hourly factory wage was $2.53 while the average cost of operating an industrial robot was about $5.00. By 1984, the situation had reversed. The average hourly wage for factory workers had climbed to over $8.00 while the average operating cost per hour of a robot was only $6.50. It is not hard to see why American companies have become increasingly aware of the need for and promise of robotics.

Such information on the economics of robotics helps us understand why General Motors paid billions of dollars for H. Ross Perot's Electronic Data Systems Corporation. The move into electronic data processing—along with purchases of interests in artificial intelligence companies plus a joint venture with Fanue, Ltd., one of Japan's leading robot manufacturers, and the consequent formation of GMFanue Robotics Corporation—makes GM's strategy clear. General Motors is betting on a technology driven future in the automobile industry, and it plans to be ready when the changes occur. Perhaps GM can even direct some of those changes.

General Motors is only one of many large corporations to become involved in robotics. Others include Caterpillar Tractor Company, John Deere, Apple Computer, and foreign industrial conglomerates such as ASEA in Sweden.

It is, of course, computer technology that has made all this possible. The economics of replacing high-cost skilled labor making as much as $20 or more an hour with wageless robots makes such automation more appealing. As one observer noted, American industry has few choices: it must "automate, emigrate, or evaporate" (Halberstam, 1983, p. 19). With advancing computer technology, robots are becoming more practical. It has been said that if "the price of cars had come down like the price of computers over the past fifteen years, the price of a new Cadillac today would be $19.95" (Halberstam, 1983). Advances of this nature could make robots and the computers that drive them even more appealing in the future.

There is no doubt that advances in specialization and automation—the most basic of all lessons of the factory system—have made thousands of products available to the masses and have freed human beings to do more creative work. The discov-

ery of interchangeable parts not only made possible large quantities of muskets but Model-T Fords as well. Mass production responded well to the demands of mass consumption (Whitsett
and Yorks, 1983).

Economic and social gains have resulted from our ability
to specialize. We now work more efficiently and as consumers
enjoy the rewards from this increased productivity. In some
areas quality has even been improved. Medical specialists, for
example, can often diagnose problems that general practitioners
know little about and even less how to treat.

Specialization, like everything else, has its cost, and those
of us who enjoy the benefits must pay the price. Increased efficiency has been purchased at the expense of more boring tasks.
The worker who used to make an entire bicycle now assembles
only one minor part as the mass-produced cycle moves down a
mechanized production line. The monotony, boredom, and
stress that result from highly mechanized and specialized tasks
and, as we will see in Chapter Nine, the need for job enrichment
have become major challenges for motivation experts in many
industries.

In a very real sense, much of the meaning has been taken
away from work. The factory made the apprentice a tender of
machines; the moving assembly line made the journeyman a machine operator; and the automated factory of today places the
robot at center stage while the human being designs, repairs,
and maintains this loyal servant that requires little more than an
occasional tuneup.

It is a long way from the analytical engine and steam-
operated factories of Babbage and Ure to the "servomanipula-
tors" of Hitachi, but the connection is clear. What started out as
a means of improving efficiency through the development of
expertise in performing a task has all but eliminated the unskilled
worker in key industries. It has inflicted considerable damage
even on skilled craftspeople.

As specialization and automation have increased, small
parts of total products and services are being produced at ever-
increasing rates. The manager's job is to coordinate the diverse
specialists and ensure that something of value results. This is
no small responsibility, and the management challenge is clear.

Even the manager is not protected from the potential use of computerized systems. Babbage's observation about the need to specialize mental as well as physical labor is gaining momentum in areas such as artificial intelligence and expert systems.

Expert systems presently exist that can "capture" the diagnostic process of the physician and aid in systematically classifying symptoms. They can even suggest possible causes and cures. Engineering chores such as drilling oil wells and designing bridges can be partially simulated through the use of an expert system.

It is unlikely that such systems will eliminate the need for doctors, engineers, and accountants. However, the availability of these aids will likely increase the productivity and efficiency of high-paid professionals. Increases in efficiency will, in turn, directly affect the demand for and ultimately the remuneration of most occupations.

These changes in our information- and knowledge-based society will not end with the impact on skilled and unskilled factory workers. All of us must learn to live with and adapt to the potential changes resulting from greater levels of specialization, automation, and computerization. Managers, in particular, cannot escape the changes and challenges. People will always be an important concern of managers, but the types of people managed will change significantly. Managers of today and tomorrow will have to adapt to these changes and learn the new tools and concepts that will be necessary for making effective decisions.

Implications and Conclusions

The family farm was a nice place to work. First, one labored for oneself (really for the local bank, but it seemed like home). Second, everything seemed to make sense. No one worried about a job description, a specialty, or a classification. There was work to be done and one did it. It was irrelevant whether one milked the cow, plowed the field, planted the corn, or cleared weeds. One did what was necessary to bring in the crop.

Work does not make that much sense in a factory. Sometimes workers never really see the result of their labor. All they know is that they punch six holes in a metal plate when it passes their work station. At the same time, the worker has little if any real ownership in the factory. The workers are "we," the owners and managers are "them."

The factory, mass production, mass markets, and an abundance of relatively low-skilled labor created the need for someone or some group to coordinate all the diverse activities into some unified organizational thrust. Efficient coordination required skilled managers.

As jobs have become increasingly specialized, the need for managers has increased. However, as we enter an era of industrial robots and accelerated automation and computerization, the manager's role is changing. One of the most important changes is the need to manage information. Today we see managers in factories who not only need interpersonal skills but computer and other technical skills as well. The manager of the future must be prepared for the factory of the future, and that factory is likely to be as different from the factory of today as the family farm was from the emerging factory a century ago.

CHAPTER 3

Searching for Efficiency

The Gospel of Scientific Management

If there is one word that more people associate with management than any other, it is *efficiency*. In fact, the scientific management movement, upon which much of modern theory and practice is based, was almost called *efficiency management*.

Before discussing the concept of efficiency, it would be desirable to introduce a number of engineers who are most directly identified with scientific management. The most important, Frederick Taylor, who is known as the father of scientific management, was mentioned in Chapter One. At that time we indicated a need to wait before saying much about him. We need to wait a little longer, since he, his associate Henry Gantt, and the famous husband-and-wife team Frank and Lillian Gilbreth will be the subject of much of the next chapter. However, since efficiency was the "good news" of scientific management, it was the primary reason why such a philosophy was needed. We need to discuss efficiency before we move to a detailed analysis of science in management because the desire for efficiency was the provocation for the emergence of systematic management thought.

Birth of the Efficiency Movement

In the summer of 1910 the railroads north of the Ohio and Potomac rivers and east of the Mississippi River filed a request for a rate increase with the Interstate Commerce Commission. From September to November of that year a series of hearings was held to determine the wisdom of granting the request. Louis Brandeis, later Justice of the Supreme Court, was a leading attorney objecting to the increase. He had read some of Taylor's papers and had discussed the concepts of management with others who agreed with Taylor's conclusion that wages could be increased and labor costs reduced simultaneously if operations were more efficient. However, his recollection was vague, and until the rate cases developed he had little reason to occupy his attention with matters of management. Now, however, he needed expert witnesses to make the case convincing, and according to Drury (1922) Brandeis held a meeting at the apartment of Henry Gantt, one of Taylor's close associates.

The meeting was attended by Gantt, Brandeis, Frank Gilbreth, and a few other people. Brandeis wanted to make sure that testimonies followed a similar logic and used a common set of terms to describe the elements of Taylor's new management system. Some of the labels the group considered for this revolutionary way of looking at the problems of industry were "Taylor system," "functional management," "shop management," and finally "efficiency." (There was even an Efficiency Society incorporated in New York with the express purpose of applying the principles of efficiency to all aspects of life.)

Although there are precise definitions, *efficiency* to some means "getting more for less or at least the same amount." To others it means keeping costs low and profits high. Actually, there is some truth in both of these popular connotations. In an economic, and ultimately a management, sense *efficiency* means maximizing the output with a minimum amount of inputs. In the case of automobiles it means producing as many cars as possible while carefully keeping the inputs of land, labor, capital, and management to a minimum. By doing so, costs are controlled, and profits, if maintained at reasonable levels, are sufficient while allowing prices to be established at levels that make it possible to sell cars without being underpriced by competitors.

It was efficiency that led Adam Smith and Charles Babbage to advocate the division of labor, or specialization. It was the same motivation that has driven the General Motors's Saturn strategy that was discussed in Chapter Two. The Saturn strategy is designed to make the largest American automobile company competitive in the international market. The Saturn, according to GM's chairman, Roger Smith, will be "less labor intensive, less material intensive, less everything intensive than anything we have done before" ("Saturn Makes Its Debut . . . ," 1985, p. 50).

The goal of GM is to use the latest automated technology, preassembled parts, and very short assembly lines that will enable more cars to be produced with fewer employees. The company estimates, for example, that only 6,000 employees will be needed in the Saturn plant, compared to 21,000 in the Oldsmobile plant in Lansing, Michigan. This is the type of efficiency, many observers believe, that will be necessary to make the United States competitive once again in the world automobile market (Wheelwright and Hayes, 1985).

Management's High Priest of Efficiency

Frederick Taylor was concerned about efficiency, and so were Gantt and the Gilbreths, but no one devoted himself so completely to the subject in early management thought as Harrington Emerson. The editor of *Engineering Magazine* once stated that Emerson's "efficiency system was large enough to become a philosophy—hopeful enough to be called a gospel." In fact, the final chapter of Emerson's first book was titled "The Gospel of Efficiency."

Looking back, it is difficult to understand what there was about efficiency that could so completely capture the attention of a man like Emerson. He was born in Trenton, New Jersey, in 1853. His father was a professor of English literature and a Presbyterian minister. The younger Emerson studied in Germany, England, France, Italy, and Greece. It is said that he could speak nineteen languages, so it should be no surprise that he became the head of the modern foreign languages department of the University of Nebraska when he was only twenty-three years old. After little more than five years, however, he tired of university life and resigned to pursue business interests. Over the next twenty years he did economic and engineering research for the Burlington Railroad and was a consultant to firms around the world. As a consulting engineer, he completely reorganized the Atchison, Topeka, and Santa Fe Railroad, where he introduced a number of cost-accounting, record-keeping, and bonus systems. These types of contributions earned him the distinction of being the first "efficiency engineer."

His experience with railroads placed him in a unique position to become one of the primary witnesses in the Eastern railroad rate cases. When Mr. Brandeis called, Emerson quickly and effectively responded. Emerson's fame grew and his talents were sought by industry and government. He was aware of the work of Taylor's group and the contributions of the Gilbreths, even though Taylor never really trusted Emerson's new breed of efficiency engineers. Therefore, Emerson's contributions were independent of the other champions of scientific management despite the fact that he shared many, if not most, of their commitments.

Of particular importance to Emerson was the need to justify the concepts of scientific management to the worker. In 1921 he was appointed a member of the Hoover Committee for the Elimination of Waste in Industry (Urwick, 1956). (This membership was shared with another important contributor to the efficiency movement, as we will soon discover.)

Fundamentals of Efficiency. Emerson wrote *Efficiency as a Basis for Operations and Wages* in 1908. He began the book with a shocking contrast between the inefficiencies of human actions and the efficient methods of nature. He used the example of "nature's pump" to illustrate his point. Water is drawn from the ocean to tremendous heights, carried thousands of miles, and deposited on mountains and plains with no pipes, no friction loss, no mechanical parts. If humans could be so efficient, according to Emerson, there would be no bread lines, no poverty. In fact, all would be wealthy. Our inefficiency, according to Emerson, causes our poverty.

The problem of human inefficiency, Emerson believed, could be addressed in two ways. First, to be efficient we must devise methods of enabling people to accomplish the most they possibly can relative to the task or established goals. This requires careful analysis of the elements of work and teaching workers the best way to do each job. He shared these ideas with the Gilbreths and probably with Taylor as well. Emerson believed that most people are only about 60 percent efficient in accomplishing their work goals.

Second, we must develop ways of setting goals that require the best performance of which we are capable. In this regard, Emerson believed that our efficiencies are so far below 1 percent of what we are capable that they do not warrant an estimate (Emerson, [1908] 1976). This particular issue of setting challenging goals is the theme of Chapter Seven. For now, we will merely note that Emerson emphasized the importance of goal setting and task management like other writers of his day.

Emerson's travels made it possible for him to draw lessons from other nations in much the same way that we seek to learn the secrets of the Japanese today. Although he was quick to point out that all nations shared the curse of inefficiency, each country seemed to develop its own unique strengths. For example, at the time of Emerson's writing, Great Britain was the industrial leader of the world. He attributed this leadership to the British discovery of the importance of the oceans. England was always one step ahead of the rest of the world. When most other nations were building fast wooden ships, England was developing steamers.

The Germans' national treasure was their ability to use their brains. The intelligence of the German people remains a resource of economic development. A mere twenty-five years after studying the American and British systems of shipbuilding, the Germans were building the finest and fastest vessels afloat. The French emerged as logical innovators. They developed the fastest trains, the first submarine, the machine gun, and the art of photography. Americans excelled because of the great accomplishments of individuals—Edison, Ford, Westinghouse, and so on. Whether this individuality could provide industrial leadership, in Emerson's day, remained to be seen. However, Emerson's appreciation of the unique virtues of many cultures made it possible for him to think in broader terms about management and productivity and to freely accept the advantages and reject the disadvantages of many national cultures.

Efficiency and Organization. One of the most important differences between the writings of Emerson and others of the scientific management school was his insights into the relationship between efficiency and organizational design. There is little doubt from his writings that the years he spent in Germany impressed Emerson with the importance of the structure of organizations.

How is it possible, he asked, for small plants all around the country producing everything from pens to locomotives to compete successfully with large corporations? Theoretically, the economies of large-scale operations should make the larger firms much more efficient. They can purchase in larger quantities and receive larger discounts; processes can be automated because of the larger scale of operation; and dozens of other reasons can be found in elementary manufacturing textbooks. As Emerson clearly noted, this is not always the case, and the reason can be explained in one word: *inefficiency.* Much of this inefficiency results from a lack of organization.

Inefficiencies have become excessive in some industries, where terms such as *diseconomies of scale* are used to describe the conditions resulting from extremely large organizations. In recent years we have seen a large company like General Electric shift manufacturing in its Aircraft Engine Division to smaller satellite plants and reduce employment in its Major Appliance Business Group. Although this seems at odds with the point made in the previous chapter about economies of scale, it is important to note that in many cases downsizing has taken place in terms of numbers of employees but not in the actual scale of operations.

Increased automation, for example, has allowed GE, among other things, to reduce its rate of rejection of inferior products by 80 percent. In other words, quality has been increased, and at significant cost savings ("Why Image Counts . . . ," 1987). The "bureaucracy" of the large factory has been discarded in favor of more decentralized operations. Emerson Electric has always maintained the reputation of being a company that succeeds by keeping things relatively small. Reducing layers in the plant organization has allowed Emerson and other firms to improve communication and develop team approaches that can eliminate many of the diseconomies of scale ("Small Is Beautiful . . . ," 1984). Diseconomies are an example of "too much of a good thing" when plants get so large and complex that they can no longer be effectively managed. The remedy is decentralizing and downsizing for the sake of efficiency until a new optimum plant size is found.

Size of the organization is not the only factor influencing efficiency. The way work is structured and who performs it also influence cost and productivity. For this reason, few more enthusiastic discussions can be found of the virtues of the line and staff form of organization than that presented by Emerson. Nature, the human body, and other well-functioning systems are all organized around line and staff concepts. Like Max Weber, the German sociologist discussed later, Emerson was impressed with the organizational precision of the Prussian army. Von Moltke, the army's great organizer, was one of Emerson's heroes because he skillfully combined line and staff with functional specialization. In the Prussian army, each important function, line and staff, was performed by a specialist. There were quartermasters, map readers, and gunnery experts so that in time of war there was no doubt about how something should be done— there was an expert present. The limitation, of course, involved coordinating all these specialists, and this, according to Emerson, was the responsibility of a strong executive: to control, adjust, and harmonize the line and staff toward the accomplishment of organizational goals.

If line and staff units are to work properly, their relationship must be clearly understood. The line has the authority to initiate action, but this should not be done independently of staff officers. A well-functioning staff can assist in the accomplishment of organizational goals in a number of ways. The staff, for example, are critical in the following areas:

1. *Human resources.* Staff are involved in the selection and training of employees. Emerson discussed Frank Gilbreth's example of bricklayers. When work was redesigned, and di-

rected more carefully, efficiency was tripled and the masons
were less bored with their jobs.

2.   *Equipment.* Properly installed and maintained equipment
     can greatly increase the efficiency of ordinary workers. The
     staff can offer valuable assistance in this area.

3.   *Materials and methods.* Staff employees are responsible for
     having the right materials at the right place at the right time
     for use by line employees. Line employees also rely on as-
     sistance from the staff to ensure that the best methods are
     used.

Standards and Efficiency. Standards, in Emerson's view,
are more than goals to be used in evaluating performance. Instead, he used the term in the sense of *professional standards.* In
other words, standards are predetermined sets of rules that are
"generally accepted by the majority in a given field." The standards in the line are less complex and more stable than those
governing the staff. Sometimes staff experts have complex and
divided loyalties between the organization and an external professional group.

Emerson gave particular attention to the standards of
cost accounting. The cost accountant, when developing cost
standards, must work closely with the efficiency engineer,
whose function it is to (1) provide the "industrial and operating world" with definite standards and dollar measurements for
all services, materials, and equipment operations; (2) make as-
says, as definite and precise as the assayer's determination of
bullion values of all current operations so as to establish the
current rate of efficiency; and (3) provide remedies that will
bring current efficiency up to 100 percent.

Emerson used a personal example to show how, in one of
his railroad projects, unit costs could be significantly reduced.
When he went on the job, the unit costs were $9.55. Working
closely with the auditor, he helped establish standard costs,
along with an efficient staff organization. At first the unit costs
increased to $10.31, followed by a slight decrease to $10.16.
However, within six years the unit costs were down to an "amaz-
ing $3.73."

The final point discussed by Emerson was the idea of standard times and bonuses. For any job, Emerson and Taylor believed there must be a standard time to accomplish it. The example of an auto mechanic is used to illustrate the point. If the mechanic completes a four-hour task (standard) in less than the standard time, he is paid the price of the four-hour task and considered efficient. If he takes longer than four hours, his company loses money on the four-hour charge and the mechanic receives a poor efficiency rating. The mechanic clearly has an incentive to work at 100 percent or above.

It is interesting to note that this very concept is the basis for a recently developed idea in health care called prospective reimbursement. Hospitals are paid for services delivered to Medicare patients on the basis of standard charges for diagnostically related groups (DRGs) of medical problems. Medicare has established standard charges for a broad array of medical conditions and pays hospitals according to these standards. If a patient receives a specific type of treatment, Medicare pays the hospital, say, $2,700. If the hospital can deliver the treatment for less than $2,700, it makes a profit; if treatment costs more, the hospital incurs a loss. The incentive for improving efficiency in health care delivery to Medicare patients is clear. Moreover, increasing numbers of private medical insurance companies like Blue Cross are beginning to use similar forms of prospective reimbursement, and some speculate that even private-physician fees may be structured in this manner in the near future. This system is quite different from the historical cost-based system of reimbursement wherein hospitals total their costs and add on a reasonable profit. In this system there is clearly less incentive to control costs.

The important point, from our perspective, is that an established, fair, and communicated standard cost is an effective way of improving efficiency. Most people respond to incentives, and when the incentive is to be more efficient and share in the benefits, employees are more likely to be productive. Emerson concluded *Efficiency as a Basis for Operations and Wages* by stating that "efficiency is unattainable from overworked, underpaid, and brutalized men." Efficiency is attained when "the right thing is done in the right manner by the right employees at the right place in the right time" (p. 254). There may never have been a more adequate statement of the concept of efficiency.

Emerson's Twelve Principles of Efficiency

Perhaps Emerson's most influential book was *The Twelve Principles of Efficiency*, written in 1913. The principles, Emerson argued, are simple, plain, and elementary. In fact, they have been practiced and accepted for millions of years by plants and other forms of life found in nature. Emerson makes an important point worth committing to memory: "Efficiency brings about greater results with lessened effort; strenuousness brings about greater results with abnormally greater effort." In other words, efficiency results in improvements because people work smarter, not harder. Who would not buy such an appealing idea?

Emerson's first principle calls for the establishment of *clearly defined ideals*. The importance of goals and ideals cannot be overemphasized. It is one of the most basic principles of management. The ideals of a manager should be promulgated throughout the organization, posted everywhere, and inoculated in every employee. Then and only then can industrial organizations obtain a high degree of individual and aggregate excellence. *Common sense* is Emerson's second principle. He believed that when a business lacks ideals, organization, and common sense, it tends to become overcapitalized. Unnecessary machines are purchased and installed and are employed less than full time. This adds excessive overhead and becomes destructive to the success of the organization.

The importance of common sense in improving productivity is illustrated in a *Business Week* article on Eli Goldratt, a physicist who founded Creative Output, a company that sells a packaged approach to improving factory productivity ("Boosting Shop Floor Productivity . . . ," 1984). The *optimized production technology* (OPT) approach applies objectives, organization, and common sense to the problem of industrial production. OPT schedules factory work so as to avoid bottlenecks or anything that constrains output. Bottlenecks may take the form of outdated and slow machines, unskilled or unqualified workers, limited floor space, or numerous other factors. OPT is used to identify the bottlenecks in the plant and to schedule work accordingly to maximize productivity. The ironic part of the system is that seemingly inefficient conditions must sometimes be endured in the interest of maximizing total output. However, the benefits gained in controlling inventory levels and keeping the work flowing overcome such occasional necessities as keeping workers temporarily idle to avoid backup of the process at a particular bottleneck.

As with most efficiency improvements, the OPT technique and technology are important, but the philosophy driving the use of the techniques is even more important. Goldratt makes the point by stating that the software and simulations of OPT are only tools managers use in building productive efficiency. The real determinant of success is the management philosophy used in achieving the goal of profitable operations.

In his third principle, Emerson returned to the theme developed in his previous book and recommended the use of *competent counsel*. Early business leaders in America relied on personal skill and knowledge even to the extent of scorning the need for expert advice from lawyers, accountants, consultants, and engineers. However, the increasing complexity of business requires the frequent use of technical experts. No single manager can become competent in all the areas necessary to run a successful business. Therefore, to ensure that the "best practices" are used in all areas, competent counsel should be employed and the manager should be receptive to the advice offered by such advisers.

Emerson's fourth principle is *discipline*. Working toward common ideals in a disciplined organization results in cooperation. In this regard, Emerson provided another of his useful examples from nature. He contended that the fundamentals of discipline are better learned from the "governance of a bee hive than a college textbook." No bee appears to obey any other bee, yet the "spirit of the hive" is so great that every bee works hard at its special task and fatalistically assumes that every other bee is also conscientiously working as hard as possible for the good of the hive. When the drones fail to be useful, the worker bees "make away with them" (p. 150). The spirit of the hive, like other examples from nature, fascinated Emerson and was frequently used as an illustration of the most pure form of efficient processes. Emerson's memorable statement is that "cooperation is not a principle, but the absence of it is a crime." If more organizations had the spirit of the hive, the task of management would be much easier and more enjoyable.

Emerson was a believer in preventive control when it came to discipline. He believed the hiring decision to be a critical point for initiating discipline. Before a prospective employee is hired, the individual should be instructed about the ideals of the firm, its philosophy of organization, and its performance expectations. Emerson believed that 90 percent of the "harder" discipline should be applied before people are hired. This would ensure that those who are unfit for the organization because of bad character, bad habits, laziness, or destructive tendencies would never be hired in a "high class organization." He believed that one of the worst faults managers can commit is to hire people for jobs for which they are unfit. Both the organization and the individual lose. Just as the bee depends on the spirit of the hive, the worker depends on the "spirit of the organization." Under the best forms of management there are few rules and even fewer punishments. Instead, there are standard practice instructions and every person knows her or his part in the success of the organization. Everyone has definite responsibilities, and reliable, timely records are kept on all important aspects of the business. Conditions and operations are standardized and efficiency rewards go to those who excel.

The fifth principle is *a fair deal.* Managers need three important qualities, according to Emerson: sympathy, imagination, and above all, a sense of justice. The greatest problem in ensuring a fair deal is the failure to establish parity between pay and performance. Wage systems should be developed in a way to ensure that today is made bearable without taking away the hope of a better tomorrow. Such reward systems provide excitement and incentive.

Keeping reliable, immediate, adequate, and permanent

records is Emerson's sixth principle of efficiency. Records make us aware of more information than is immediately available through the senses. They give us warnings, allow us to recall the past, and make projections into the future. Emerson's discussion of records illustrates the importance of cost-accounting data in his system of efficiency. His contention was that no manager could know how well things are operating unless there are records that show standards for materials, material prices, wage rates, and so on. Then and only then can the manager monitor actual performance and determine the degree of efficiency compared to standards.

The seventh principle is *dispatching*. Emerson used the term to describe that aspect of planning that involves scheduling. The terminology no doubt results from his extensive involvement with the railroad industry. The eighth principle covers *standards and schedules*. Standards and schedules may be a matter of precise mathematics, or they may defy quantification. Both are important in building and maintaining efficiency.

Standardized conditions is the ninth principle. It is often tempting to skip the present and plan strictly for the future while depending on past techniques and rules of thumb. Emerson stated that even in great American industrial firms conditions imposed by an ignorant and inefficient past are accepted, schedules are toned down, and painful effort crowds out intelligent control.

Standardization of operations is the tenth principle of efficiency. Good results are never achieved by chance. The standardization of operations makes good outcomes a possibility. High levels of efficiency, according to Emerson, require only proper intelligence, spirit, and organization.

The eleventh principle states that merely having standard practice instructions is not enough—they must be *written*. These instructions are the permanent laws and practices of the plant. They offer the promise of organizational learning and the opportunity to become progressively better in performing the tasks. Unfortunately, this is time-consuming, hard work, and the American weakness is to be discouraged by difficulties and to retreat instead of overcoming troubles and moving forward.

The twelfth and final principle is *efficiency reward*, or a reward that enables the worker to see and grasp, while the work is being performed, how important his or her job is to the company. Efficiency reward is paid-for individual excellence in the area for which the individual is accountable. The best standard of efficiency is not the maximum muscular effort for a short time but a combination of mental and physical efforts that leave the worker in the best condition possible to make future contributions (Emerson, 1913, p. 363).

When all twelve principles are practiced together, the outcome is the elimination of waste. Dreaded inefficiency can exist for only one of two reasons. First, it is possible that in a given plant the principles are simply not known. Second, they may be known but not practiced. In either event, efficiency suffers. If the principles are not used, efficiency is not possible. Nor is it possible if the principles are not known. They must be known and applied in real settings.

Emerson believed that work should be a blessing rather than a curse. It should be a pleasure, a game, not merely a task. He ended his book with the observation that a person of supreme ability is the one who can create and control an organization founded on and using principles to attain and maintain ideals.

Other Important Contributors

Besides Emerson, several other engineers were interested in efficiency. Two of the more important contributors were Morris Cooke and Wallace Clark. Cooke was responsible for applying concepts of efficiency to organizations outside the industrial sector. Clark was responsible for sending many of the ideas of American scientific management into the international arena.

Morris L. Cooke: Municipal and University Management. Morris L. Cooke was one of only four men, including Gantt, that Taylor acknowledged as true followers who were authorized to teach his system. Born in 1872, Cooke was trained as an engineer at Lehigh University (Lee Iacocca's alma mater).

Even before he met Taylor he questioned inefficiencies in industry and attempted to apply scientific methods to the elimination of waste. Taylor was duly impressed with the young engineer when they met and recommended him as being capable of major consulting responsibilities. In fact, Cooke was commissioned, at Taylor's recommendation, to study the American Society of Mechanical Engineers itself.

Taylor also recommended Cooke as the man to study the efficiency of higher education administration under the sponsorship of the Carnegie Foundation for the Advancement of Teaching (Arnold, 1966). The comprehensive report, published under the title *Academic and Industrial Efficiency* in 1910, provided its author with great notoriety. Predictably, the scrutiny of an efficiency engineer was not welcomed by professors and college administrators. The report told them what none wanted to hear—that their committee decision-making structure was cumbersome, that their tenure system protected too many unproductive colleagues, and that their departments were uncooperative. Cooke's recommendations called for the establishment of "student credit hours" as the unit of efficiency measurement, for rewarding professors on the basis of efficiency, and for a university system that more critically looked at itself rather than believing it was somehow beyond the criticisms of the society that supported it (Trombley, 1954).

Cooke was not through. When he finished with the university, another opportunity presented itself with the help of Taylor. In 1911, the new mayor of Philadelphia invited Taylor to become his director of public works. Taylor refused but recommended Cooke, who was happy to receive a chance to try out his ideas on efficiency in the public sector. His book *Our Cities Awake* (1918) presented his case for the improvement of municipal management. Over the course of four years he saved over $1 million in garbage collection alone, and he personally sued the Philadelphia Electric Company in an attempt to force it to reduce its rates. The out-of-court settlement resulted in payments of over $1 million and a retroactive payment of nearly $200,000 to the city.

The push toward efficient productivity in the public sec-

tor, while mixed in terms of outcome, has emerged again in recent years. The city of Phoenix, for example, initiated a work
planning and control productivity improvement program in
1970. The program was a rather standard efficiency-oriented
program when it was implemented. Work methods were simplified and procedures were established. Standards of performance
or goals were developed for each department in city government,
and a reporting system was designed to ensure the efficient allocation of human and nonhuman resources. The information
system that resulted was helpful to supervisors in planning and
balancing the work of different groups (Aranda, 1982).

The results were impressive. For the decade of the 1970s
Phoenix realized savings and cost avoidances of over $2 million
a year, or $23 million over the period. In the 1980s the favor-
able trends continued and the morale of employees significantly
increased. Cooke would have been proud of these achievements.

When World War I erupted, Cooke proposed to Secretary
of War Newton Baker that an efficiency organization was needed
to ensure that the war be "managed scientifically." The secretary
adopted the suggestion, and the little-known efficiency engineer
became a prominent figure in Washington, D.C. At one point
President Hoover appointed Cooke to a committee to eliminate
waste in industry; another familiar member of the committee, as
noted previously, was Harrington Emerson (Drury, 1922).

Cooke's contribution to the efficiency movement was significant. Until he came on the scene, manufacturing industries
were the only targets of scientific management. Cooke applied
the same principles to higher education and to government at
all levels. He was convinced that few principles of management
applicable to business could not be applied to other fields as
well.

If Cooke was not impressed with many of the professors
and administrators he found in colleges and universities, it may
have been because he recognized the critical importance of the
university of today in training the industrial leaders of tomorrow. As one IBM executive has stated, "There can be no factories of the future unless there are universities of the future

educating people now" (DeMott, 1984). The Japanese recognize this critical "town and gown" connection. Some of those who believe that the Japanese work ethic is "cracking" place a portion of the guilt on the universities in Japan. The professors and students appear to be more passive than previously, and that worries some about the future of the Japanese economic miracle (Smith, 1984).

While Cooke extended the principles of scientific management to other fields, Wallace Clark expanded the concepts to other countries.

Wallace Clark: Efficiency Goes on Tour. Wallace Clark was born in 1880 and graduated from the University of Cincinnati. He worked in various clerical positions and became the private secretary to the president of Remington Typewriter. He was associated with Henry Gantt's consulting firm before opening his own practice in 1920. Clark traveled extensively in Poland, England, and France applying the principles of scientific management (Smiddy, 1958).

An admirer of Henry Gantt and his graphical planning or scheduling techniques, Clark believed that the Gantt Chart would be useful in controlling Russia's "five-year plans" (Clark, 1922). (Gantt's ideas will be discussed in Chapter Eight.) He was associated with people like Walter Polakov, who was instrumental in taking many concepts of scientific management to the USSR (Wren, 1980). Clark also absorbed many of the ideas about the human being that Gantt espoused. He worked freely with labor unions to improve industrial efficiency, as did Cooke. However, Clark will always be remembered first and foremost for his work in taking the concepts of scientific management and industrial efficiency to many of the nations of Europe. One of the most distinguished awards given in management today is the Wallace Clark International Management Award for distinguished contributions to scientific management in the international field. Cooke carried scientific management out of the factory and into the university and city hall. Clark took the same message over the Atlantic and in so doing widened the circle of groups and people knowing American management systems.

High-Tech Efficiency

Efficiency has been identified so closely with the scientific management era that many people think of it only in terms of the "smokestack industries." Nothing could be more incorrect. Even innovation has to be efficient to some degree. That recognition makes efficiency just as relevant to today's managers as it was to the managers of the scientific management period.

Drucker (1985) argues that the process of innovation can be learned and practiced and that entrepreneurs should search purposefully for sources of innovation while applying the behavioral principles available to them. To illustrate his point, Drucker notes that McDonald's is an example of entrepreneurship even though owner Ray Kroc did not invent anything. Instead, Kroc standardized a product, designed processes and tools, based training on the analysis of work, and set the standards success demanded. In other words, he applied management concepts and techniques to the problem of creating value for the customer. The result has been an efficiently produced product that is in great demand around the world. The Golden Arches are familiar sights in Chicago, Paris, Houston, Munich, San Francisco, Geneva, Seattle, and Rio. The price is always competitive and the taste is predictable—some say it is even good.

Drucker defends his arguments with diverse actual business examples, even though high-tech industries continue to provide much of the excitement of our modern organizational society. If America is to be competitive in the international arena, it is clear that productivity improvements will have to take place in traditionally white-collar sectors of the work force as well as in blue-collar occupations.

Bolte (1986) notes that the productivity of engineers is customarily measured against a schedule by tracking milestone accomplishments. However, this is not a genuine measure of productivity or efficiency. To provide a more accurate measure, a system known as *engineering performance analysis* (EPA) was developed at Intel. The system was designed to (1) highlight problems in human resource allocation, (2) evaluate the value of alternative methods and systems, (3) balance staff and work load, (4) measure group performance, (5) forecast personnel requirements, and (6) schedule work.

One of the major thrusts of EPA has been to shift routine, technical activities that can be performed by nonengineers to less highly paid employees. In one preliminary test case the following findings were generated:

1. Almost one-third of the reports being generated could be completely eliminated, over 40 percent of the remaining reports could be produced by technicians, and almost 20 percent could be routinely developed by a clerk.
2. Over half of the engineering change orders could be written by technicians.
3. Trouble calls could be reduced by over 40 percent with better documentation, and two-thirds of the remaining trouble calls could be effectively handled by nonengineers.

The director of productivity at Intel has reported significant savings and greater efficiency in the use of valuable engineering talent through the implementation of EPA. This type of program illustrates the increasing importance of efficiency measures in nonmanufacturing, service-oriented occupations. Such applications are particularly important in view of the fact that our economy is becoming increasingly service oriented. No longer are the majority of American workers employed in the steel mills, foundries, and automobile plants. Instead, they are engineers, barbers, teachers, physicians, dentists, and custodians. Little is known about efficiency-improving techniques in professional, technical, and service occupations. No one denies, however, that this is the work force of the future, and management must be prepared to deal with the unique challenges to efficiency these occupations will present.

Implications and Conclusions

Efficiency is as important today in the sterile production laboratories at Intel as it was seventy-five years ago in the smoky steel mills of Gary, Indiana, or the assembly lines of Detroit factories. Granted, efficiency may be realized and developed in different ways, but as long as there are competitive product markets, producers will survive only if they are reasonably efficient.

Consider, for example, the different ways efficiency can be realized and the ways it can be disguised under other labels. At Eastman Kodak the top-of-the-line Ektaprint copier is a recognized standard in the industry. The copier market is highly competitive, and companies like Canon and Xerox are always working to make improvements and provide the highest levels of customer service. Kodak, however, came up with an idea that increased efficiency while taking advantage of the unique needs of workers in high-technology industries. Quality inspectors were eliminated and workers were made responsible for their own inspections before the product was passed to the next stage in the production process. Greater job autonomy was achieved and costs were significantly reduced. Company officials report that since the beginning of the program in 1983 product defects have been reduced by 300 percent and production costs have been reduced by 70 percent ("The Push for Quality," 1987).

If America is to retain its role as a world industrial leader, efficiency and related factors such as quality must be the top priority of today's managers. The world, particularly selected areas, has proven its intention and determination to compete with American firms in their own ballpark. To date, nations such as Japan, Korea, and Hong Kong have experienced remarkable success. Renewed interest in returning to the basics of efficient and high-quality manufacturing, however, indicates a determination on the part of the United States and her managers to maintain the hard-earned position of number one.

PART TWO

Merging the Art and Science of Management

It may be that one of management's greatest virtues as a field of study is its willingness to accept relevant knowledge, whatever its source. The well-known management consultant Saul Gallerman once told me that he was prepared to "dig for gold wherever he found it." If it was in old management books, that was quite satisfactory. As long as the gold was "high grade," the age of the mine did not matter. That seemed like good advice to me then and is even better advice today.

Engineering is the "mother discipline" of management. Admittedly, she was at times a reluctant—even unwilling—parent, but the legacy of engineering to management should never be ignored or forgotten. Engineering societies provided the only forums available for discussing management ideas, and engineers were the first to apply their art, science, and profession to business. However, as we will see, not all the advances in putting management on more respectable and more scientific foundations were accomplished by engineers. In fact, some of the most courageous attempts at synthesizing the field of management were initiated by people identified with the functional, process, or administrative organization tradition of management thought.

In this part we will look at three major topics. Chapter Four illustrates the importance that early engineers attached to the application of scientific methods to the study of work. Of particular significance was the value of science in making management "respectable." We will also see how, as the discipline has matured, the necessity of conventional science has been increasingly questioned. Chapter Five extends the discussion of science to the area of decision making, or, as Herbert A. Simon calls it, "the heart of executive activity." In this chapter the evolution of decision-making theory and practice is traced from the normative guidelines of management science to behavioral-descriptive models and ultimately to normative nonrational models such as muddling through and logical incrementalism.

Finally, in Chapter Six a relatively modern controversy, the nature of managerial work, is examined, because it relates directly to the issues of art and science in management. Although this final issue of Part Two does not have the history of the other issues discussed to this point, it is so fundamental to the future of management that it is included as a means of synthesizing much of the foregoing discussion.

CHAPTER 4

Science and Management

The Quest for Legitimacy

The factory system and the agrarian society that preceded it faced a similar problem: the problem of continuity, or how successive generations of farmers, skilled craftspeople, and artisans would be trained. For centuries training was accomplished by apprenticeships. The aspiring farmer worked with an experienced planter and observed successful behavior; the prospective merchant signed on with a person trained in accounts; future lawyers willingly served as clerks to those already practicing law. It should not surprise us that factory workers were trained the same way. Journeyman machinists, bricklayers, tool-and-die makers, and welders were expected to serve the familiar apprenticeship.

Apprenticeships were an effective means of ensuring an adequate supply of skilled workers. Learning by doing was the official teaching method, and the accomplished worker was an adequate teacher. It was an interesting system when viewed from the biases of today. We, for the most part, teach theory and delay practice. Historically, by contrast, theory was inferred from successful practice. Because practice preceded theory, the skilled and observant barber could learn enough anatomy to perform routine, although rarely successful, surgery; the literate and ambitious student could independently read enough books to pass the bar examination; and the well-intentioned minister and schoolteacher could preach the gospel or teach reading with little understanding of theology or psychology.

It was not until the application of science and the use of the scientific method in medicine that the surgeon became a physician. It was not until the "science of jurisprudence" was widely applied that the practice of law became a learned profession, and it was not until science was applied to engineering that engineers gained significant social status.

The precedent was clearly established that if management was to acquire professional status it would have to apply scientific methods to the study and practice of organization. If only management could be recognized as an applied science, advocates reasoned, it would be accepted as a legitimate field of study. That was the thrust of Henry Towne's appeal more than a hundred years ago and one of the primary reasons the American Society of Mechanical Engineers was selected as the forum. Engineering was already legitimate.

Science and Scientific Management

An examination of the significance of science in management requires immediate reference to Frederick Taylor. At last we are able to introduce this one about whom so much has already been said. Babbage was a mathematician and Ure was a doctor. Both were trained in science and appreciated its power. Neither, however, had a vision of how science could improve the reputation as well as the practice of management. This distinction was reserved for Taylor and a few other engineers, such as Gantt, Cooke, Clark, and others who were active in the early formation of scientific management and the efficiency movement. From the time of Taylor, the importance of science is a recurring theme in management.

Frederick Taylor and the Role of Science. Taylor was born in Philadelphia in 1856. He was fortunate to have been born into a relatively wealthy family and to have the leisure to theorize about the factories that were so much a part of his surroundings. His inclination toward mechanics was evidenced early in life by his fascination with taking things apart and putting them together again (already Taylor sounds a lot like Babbage). This fascination led to an interest in science and eventually to the application of science to management. For example, his stated purposes for writing *The Principles of Scientific Management* (1914, p. 7) were as follows:

1. To show through simple illustrations the loss taking place in this country through inefficiency.
2. To convince the reader that the remedy for this loss lies in systematic management, not a futile search for extraordinary workers.
3. To prove the *best management* is a true science resting on defined laws, rules, and principles. To further prove the principles of scientific management are *applicable to all human activities* and when used correctly will result in astounding results.

An appreciation of the importance of science in Taylor's system requires some background knowledge. First, Taylor believed that the legitimacy of management rests on its ability to maximize the prosperity of both employers and employees. This, he believed, is necessary for success because the self-interest of the two groups is mutually reinforcing. Over the long run it is impossible to have one without the other. If, however, workers are to achieve their maximum productivity, they must perform work in the best way possible, which requires that managers scientifically study work and train laborers in the optimum way of accomplishing jobs.

Even though Taylor believed that the interests of workers and employers are mutually reinforcing, he was a realist. He knew that years of doing work the same old way would make change difficult. Workers believed that it was in their own self-interest to "soldier," or work at less than their maximum pace, and, in fact, existing management systems made it to the workers' best interest to soldier. Procedures used in most trades were based on inefficient rules of thumb rather than scientifically determined methods. The most effective management systems of Taylor's day, or the "finest type of ordinary management," were those that provided an incentive for the greatest personal performance. Taylor called this *management of initiative and incentive.*

The problem with these systems resulted from the fact that the responsibility for productivity was placed almost exclusively on the worker. Taylor believed that managers should share in this responsibility. Managers should gather, tabulate, and classify information and, through the use of science, reduce it to principles, rules, laws, and formulas that summarize all the workers' experiences and that can be used as guides for better performance of daily tasks. The practical guidelines developed from this activity of management should then be taught to workers, and measures should be taken to ensure that the proper principles are followed. Managers, under Taylor's system, were expected to perform a new, vital, and highly respectable task. Their duty was to develop a science of each element of human work and replace old rules of thumb. In the process they were to scientifically select, train, teach, and develop workers to their maximum potential. A critical part of the developmental process was training each worker in the proper way to accomplish different tasks.

It would have shocked Taylor to learn that in one of Ford's "better" plants, making two engines a day takes a work force made up of almost 200 job classifications, an inventory backlog of three weeks, and 800 square feet of floor space to support one worker. In a Toyota plant in Japan, one worker can make more than four times as many engines a day with almost half the floor space, a one-hour backlog of inventory, and a supporting work force composed of only seven job classifications (Murrin, 1984). The difference has to be more than the Japanese worker.

Taylor advocated the scientific approach as the solution for this type of productivity problem because he respected its power in improving industrial efficiency. He also recognized the dangers that the mechanistic application of science could entail. He was emphatic in stating that the "mechanisms" of scientific management should never replace its philosophy. The philosophy was a scientific attitude that insisted on data collection, tabulation, and the application of knowledge to problems of an industrial society. The mechanisms were techniques such as time studies, functional foremanship, instruction cards, differential piece rates, and cost systems. These were merely techniques. Scientific management, on the other hand, was a "mental revolution" that advocated an entirely new way of managing work. An earlier book by Taylor, *Shop Management* (1903), had dealt with the techniques or mechanisms. In *The Principles of Scientific Management*, his goal was to present the elements required by the mental revolution.

It is clear that Taylor looked at science as an important aspect of good management. Without data, theory, principles, and laws, no one was likely to take management seriously. However, true science, the kind that leads to informed professional practice, is more than technique, formulas, and laws. It is a mental revolution, a way of looking at the world and a method for problem solving. In view of this, Taylor knew that if his system was to be widely practiced, success stories were essential. His quest for such illustrations began early in his career.

Trials and Triumphs of Taylor's System. It was not an easy road Taylor chose to travel in his attempt to prove the superiority of his science-based system of management. Industry had functioned for centuries without the application of science, and not many people were willing to try something new—especially something as radical as scientific management. Taylor was, however, committed to science and to the system he had developed to apply it to work in factories.

I will not attempt a psychoanalytic probe of Taylor's motivations at this point, although such studies are available. However, at least a passing understanding of Taylor's personality is necessary to understand his obsession with efficiency, time, and order (Kakar, 1970).

Taylor was born to a strong Quaker tradition. It may have been his fear of disappointing his demanding mother that caused him not to enroll at Harvard or to follow his father in the practice of law. It could have been his failing eyesight, his fascination with mechanical things, or one of many other reasons that prompted him instead to become an apprentice patternmaker and machinist at the Enterprise Hydraulic Works. Little of consequence happened on this job, and Taylor left to accept employment at Midvale Steel Company. Taylor was known to the owners of Midvale Steel, and he learned the ropes of the steel business from two demanding supervisors who taught him both character and self-control. During this time he displayed an incredible amount of creativity in the mechanical arts, completed his degree in mechanical engineering through evening classes and home study at the Stevens Institute of Technology, and secured a number of patents for a variety of inventions. He was no stranger to science and he practiced it well.

By the time he was thirty-five years old, he had become a famous management consultant. He left Midvale Steel to accept a job offered by an admirer. This time he failed in his work as general manager and began to move from job to job. In some cases his ideas would be successful; in others, his ideas would fail. Because of his determination and personality, Taylor could not deal with these ups and downs and experienced two nervous breakdowns.

Just when things seemed hopeless, one of his former bosses at Midvale Steel who had been promoted to vice-president of Bethlehem Steel Company offered him a job. Things were better at Bethlehem. Taylor surrounded himself with admiring disciples such as Henry Gantt and was given substantial freedom in implementing his ideas. Success, unfortunately, is sometimes an enemy. It certainly was to Taylor, who became dogmatic when any aspect of his system was questioned. When he left on a short vacation, his enemies seized the opportunity and "changed the lock on his door." He was no longer welcome at Bethlehem Steel, and his loyal colleagues were fired. Even the vice-president who had hired him was forced to resign.

After this incident Taylor could no longer "afford to work for money." He consulted, wrote important papers on shop management and the mechanical arts and sciences, and enjoyed life a little more than in the past. In 1910 his testimony in the Eastern rate cases, involving the railroads and their inefficiencies, sent his ideas throughout the country as headlines on all the major papers. Taylor was in the process of showing how, through the application of scientific principles to the management of work, freight rates and labor costs could be reduced while at the same time the wages of workers could be increased. He made his point even though his performance under questioning once again revealed his emotional problems and his dogmatic attitudes.

Taylor produced compelling data in support of his system. At Bethlehem Steel his studies on pig iron shoveling reportedly increased labor productivity by almost 400 percent, accompanied by a 60 percent increase in wages. Taylor's solution to the problem of inefficiency (as he called it, the "greatest evil" of his time) was the application of scientific methods to the study and improvement of work. This type of study and improvement, it should be remembered, was the responsibility of management in Taylor's system.

Taylor's recommendations came at a particularly critical time. Yet, he also had his critics. Some of the criticisms were directed at his character and personality, while others focused on his work. For example, Hoagland (1957) argued that experiments on pig iron shoveling could be traced to 1699 and that Charles Babbage conducted experiments of this nature long before Taylor. Hoagland lists twenty people who studied shoveling between the end of the seventeenth and the beginning of the nineteenth centuries. None was acknowledged by Taylor, even though he stated in *The Principles of Scientific Management* (1914, p. 54) that he had hired a college graduate to review all the works on shoveling in English, French, and German.

Wrege and Perroni (1974) are even more severe in their criticism of the pig iron shoveling research. They contend that the entire experiment was "more fiction than fact" and present examples of how Taylor's various accounts of the details of the study were inconsistently presented. Taylor's discovery of the "law of heavy loading" and pioneering work on rest periods were, according to these authors, largely a hoax.

It is confusing to read the criticisms of Taylor, especially those that reflect adversely on his character and integrity (Wrege and Stotka, 1978). His obsession with his reputation would seem to preclude the actions for which he is frequently

criticized. We cannot, however, disregard the criticisms as un-
founded, since they are, for the most part, well documented
(Bluedorn, Keon, and Carter, 1985).

Taylor also has his champions. Copley's (1923) two-vol-
ume work on Taylor as the father of scientific management is
largely complimentary. Boddewyn (1962) maintains that most
of the criticisms result from quotations taken out of context
and from the overzealousness of Taylor's followers. The most
systematic defense of Taylor, however, comes from Locke
(1982), who states that many of the criticisms have been "in-
valid or involved peripheral issues, and [Taylor's] ideas and contributions often have gone unacknowledged" (p. 14). When we
look closely at what has been used by managers, it is evident
that many, perhaps most, of Taylor's ideas have stood the test
of time (Frey, 1976). This is particularly true of his advocacy of
science and the role it can play in the practice of management.
Taylor's character was questioned, but few doubted the potential improvements that the application of science to the problems
of industry could make when used according to his guidelines.

Taylor was not the only one who advocated the application of science to problems of management. His willing followers were many, but few were more devoted than Henry L. Gantt,
the person who hosted the meeting with attorney Brandeis in
preparation for the Eastern rate cases.

Other Advocates of Scientific Management. Henry L.
Gantt was born just five years after his mentor but was reared in
a completely different setting. Gantt's family owned a planta-
tion in Maryland but lost their fortune after the Civil War. Even
though he was later able to go to Johns Hopkins, his childhood
was characterized by austerity. He enjoyed little of the "good
life" that was familiar to Taylor. After qualifying as a mechanical engineer at the Stevens Institute of Technology while teaching school, he became the assistant to the chief engineer (Frederick Taylor) at Midvale Steel. Gantt and Taylor worked well
together in their early years and jointly held six patents. Their
work was so successful that Gantt followed Taylor to Simonds
Rolling Company and then Bethlehem Steel, where both were
fired. Gantt was a successful consultant on his own and com-

pleted many challenging assignments that provided him with a degree of personal fame (Alford, 1934; Peterson, 1986).

In Gantt's later writing (1919) his appreciation for and advocacy of the scientific method in management were less a theme than in his early work. In *Work, Wages, and Profits* (1910), his first chapter addresses the importance of science to management. Gantt believed that in order to achieve high levels of industrial efficiency, managers would have to apply the same careful scientific analysis to every detail of labor as chemists and biologists apply in their work. In his view, careful scientific analysis of management problems "never fails" to show feasible improvements in work methods that were previously unsuspected. Gantt believed that there is no way to develop general laws other than through scientific analysis and that sufficient evidence exists to suggest that such analysis is applicable to problems of work and labor.

According to Gantt, improvements in management require the elimination of chance and accidents. Successful management is the accomplishment of goals through the use of knowledge derived from scientific analysis. He made it clear that the legitimacy of management rests to a great extent on its ability to accomplish results through the use of scientific methods. This requires applied research into the problems of industry and elevates practical research activities to the status of more "pure" forms of scientific reasoning (Spriegel and Myers, 1953).

It is particularly interesting how Gantt accepted the idea of analysis and synthesis proposed by Lillian Gilbreth. He advocated studying complex operations by breaking them down into their simple components and analyzing each (*analysis*). When the analysis of each element is complete, the complex whole is then reassembled by adding successive simple components (*synthesis*) until the most efficient form of the complicated operation is recognized and used.

Gantt stated that the attempt to substitute scientific knowledge for opinion was the true meaning or spirit of scientific management. In his view, we might even choose a better phrase, like "the scientific method applied to management"

(Rathe, 1961). Taylor's system was built on the application of science to problems of industry, and Gantt agreed with almost all of Taylor's ideas except his system for rewarding labor.

Although he never worked directly with Taylor, Frank Gilbreth enthusiastically agreed with Taylor's scientific approach and extended it into the area of motion study. Taylor had focused primarily on time studies and the determination of the amount of work a "first-class" worker could do in a specified period. Gilbreth supported the notion of time study but only after one was sure that the motions involved in work had been reduced and that the "one best way" to do a particular job had been established.

The similarities between Taylor and Gilbreth were much greater than either shared with Henry Gantt. Taylor had an opportunity to attend Harvard and chose to become a machinist instead. Gilbreth qualified for admission to M.I.T. but decided to be a bricklayer because masons were considered "kings of mechanics" (L. M. Gilbreth, 1973). At the age of thirty-six he married Lillian Moller, who completed her Ph.D. in psychology and became Frank's close associate in the work of scientific management for the remainder of his life.

Scientific management to the Gilbreths was based on measurement. Its aim was to eliminate waste and reduce the amount of fatigue a worker experienced doing a job. To be respectable as an art and science, management needed to consider problems according to the scientific method—that is, by dividing the problem according to its elements and submitting each element to detailed study (Gilbreth and Gilbreth, [1917] 1973). Through careful analysis of the motions involved in bricklaying, Frank Gilbreth was able to increase the number of bricks a single man could lay from 175 to 350 per hour, thereby increasing productivity by 100 percent.

In much of the work of the Gilbreths, problems were stated in precise scientific terms. They treated the amount of work, for example, as a dependent variable, while they measured the influence of such independent variables as those relating to the worker (brawn, experience, fatigue, etc.); the surroundings, equipment, and tools (clothes, lighting, union rules, etc.); and motion (acceleration, speed, etc.). Management systems were characterized on the basis of how scientific they were in their approach to problem solving. *Traditional management* was the term applied to management systems based on rules of thumb and passed down from worker to worker and supervisor to worker. *Transitory management* was used to describe systems that attempted some but not all of the improvements recommended by Taylor's mental revolution. *Scientific management*, or the "ultimate management system," was the type recommended by Taylor (F. B. Gilbreth, [1912] 1973).

Lillian Gilbreth ([1914] 1973) used the same classification system but defined the ultimate system more specifically as a type of management that "is a science" and has been developed through studies and experiments. In her view, any study of management that proposes to be scientific must use investigations based on analysis and synthesis. Through analysis an aspect of management such as work is taken apart and broken down into its essential elements. Through synthesis it is put together again, including only those elements that are absolutely necessary for the performance of the task. This approach clearly provides the logical foundation for motion study. When properly conceived, scientific management contains within it a substantial improvement for the welfare of workers through higher wages, reduced fatigue, and generally improved working conditions.

Management emerged in response to a call for the application of scientific methods to the problems of a factory system. Science was recognized from the beginning as the only real approach to building legitimacy and professionalism. The scientific management writers, particularly those we have discussed— Taylor, Gantt, and the Gilbreths—did much to gain recognition for management and the scientific approach. They also convinced many highly qualified advocates, such as Emerson, Clark, and Cooke, who made their own unique contributions in eliminating waste and inefficiency. However, they did little to unite management into a theory that could be taught in a holistic manner. Experiments could provide principles and laws that could be taught to a particular worker about the best way to do a specific task. But if management was to become genuinely respectable, it had to have a theory or theme that would unite many of the isolated fragments of information generated by the engineer.

Administrative Organization and the
Unification of Management

The scientific management writers recognized the importance of analysis and synthesis in developing a respectable science of management. However, they were much better at analysis, or breaking complex processes such as work into individual elements, than at synthesis. Developing a unified theory became the quest of another group of writers who helped establish the administrative organization, or functional, view of management.

Toward a Unified Theory of Management. Management history most often remembers Henri Fayol and other proponents of administrative management and organization for the functions, principles, and tasks they identified and isolated. One of their most significant contributions, however, was their ability to synthesize the contributions of their contemporaries and predecessors.

If writers for the popular business press today knew much about Henri Fayol, they would, no doubt, compare Lee Iacocca to this French industrialist. Both accomplished something that few managers are able to achieve: saving a giant corporation from bankruptcy. Fayol was born in 1841 and was the youngest student in his graduating class at the National School of Mines. When he was only nineteen, he was hired as an engineer at the Commentary pits of the Commentary-Fourchambault Company. He remained with the firm for his entire career and after retirement retained the title of managing director until his death in 1925 (Breeze, 1985).

When Fayol arrived at Commentary-Fourchambault, the company was in the red. By the time of his retirement the firm was in sound financial condition. It is said that Fayol would accept no position of any type unless it directly contributed to his duties at Commentary. Fayol's most famous writing on management was *General and Industrial Management* (1949). The book was first published in bulletin form in 1916, but translation difficulties restricted its influence in the United States until its second English translation (Urwick, 1972). Fayol viewed management as a series of activities or functions. He offered a definition of management that applied to any type of industrial undertaking. Regrettably, Fayol was not able to complete the entire book before his death.

   An Attempt at Integration. Fortunately, much of Fayol's work has been preserved and expanded by Lyndall Urwick. Urwick published a masterpiece of synthesis and integration titled *Elements of Administration* (1944), which was a collection of five lectures presented in London at the Polytechnic College. The primary point underlying the lectures was that a logical scheme existed among the "principles of administration" formulated by various authorities. Urwick illustrated precisely how the different principles that had been worked out by people from different countries, with a variety of experiences and with no knowledge of each other's ideas, were "susceptible to logical arrangement" (p. 7). He believed that a technique of administration was in the process of being developed and that managers who attempted to operate without administrative principles ran the risk of appearing increasingly "amateurish." Urwick considered the phrase *scientific management* merely an affirmation that the methods of thought and respect for natural law that had led to developments in chemistry and engineering could and should be applied to human arrangements such as administration. *Elements of Administration* cautions us that there are no easy answers to complex management problems. Certainly, there is no "quick fix" (Kilmann, 1984).

   The format for synthesizing the concepts presented by Fayol and other writers on management was originally developed by Mooney and Reiley (1931), who stated that every principle in management has its process and effect, and when these have been correctly identified, they will, in turn, each have a principle, process, and effect.

   Urwick proposed the idea of *logical squares* as a way of comparing and organizing the concepts of management. Research is the principle underlying the entire process of administration, and when research is properly conducted logical squares can be formed for each principle. Note in Figure 1 how a logical square is constructed. The principle of investigation (research) facilitates the process of forecasting, which results in the effect or the plan. Forecasting is based on the principle of appropriateness and enters into process with organization. The effect is coordination. Planning is based on the principle of order, enters the process with command, and results in control.

Figure 1. Logical Square and Principles of Administration.

1. Principle	2. Process	3. Effect
Investigation	*Forecasting*	*Planning*
All scientific procedure is based on investigation of facts.	Investigation enters into process with forecasting . . .	and takes effect in a plan.

↓
Forecasting

Forecasting must be in terms that correspond with the realities of the situation, that is, with the general objective and broad policy of the undertaking. It therefore finds its underlying principle in appropriateness.

Appropriateness	*Organization*	*Coordination*
Is the organization suitable for the situation?	Forecasting enters into process with the provision of a suitable organization . . .	and takes effect in coordination.

↓
Planning

The purpose of planning is to secure systematic action in accordance with the general objective and broad policy.

Order	*Command*	*Control*
Planning imposes human and material order.	Planning enters process with command . . .	and takes effect in control.

Source: Adapted from Urwick, 1944.

The bulk of *Elements of Administration* is devoted to carefully constructing a pattern of administration and a unifying model for the elements of administration. The complexity of the synthesis can be appreciated only after it is recognized that the model makes a heroic attempt to relate Fayol's administrative principles, duties, and aspects of administration; Mooney and Reiley's principles of organization; Taylor's principles; and selected ideas of other writers. Urwick's work is a compelling argument in favor of a unifying theory of administrative science. His work contributes greatly to the legitimacy of management as a systematic field of study.

Other attempts were made to illustrate the consistency among the concepts and principles of various writers on the subject of administrative organization (Gulick and Urwick, 1947). Some were collections of essays brought together for the first time, but none compared to Urwick's *Elements of Administration*, which remains an outstanding attempt to integrate the field of management.

Science and Modern Management

Management as a recognized field of study is a century old, yet it is far from mature as either a theoretical or empirical science. The immaturity is a major cause of its limitations as a practical art. In spite of the pioneering works of engineers such as Taylor, the Gilbreths, and Gantt, and the courageous theoretical labors of people such as Urwick, management continues to seek legitimacy, and the arguments are basically the same as in the past.

The dedicated quest for a science of management evident in the work of the engineers and the great synthesizers like Urwick was interrupted somewhat during the human relations period. Although much attention was given to the virtues of scientific methods, one gets the impression in reading the emerging human relations thought during and after the Hawthorne studies of the 1930s that scientific methods became somewhat less important—at least scientific methods in the experimental sense so evident among the engineers. However, the tradition emerged again with the modern behavioral science movement in management.

Continued Quest for a Science of Management. In recent years the primary advocates of a traditional science of management and organization have been applied behavioral scientists—

in particular, psychologists. The most outspoken are those who advocate the application of natural science methods to the study of behavior in organizations. Behling (1980) examines five objections that are often raised to the application of natural scientific techniques to human beings and problems of management. He agrees there is some validity to objections such as that each individual, group, and organization is unique; that behavioral events are transitory; that human beings do not always behave the same way when they are being observed; and that natural science controls reduce realism. However, he argues that none of these limitations is sufficient to invalidate traditional scientific methods in understanding human behavior. He concludes his defense with an interesting play on Churchill's comment on democracy by stating that the natural science approach to understanding organizations and management "is the worst possible way to study organizations—except for all the others" (p. 489).

Other writers have indicated more directly the importance they attach to the use of traditional scientific approaches in management research. Scott (1975) contrasts modern behavioral scientists who have developed useful knowledge about human behavior in organizations with the "human relations saws of an earlier time" (p. 142). He agrees with the "amateurish" label of Urwick by indicating that unless managers today equip themselves to read, understand, evaluate, and use scientific reports of behavioral studies in organizations, they will soon find themselves outdated and incapable of dealing with the complexities of their jobs. The argument is extended by blaming the lack of management interest in the behavioral sciences on the general uselessness of prescientific conceptions of human behavior in organizations. In other words, managers have not been interested in earlier behavioral concepts because such concepts have not been useful in practice. This uselessness, in turn, is the result of a lack of scientific sophistication (Scott and Podsakoff, 1985).

Operant Conditioning and Management Science. One of the most familiar contemporary examples of the application of traditional science to management is *operant conditioning* in motivation theory and practice. The advocates of this approach in management trace many of their ideas to behaviorism in psychology and specifically to the ideas of B. F. Skinner (1974). Skinner's ideas about the proper way to study human behavior are based in his abiding faith in the scientific method. As he states, "The methods of science have been enormously successful wherever they have been tried. Let us then apply them to human affairs" (Skinner, 1953, p. 5). In perhaps his most challenging, and to some his most frightening, writings he advocates the development of a "technology of behavior" that would allow us to adjust the growth of the world's population as rapidly as we correct the course of a spaceship. This behavioral technology should be, according to Skinner (1971), as powerful as our present physical and biological technologies.

The most complete development of behaviorism in management is the subfield known as behavior modification, or organizational behavior modification (O.B. Mod.) as it is often called (Luthans and Kreitner, 1975). The theory underlying O.B. Mod. is the Skinnerian concept of positive reinforcement.

Familiar theories of motivation such as that of Maslow (1970) take an internal view and concern themselves with things like needs, desires, attitudes, and aspirations. Approaches to motivation such as that of Skinner are external in the sense that they describe and attempt to explain human motivation in terms of its consequences. The key to understanding Skinner's views and the managerial prescriptions that can be deduced from them is the *schedule of reinforcement*, or how desired acts are rewarded or not rewarded.

Emery Air Freight was one of the early business firms to receive a great deal of press coverage for the results it achieved through the practical use of positive reinforcement techniques ("At Emery Air Freight . . . ," 1973). Some estimate that Emery benefited by more than half a million dollars in the first year of its reinforcement program. Another, more recent, example of the use of operant conditioning principles in management is an experiment by Scandinavian Airlines. The airline selected a group of reservation sales personnel and through the principles of positive reinforcement significantly increased performance of the agents in the direction desired by the organization (Feeney, Staelin, O'Brien, and Dickinson, 1982).

The development of a successful behavior modification program relies on the skillful use of operant conditioning principles. The manager first identifies the target or desired behaviors she or he wants to achieve. Baseline measurements are then taken to provide a reference point against which change can be measured. For example, in one case at Emery, the goal was improvement in the utilization rate of the standardized containers into which smaller packages were placed. Managers and employees initially believed the containers were in use 90 percent of the time, but careful measurement revealed 45 percent was a more accurate figure. Care was taken to analyze the factors that led to the improved utilization rate of containers (antecedent conditions) and the consequences of a higher utilization rate. The behavior change program was implemented by providing positive feedback to dockworkers each day the utilization rate fell between 45 and 95 percent. Many companies have found that both tangible rewards and information feedback increase the rate of progress toward target levels of accomplishment. As with all good change programs, it is important to frequently evaluate and update the use of behavior modification programs.

Although some people fear that overzealous use of O.B. Mod. and other operant conditioning programs could become a new form of social engineering, advocates point to their effectiveness as proof that scientific principles and programs can be applied with precision to human behavior in organizations.

Final Update on Science and Management. There are many indications of the maturity of an academic field and the professionalization of a practical art. Unlike the applied psychologists, some highly influential writers in management believe there is little need to be constrained by the conventions of traditional science in our search for organizational understanding. Some even argue that management has attained enough legitimacy to enjoy the freedom of using relatively unorthodox methods in the study of organizations. Perhaps the most familiar deviations have come in the areas of organizational culture and symbolic management.

Weick (1979), in presenting his view of organizing, states that his "sympathies in inquiry lie with people who can think deeper than a fact" (p. 25). He declares himself free to seek knowledge wherever it may be and to pursue it using whatever techniques seem appropriate. This, according to him, is legitimate because all "slants on organization are partly true, partly false, partly incomplete, and partly irrelevant" (p. 26).

Frost (1985) reinforces this approach by arguing that organizations are not nearly so rational, logical, and objective as models of organizational behavior would suggest. In this light, it is essential that managers and administrators in all types of organizations be perceptive to the subjective aspects of organizations. Managers need to recognize the meanings that different employees attach to events and actions in organizations. To do so requires an increased appreciation of the symbolic nature of human actions in organizations and an understanding of unconventional means of gaining insights into the subjective side of organizational behavior.

It is not likely, or even desirable, that managers will approach their work from an analytical and objective perspective. There is a considerable subjective aspect of management that is equally real and worthy of attention. However, science and the scientific method offer managers a resource that should be freely used when appropriate.

The purpose of the application of scientific approaches is no longer merely to build respectability for management. Today science is not only a way to manage but also a phenomenon to be managed. High-technology industries that are directly or indirectly built on the application of science require increasingly effective management if they are to realize their potential contributions at competitive costs. This reality alone will ensure the continued trend of a closer association between management and science.

Implications and Conclusions

Management has made a great deal of progress scientifically since its beginning more than a hundred years ago. The engineers appreciated the power of science and resolved to use the methods they knew best in attacking the problems of the factory system. They emphasized facts, data, and technique. As far as analysis was concerned—that is, the breaking down of complex problems into simple elements that could be systematically studied—the engineers had no equal. They were not, as a rule, very good at synthesis, or putting the elements back into a coherent whole. Administrative organization writers such as Urwick were masters at synthesis. It was for them to build the theory on which much of modern management practice is based.

While it may be true that in some circles science has been taken too far, most objective observers agree that the legitimacy of management has been greatly improved by the application of scientific management. Young management graduates are frequently criticized as being too involved in "counting beans," building models that are incomprehensible to traditional managers, and generally projecting the image of planocrats and technocrats. However, they remain in demand in many large, well-managed organizations because they have learned better than their counterparts of a short generation ago the benefits of the scientific approach to problem solving and decision making.

It is not uncommon to have physicians, lawyers, and even engineers enroll in graduate management courses. That is something that rarely happened even a decade ago. The reasons for this new respectability are complex and certainly involve more than the use of the scientific method. However, we should not minimize the importance of this factor in the improving image of management as a field of study and as a practical art. Not all the problems of organizations have been solved. Of those that have been solved, not all were resolved through the use of science. However, many were, and science offers the potential for solving many more in the future. We should, as Weick stated, not be constrained totally by facts and should solve management problems using any and all approaches at our disposal. At the same time, we are forced to agree with Behling (1980) that to date, no approach to the study of management and organizations has provided better results than traditional science. Things may change in the future, but until they do credit must be given where credit is due. Science has done much for management.

CHAPTER 5

Decision Making

The Heart of Executive Activity

The primary function of management, says Akio Morita (1986), chairman of the board and chief executive officer of Sony Corporation, is decision making. Decisions are required for making the hamburgers at McDonald's, assigning beds to the medical departments at the local hospital, and loading and unloading airline passengers at O'Hare Airport. Unnoticed decisions are a part of almost every activity in our lives, personally and professionally.

In the previous chapter we reviewed the importance of science to the legitimacy of management. The controversy there provides an opportunistic lead-in to an analysis of decision making because the two issues are similar. Of all the areas of modern management, scientific methods have been applied more to decision making than any other. There are many who think of decision making as a rational, logical, and entirely systematic process. Others lean more toward a less rational view and see decision making in more behavioral and relatively unsystematic terms. Yet most informed observers agree that decision making occupies much of all managers' time, even if they do not agree that it is their only function. In fact, some believe that the one thing "generic" to the job of management is decision making. Herbert A. Simon (1960) has called it the "heart of executive activity."

The important controversy surrounding management decision making involves the more exacting question of how choices are actually made under conditions of uncertainty. Managers are people who earn their living in high-pressure, uncertain, and unforgiving environments. The result is often an inability to engage in reflective calculations and well-structured work schedules. How, then, can a person be an effective decision maker under such unpredictable conditions?

Rational Decision Making and Management

We have already demonstrated the impossibility of managers acting in a totally logical manner. If they could, the application of conventional methods of science to almost all areas of management would be greatly simplified. Decision making, however, has always been considered an exception to this lack of logic, since it is the closest thing management has to "real science." The systematic nature of operations research and applied optimization theory has been guarded carefully, although the idea of logical human choice, interestingly, did not emerge from management but from philosophy, sociology, and economics long ago.

One of the relatively recent and certainly one of the most influential advocates of the idea of rationality in decision making had little knowledge of and even less interest in management, although he was the foremost social scientist of his day—perhaps of the century (Weiss, 1983). Max Weber was born in Germany in 1864. His father was a lawyer and active in politics. His mother was deeply religious and dedicated to humanitarian causes. After distinguishing himself as a legal scholar at the University of Heidelberg and the University of Berlin, Weber became a professor of political economy at the University of Freiburg and later at Heidelberg.

Like Taylor, Weber was given to episodes of nervous illness. While he was still a young man, the illness became severe and forced him to resign his position at the university and spend years doing little more than traveling. After being drafted and serving time in the army, Weber accepted his first teaching job in twenty years at the University of Munich. At the age of only fifty-six and at the height of his career he died in 1920.

Throughout his brief and difficult life, Weber wrote on a variety of topics, including the sociology of religion, the effects of assembly lines on workers, and the theory of social and economic organizations (Kronman, 1983). His contributions are so far reaching that he is claimed by a number of academic disciplines, including sociology, economics, and philosophy. However, it is his ideas on the rational nature of human beings and organizations that concern us here because of the implications they suggest for decision making.

Rationality and Common Sense. The world observed by Weber was not just. It was dominated by class consciousness and nepotism. To be an officer in the Prussian army, for example, presupposed an aristocratic birth. Leadership in government and industry was no different. To Weber such things appeared as a ridiculous waste of human resources. Was it not possible for the working class to produce leaders as well as followers? This type of injustice resulted for the most part, in Weber's view, from the imperfection of human judgment. It was unfortunately a characteristic of human nature to hire relatives and preserve the wealth of the rich even if it disadvantaged society in the process. Weber's solution, perhaps surprising for a social scientist, was to free the individual as much as possible from the judgments that were so often clouded by emotion. This could best be accomplished through the organization of work in ways that followed Weber's "ideal bureaucracy." The ideal bureaucracy does not exist in reality but provides a basis for theorizing about work and how it is done in large groups. It is, according to Weber, a "selective reconstruction" of the real world.

In the ideal bureaucracy, selection and tenure are based on competence—*what* you know, not *whom* you know. Rules, regulations, and procedures that are tried and shown to be valid are the basis for decision making, and authority is distributed according to position and rank rather than divine rights and traditions (Weber, 1947). This organization has another compelling characteristic that makes it superior to all other known structures. The administrator at the top of the hierarchy cannot know everything about the choices he or she is required to make, but help is available. Qualified specialists assembled at lower levels can filter the most appropriate information and send it to the top. Since, in the ideal form of organization, these experts are not motivated to protectively screen information, it is possible, at least theoretically, for top managers to become better informed while dealing with only a portion of the total information.

The result of Weber's ideal bureaucracy is a form of rationality that has become the standard in much of modern decision theory—not a rationality in terms of psychological normality but in terms of information. Thus, the rational manager is the manager who is informed. The nonrational manager merely lacks knowledge. The rational manager has a purpose, a goal. The nonrational manager does not. On this basis Weber spoke of rationality as a means of differentiating one type of action from other types. Rational behavior is directed toward unambiguous goals, and the means of achieving the goals are selected on the basis of the best available information (Weber, 1947).

Logic of Normative Decision Theory. The legitimacy of what has become known as rational, normative, or mathematical decision theory was established during World War II. The Operational Research Unit of the Royal British Navy and a similar group attached to the American Tenth Fleet known as the Antisubmarine Warfare Operations Research Group (ASWORG) were spectacular in solving some of the most troubling problems of the war. Using a combination of mathematics and other sciences, these groups were instrumental in improving the odds of survival for Allied convoys crossing the North Atlantic and in selecting "optimal" depth-charge patterns for aircraft and surface vessel attacks on U-boats (Pitt, 1977). After the war, Henry Ford II reasoned that if problems of war could be solved by mathematics and statistics, so could the problems of management. Attention turned to helping managers make complex decisions, and in the process *normative decision theory* was born.

Normative decision theory, as the name implies, is designed to assist managers accomplish the goals (norms) they set for organizations. Decision rules become prescriptions for maximizing profits and revenues—or, if one is comfortable with such abstract measures, decision theory can even maximize one's "utility function." In its purest sense, normative theory assumes that managers are utility (satisfaction) maximizers who know all their options and the outcomes associated with the various options and can rank their preferences among the alternative choices they face in a particular situation. They are, in other words, rational in the Weberian sense of being informed.

Operating from the assumption of rationality, even strategic decisions can be structured in a manner that appears rational. Strategic decisions become defined processes consisting of setting goals, scanning the environment, identifying one's strategic capacity (that is, evaluating strengths and weaknesses), formulating alternative strategies, choosing a strategy, implementing the choice, and following up to ensure that goals are achieved (Ginter, Rucks, and Duncan, 1985).

As impressive as results of this approach have been, there has always been a recognition that somehow the assumption of the perfectly rational decision maker is out of touch with reality. Uncertainty is the rule, not the exception. Whereas Weber knew that his ideal bureaucracy was an abstraction, a simplification, a model, others have suspected that operations researchers and management scientists have placed more faith in decision matrices than is warranted. No one is as logical as the decision trees make one appear (McKean, 1985).

A Closer Look at Rationality

Weber introduced us to the importance of rationality, but Herbert A. Simon applied it to administrative behavior. Simon's analysis of rationality in decision making initially appears strange. After all, in a time when knowledge is so specialized that we can scarcely master a small part of even a highly specialized field, Simon emerges as one who has excelled in several. He was trained in political science at the University of Chicago, where he received his doctorate in 1943. He worked at the International City Managers Association and at the Bureau of Public

Administration at the University of California and taught at the Illinois Institute of Technology before going to Carnegie-Mellon University in 1949. He currently serves as the Richard King Mellon University Professor of computer science and psychology.

Simon has studied decision making, problem-solving processes, and artificial intelligence for over thirty years. His unusually significant research has been recognized by his election to the National Academy of Science and by awards from the American Psychological Association, the American Economic Association, and the Institute of Electrical and Electronic Engineers. In 1978 he received the Alfred Nobel Memorial Prize in Economics. Perhaps more than any other person, Simon has increased our understanding of human problem solving and decision making (Neuhaus, 1981).

Simon began developing his ideas on decision making and management in his first book, *Administrative Behavior* ([1946] 1976). The book was written for scholars interested in research, managers interested in practical aids for improving their performance, and students interested in learning more about management and decision making. The decision-making orientation of the book is established early when Simon notes that any practical activity consists of "deciding" and "doing." Management and administration should, therefore, be thought of as decision processes as well as processes involving action.

Simon looked at decisions in terms of a hierarchy. Each lower-level decision is concerned with implementing the goals set forth in the decision just above it. The decisions of the production superintendent in a steel mill, for example, directly involve the implementation of decisions made by the production vice-president. Supervisors under the authority of the superintendent will make their decisions and direct them toward implementing the decisions made by the superintendent. Decisions are logical means-ends relationships whereby the ends (goals) of one level become the means by which the next-higher-level goals will be accomplished. Decision-making behavior is purposeful when it is goal directed. It is rational to the extent that alternatives are selected that are directed toward the accomplishment of previously established goals.

Rationality, as Simon notes, is more complicated. The rationality envisioned by the operations researchers and classical economists is *objective rationality.* It results in decisions that maximize the values of the manager or the organization. This objective rationality never occurs, however, because it requires complete knowledge of all possible choices and their outcomes, and some means of supplying knowledge resulting from a lack of experience (Simon, [1946] 1976). If not objective, perhaps we can attain *subjective rationality,* whereby we maximize the outcome subject to the limited knowledge we possess about the decision situation. Upon investigation, however, we find that not even this "rationality" is possible.

To illustrate, Simon defines the general concept of *rationality* as "concerned with the selection of preferred behavior alternatives in terms of some system of values whereby the consequences of the behavior can be evaluated" (p. 75). The economic man or woman of classical economics could achieve the state of objective rationality but not the administrative man or woman who populates the real world of decision making. This person has limited knowledge, or *bounded rationality,* rather than perfect knowledge. In solving organizational problems this individual conducts a *sequential search* for randomly generated alternative solutions and achieves satisfactory rather than maximum outcomes. In other words, the person makes satisfactory decisions because he or she does not have, in Simon's words, "the wits to maximize" (p. xxvii). Even subjective rationality is denied, because maximizing choices within the bounds of knowledge is influenced more by the order in which alternatives are generated than by the preexistence of some clear guidelines for ensuring maximizing behavior (Cyert, 1979; March, 1978; Roach, 1979).

To illustrate, the administrative person in Simon's theory of decision making has, through experience, a sense of what constitutes satisfactory performance. If investors earn, say, 6 percent on their investment, the decision maker notices that employees do not complain that excessive profits are being made at the expense of lower wages, customers do not complain that the profits are being sustained by exorbitant prices, government regulators leave the company alone, and not one investor ever asked whether 6 percent is the absolute maximum that could have been earned. The decision maker thus focuses on this satisfactory return and abandons objective rationality. Next the decision maker searches within the bounds of rationality (that is, limits of his or her information) by randomly selecting alternative solutions in a sequential manner until an option promises a return of 6 percent or more. In the process, subjective rationality is sacrificed. Simon concludes that "what managers know they should do . . . is very often different from what they actually do" (Simon, 1987, p. 62).

The fame of Simon and others at Carnegie-Mellon University attracted many scholars to Pittsburgh who shared an interest in decision making. Richard Cyert and James March were two of the more famous, and in 1958 March and Simon collaborated in the publication of *Organizations.* The focus of this book is broader than the subject of decision making in a technical sense. It is, as the name implies, a book about organizations and management. However, the perceptive reader soon realizes that the ideas developed in *Administrative Behavior* occupy a place of more than passing importance in this book.

Cyert, Simon, March, and others of the so-called Carnegie school of thought likely did not anticipate the importance of their work on management and decision making. With the use of ideas such as satisficing (pursuing a satisfactory rather than a maximum outcome to a decision problem), bounded rationality, and sequential search, they did much to legitimize the view that managers are not rational problem solvers or reflective calculators. Decision makers do not operate under conditions of perfect knowledge, so uncertainty is the normal state of affairs. So confident did the researchers become in the accuracy of their ideas that they even suggested such things as "garbage can models" of decision making (Cohen and March, 1974; Cohen, March, and Olsen, 1972).

The garbage can model applies to a special type of organization known as the *organized anarchy.* Organized anarchies are illustrated by universities, think tanks or research organizations, and perhaps some health care organizations. In this type of organization, preferences are ill defined and often inconsistent. Technologies are unclear, and participation is fluid, with numerous examples of temporary personnel changes through "going and coming" as well as some degree of permanent change through turnover. Preferences or goals are found through action rather than the manager beginning with a set of predetermined goals and pursuing them. The mode of operation of the organized anarchy is best illustrated by the following quotation:

> [These organizations are] collections of choices looking for problems, issues and feelings looking for decision situations in which they might be aired, solutions looking for issues to which they might be the answer, and decision makers looking for work [Cohen, March, and Olsen, 1972, p. 2].

Humorous as this may sound, there is much truth to the idea of garbage can models of decision making. For our purposes it can only be looked on as one of several nonrational models of decision theory. These models add an important dimension to be considered by managers as decision makers. Yet the writers of the Carnegie-Mellon tradition of thought always seemed to stop short of actually advocating nonrationality. The credit for legitimizing nonrationality goes to other writers who agree that managers "do not have the wits to maximize" and who believe that that, in itself, is a virtue.

Science of Muddling Through

Charles Lindblom (1959) accelerated, at least in terms of public policy, the interest in nonrational models of decision making by introducing the idea of *muddling through*. This idea may have been formulated with reference to the public sector, but it has implications for all types of strategic decision making.

Like March and Simon, Lindblom begins with a rational view, which he calls the *rational comprehensive model*. This approach progresses logically from goal setting to implementation and follow-up or control (Lindblom, 1979). Somewhere between

the impossible (rational-comprehensive model) and the unaccept-
able (grossly incomplete analysis) lie Lindblom's "feasible" approaches to strategy. All the feasible approaches share one thing
in common: they are *incremental*, or proceed step by step from
what is unknown to what is known and desirable.

Although Lindblom defines at least three types of incremental analysis, the most important for our purposes is simple
incremental analysis. In all forms of incremental analysis the decision maker uses the method of *successive limited comparisons*
(SLC), whereby goals are never clearly established and pursued
as implied under normative decision theory. Instead, the decision maker simultaneously chooses a policy to attain an objective and the objective itself. Relationships between means and
ends in decision making are difficult, sometimes impossible, to
establish. In normative theory, policy decisions are "good" if
they accomplish a specified goal. In SLC, good policies are
those that are agreed on by the "key actors" in the organization.

In the rational-comprehensive method everything important is analyzed only when *important* is so narrowly defined
that it becomes meaningless. SLC simplifies this situation in two
ways. First, only policy alternatives that differ little from those
currently in effect are considered, thereby reducing the number
of options that must be weighed by the decision maker. Second, potentially important consequences of options are excluded
from consideration. Policies arrived at through SLC are not
once-and-for-all decisions but products of successive approxima-
tions. Theoretically, this method reduces errors because (1) past
outcomes provide the knowledge for constantly defining and
refining an organization's direction; (2) as a result of this constant redefinition, there is no need for "big jumps" toward new
and different goals; (3) previous predictions and forecasts can
be tested before proceeding; and (4) correcting past misalloca-
tions of resources is made easier since small steps in decision
making ensure that mistakes are corrected before major errors
occur.

Process of Muddling Through. There are many forms of
incrementalism, but a simple case will be sufficient to illustrate
the nature of the process. Unlike the decision maker pictured

by the operations researchers, the strategist in the process of muddling through does not behave in a totally predictable manner. As with the case of the satisficing manager (seeking a satisfactory outcome), the decision maker begins muddling by formulating a few equally simple goals that encompass the values, power, and overall interests of a few groups in and out of the organization. Next, the decision maker formulates an array of alternative options or strategies that will accomplish the goals. All of these strategies represent small, incremental movements from the present strategy or the status quo. Because only small, incremental strategy options are considered, they are familiar, drawn from the decision maker's past experience. Finally, the manager selects an option, even though the choice is not necessarily assumed to be the "best" way of accomplishing predetermined goals. The incrementalist never expects a goal to be fully achieved. Rather, he or she expects decisions merely to bring the desired outcome closer and closer.

While the details differ slightly, Lindblom's process is not unlike Simon's—at least not in principle. Both picture the decision maker as a nonmaximizing, compromising, and satisficing individual. The thing that distinguishes Lindblom's argument is that he does not advocate muddling through as a realistic, "second-best" approach to decision making but as the preferred way to make decisions. He makes it clear that muddling through can and should be constantly improving but that in almost all its forms incrementalism results in better decisions than the most feasible form of the rational-comprehensive model (Lindblom, 1979).

Systematic Muddling: Logical Incrementalism. James Brian Quinn (1980a) agrees with Lindblom to a point. He finds no argument with the contention that managers are less than perfectly rational. In fact, he states that decisions are an "artful blend of formal analysis, behavioral techniques, and power politics" (p. 3). Decisions, according to Quinn, are "typically fragmented, evolutionary, and largely intuitive" (1978, p. 7). However, he protests the contention that muddling is either nonrational or illogical. Instead of calling the process muddling, Quinn prefers to see it as "a purposeful, effective, proactive

management technique that is capable of improving and integrating both the analytical and behavioral aspects of strategy
formulation" (p. 8).

Logical incrementalism (LI) begins with the assumption
that goal setting is vague. The manager has an idea of where the
organization should go, but the objectives are not formalized—
for several reasons. Announcement of a set of formal goals
would tend to centralize decision making and give both loyal
and disloyal opposition an opportunity to see what one is "up
to," making it easier for them to rally around defeating one's
plans. Formal goals also increase the rigidity of thinking and
create the impression that goals are carved in stone. Finally, formalized goals can help competitors discover what the manager
hopes to accomplish, thereby aiding in the formulation of their
defensive strategy.

Rather than beginning as formal goals, strategic concerns
arise because the manager confronts some problem in relating
the firm and its current way of operating to the larger environment. Often systems for scanning the environment are not present or are ineffective, so the decision maker builds informal networks with people inside and outside the organization (Kotter,
1982; Luthans, Rosenkrantz, and Hennessey, 1985). These networks, however, do more than supplement information from
the formal lines of communication. They are built to ensure
that people at the top hear what they need to hear rather than
having important data filtered or screened out as information
flows up the hierarchy (Quinn, 1980b). The emphasis, unlike
in the case of muddling through, is not merely to make small,
nonthreatening changes but to actually find and attract effective members of the network who will offer options that go beyond the status quo. Perhaps even radical options will develop
if the network is properly constructed.

When problems develop with the organization's interaction with its environment, managers become convinced that
some type of strategic change is needed, and additional information is required before they can take actions with reasonable
confidence. Data are gathered and energy is devoted to building
support for the preferred option when it emerges. Unlike the

system described by March and Simon (1958), logical incrementalism rarely results in the selection of the first, randomly generated alternative. To the contrary, the manager consciously engages in constructing a broad array of options. A case is built to dislodge preconceived notions, even though at this point top executives are careful not to become too identified with a tentative notion that may prove to be a bad idea or to prematurely tip off competitors before a winning plan is developed. During this period of time the decision maker freely shops for ideas among trusted colleagues and employees and carefully tests them. Occasionally, a task force is commissioned to study the options. After a matter of time, and only after satisfying herself of the likelihood of success, the decision maker acts (Quinn, 1980b).

When the option is selected, implementation begins. At this point Quinn makes one of his greatest contributions to decision making by emphasizing the behavioral and political nature of implementation. The culture of the organization becomes a critical factor in employee acceptance of strategic change, and symbolic acts on the part of the decision maker take on important meanings. The CEO's presence or absence at a meeting, for example, may be interpreted as a signal regarding the importance attached to a new strategic direction.

Initially, the experienced executive is likely to introduce strategic changes as little more than tactical adjustments and to allow the time necessary to build support for the new direction. He takes particular care not to alienate allies or supporters and to build as much flexibility as possible. Always the decision maker is waiting for just the right time to announce the decision. Key events sometimes provide "windows" that briefly open and offer the opportunity to take the initiative. These windows may be created by the retirement of a strong opponent or a similar event.

Even when the decision maker attempts to "lay low," he or she is quite active in the strategic change required by new decisions. As Quinn (1980a, p. 11) notes, managers frequently use the hidden-hand approach but keep their hands busy even though they cannot be seen. Thus, Quinn makes the case for logical incrementalism not as muddling through but as an attempt to adapt to "the practical psychological and informational problems of getting a constantly changing group of people . . . to move together effectively in a constantly changing environment" (1980a, p. 12).

Quinn offers no apologies for the nonrational process of logical incrementalism. In the case of normative decision theory, making better decisions always implies moving from a second-best approach such as incrementalism to the rational, complete, normative model. To incrementalists, better decisions means practicing incrementalism more effectively while rarely, if ever, turning away from it to another technique (Lindblom, 1979).

When Necessity Becomes a Virtue

Cyert, March, and Simon talk of such behaviors as satisficing, bounded rationality, and sequential search as things decision makers do in an attempt to deal with the extreme complexity of the problems they face. These theorists have attempted to describe how decisions *are* made, not how they *should* be made. That is why their approach is appropriately referred to as *behavioral-descriptive theory.* It attempts only to understand and describe decision-making behavior. Lindblom and Quinn, by contrast, have sought guidelines managers can learn to aid in accomplishing organizational goals. Thus, their approach is normative because a norm is pursued, whether that norm is revenues, market share, profits, satisfaction, or a number of other outcomes.

In the sense that they are descriptions of how managers make decisions, logical incrementalism and muddling through share much in common with the work of Cyert, March, and Simon. However, in the sense that both Lindblom and Quinn believe their processes result in better decisions, their work is positioned closer to traditional normative models. However, there is little to suggest that nonrational decision theories result in better decisions than more rational theories (Duncan, 1987). Some of the problems are apparent.

First, neither logical incrementalism nor muddling through insists on clear, concise, and understood goal statements. To measure, monitor, and correct actions there must first be a standard, goal, or reference point from which deviations can be charted. Locke and Latham (1984) note that without understood, communicated goals and a timetable for reaching them, planning is reduced to "hollow rhetoric that leads to nothing but inaction" (p. 27).

Effects of Nonrational Models of Decision Making. Adams (1979) presents a convincing argument regarding the kinds of problems that develop when the impossibility of rationality is accepted. Some of the more important are:

1. Where quality and quantity are difficult to measure and goals are not properly developed, quantity sometimes becomes the substitute measure for organizational effectiveness. The manager may believe he is productive because meetings, telephone calls, and answering mail consume most of the day. Perhaps this explains why Mintzberg (1973) found managerial work to be so fragmentary.
2. Statistics make it obvious to anyone who reads the facts that managers are busy people who arrive at work early and go home late. They rarely have time to read and stay informed about the important events that could affect their business. Instead, they fight fires, respond to emergencies, and deal with crises most of the day. Even though everyone works hard, unless the effort is directed toward clearly defined goals, productivity is not likely to increase.
3. Symbols replace substance as measures of achievement. Appearances may become particularly important. Where people sit at meetings, where their offices are located, and the kind of car the company furnishes may become the real indicators of performance and success.
4. When managers are rewarded for taking the course of least resistance, others will follow. Managers especially must know what they are doing if they are going to supervise others in pursuit of organizational goals.

The results of all these deviations from the rational, complete method of decision making, even if the latter is recognized as impossible, can be disastrous. An appropriate example might well be the *Challenger* space shuttle tragedy on January 28, 1986. Just over a minute after the shuttle lifted off, people all over the nation and the world were stunned to see it explode before their eyes, killing all seven occupants. Tragedy had taken the lives of three other American astronauts in 1967, but that accident had not been witnessed by millions on television and the loss seemed less personal.

While the immediate cause of the explosion was determined to be leaking O-rings, the true cause of the tragedy, many believe, was the faulty decision-making processes at NASA. Since the tragedy numerous theories have been presented to explain how something so horrifying could have occurred. Some have blamed the temperature on the morning of the launch, while others have placed the fault with a failure to adequately assess the risk; but all informed observers of the event and its aftermath have been confused at how NASA decision makers could allow such a thing to happen. To better understand, consider the events from the standpoint of decision making.

Perrow (1984) argues that machines and processes have become so complex that even the best scientists, engineers, and managers with the best available equipment cannot anticipate, design for, or allow for all the possible quirks of such complex systems. Serious failures of technology and judgment are capable of leading to disasters like those with the *Challenger*, Three Mile Island, and Union Carbide's Bhopal, India, chemical plant. Decision makers, whether scientists, engineers, or managers, cannot deal effectively over long periods with the tremendous number of relationships and systems that are necessary to operate high-risk technology. To some extent, these "normal accidents" are even predictable.

Usually disasters begin with small events and trivial failures in the system. As far back as 1980, NASA officials knew there was a problem with the O-rings. In December 1982, after five successful shuttle launches, seal (O-ring) failure was put on the critical list of dangers and its effects were described as "loss of mission, vehicle, and crew due to metal erosion, burn-through, and probable case burst resulting in fire and deflagration" (Biddle, 1986, p. 42). Out of the first twelve shuttle flights investigators found four incidents of seal burn-through on the primary seal. Seven occurred on the first four flights in 1984 and even some secondary O-ring erosion was found. The danger was clearly alarming. However, in the interests of not slowing down the launch schedule, the normal safety standards of NASA were waived in 1983 in the case of the O-rings and were not reinstituted.

Next, Perrow believes that accidents often happen because of production pressures. NASA obviously wanted to prove the commercial value of the shuttle through frequent flights, support for which involved gaining citizen backing through the inclusion of government officials, teachers, and journalists on the flight crews. Cost containment efforts frequently encourage compromise of safety standards and controls unless policies are monitored to assure otherwise. Finally, and perhaps most frightening, there is little evidence to suggest that investigations of normal accidents do little to prevent future mishaps. Decision makers, in Simon's words, do not have the wits to ensure the perpetual safe operation of the machines they create.

If we cannot ensure safety of future flights, can we assess the risk so that crew members know the chances they take each time a shuttle is launched? The answer here is an emphatic yes. NASA certainly had this type of information, but the mere possession of data does not ensure that decision makers will act in accordance with it. McKean (1986) states that during the days of the Apollo program engineers calculated the risk of successfully sending a person to the moon based on the best technical information. The odds were not very good—the engineers estimated that the chance of an Apollo astronaut returning alive was only one in twenty. Supposedly, the engineers' manager said the figures were so ridiculously low that he wanted the numbers buried; the risk analysis group was disbanded, and risk analysis was rarely mentioned again.

In spite of NASA's reluctance, the science of risk analysis has continued to develop. Such sophisticated techniques as fault tree analysis, event analysis, and failure mode and effects analysis (FMEA) are available to decision makers in all industries.

The failure of NASA to fully utilize the available technology in this area hints at a form of decision making that was clearly nonrational. Throughout the modern history of the space agency, the risks have been acknowledged, but the accepted assumption has been that test pilots are used to danger and their experience makes them aware of the risks. However, the same is not true of congressmen, teachers, journalists, and payload scientists not trained or experienced as members of flight crews.

There is evidence that Morton Thiokol, the manufacturer of the shuttle's solid fuel rockets, performed FMEA on the O-rings before 1982 and assessed the probability of a failure at between 1 in 500 and 1 in 5,000 launches. The result was the installation of a secondary seal to provide a redundant safety factor. Yet NASA demonstrated an unusual type of certainty in the face of disturbing data. Perhaps it was the macho culture, the can-do attitude so evident among paratroopers, test pilots, and rocket experts. After all, the space program had been extraordinarily safe. Can anything less than overconfidence be expected after twenty-four relatively eventless launchings, in spite of the fact that one engineer expressed all our fears by saying that every time a "rocket goes up successfully, it's a miracle . . . something always happens that makes you think they will never fly again" (Biddle, 1986, p. 40)?

Relating All This to Management. The *Challenger* tragedy seems far removed from management. Yet to some it seems too close. It is indeed ironic that throughout the history of the American and Soviet space programs little has been said about the tremendous managerial challenge presented by both manned and unmanned flights. In spite of this challenge, the scientific accomplishments have consistently kept the spotlight and relatively little has been said about management. Little, that is, until the shuttle disaster. Since then, management has been targeted for a great deal of the blame. Perhaps the condemnation is justified. There is no denying that a serious breakdown in the decision-making and communication processes at least contributed to the disaster. Perhaps administrators did place too much attention on budgetary and cost pressures at the expense of safety. Perhaps ceremonies and rituals did replace substance in the management of NASA. It is certain that the risks everyone knew were present should have prohibited any degree of over-confidence. However, can any of this be justified simply by ac-knowledging the impossibility of certainty? Should we tolerate uninformed and nonrational decision making merely because it is impossible to acquire all relevant knowledge? Fortunately, the choices are greater than we might expect.

In arriving at the best possible decisions it is important to keep rationality the goal. We cannot obtain rationality but we can try, and by trying we can become more informed than would otherwise be the case. Dror (1964) provides an approach that is useful in obtaining as much information as possible while recognizing that something less than perfect knowledge will be the ultimate outcome. This process involves the following steps:

1. Giving attention to the clarification of specific values, ob-jectives, and decision criteria. Rather than beginning the process of endless iterations and fine-tuning, the manager should devote time and energy to specifying the primary elements in the issue under review. This will provide direc-tion, offset uncertainty, and establish a basis for monitor-ing and evaluating performance and calculating rewards.
2. Generating alternatives in order to expand the bounds of knowledge as much as possible. Search behavior in this case attempts to exceed the "bounds of familiarity" and move significantly away from rather than remain as close as pos-sible to the present strategic direction.
3. Making preliminary projections and estimations. Here the emphasis is on projecting the outcomes that can be reason-ably expected from each alternative action.
4. Evaluating options and selecting the decision paradigm. The decision maker and the organization are required to criti-cally review the criteria upon which decisions are to be made in light of complexities and other aspects of reality. Perhaps risk should be minimized by adapting a familiar ap-proach as suggested by successive limited comparisons. Or, it might be that additional search is justified on the basis of the potential gain.

5. Testing for the optimum strategy. If additional search is deemed useful and desirable, it may be continued until an action is agreed on by different analysts and then only after frank discussion and debate.
6. Committing resources and facilities. Expanded search should take place on the basis of the best known theory, experience, and rational and extrarational information available until the best known alternative is identified and selected.

Theorists continue to attempt to identify ways of simplifying the problems facing decision makers. One such example is the search for *critical success factors* (CSFs). These CSFs are "those relatively few key areas of activity in which favorable results are absolutely necessary for a particular manager to reach his/her goals" (Boynton and Zmud, 1984; Rockart and Crescenzi, 1984; Rockart, 1982). Critical success factors help us become more rational by restricting the number of factors we should consider in making important decisions. Even here, however, rationality remains elusive, and attempts to acquire more information in a given situation are as often frustrated as they are rewarded. The fact remains that managers get paid for facing and dealing with uncertainty. Nothing less than a crystal ball will afford managers insight into the future. In the absence of such a tool we must content ourselves with something less than perfect knowledge. Management is not the field for those who cannot cope with uncertainty.

Managers do have the choice of being more informed in decision making. In fact, they have a responsibility to learn as much as is economically feasible before they make choices that influence the lives and careers of many people and the welfare of many more. Perhaps there is even an ethical obligation to do so.

It is essential that we recognize and appreciate the reality and significance of our lack of rationality. It is quite another thing to make it a virtue. Information, like all resources, has a cost, and managers must carefully evaluate its costs and its benefits. In the absence of compelling evidence to the contrary, managers should opt for more rather than less information.

If decision making is the heart of executive activity, managers must do it well. It deserves time and energy and requires a continuous quest for excellence. Necessity cannot become a virtue. It is a limitation, and an important one at that, but the goal deserves more than submission to the limitations of our wits.

Implications and Conclusions

Decision making is an important activity of all managers, but decisions cannot be made with complete certainty. Managerial choices almost always involve uncertainty. Simon and other members of the Carnegie-Mellon school of decision theory recognized the limits of rationality in their research and offered an image of the administrative man or woman who satisficed, lacked perfect knowledge, and engaged in randomly generated sequential search processes. This was quite different from the maximizing, economic man and woman envisioned by normative prescriptive theory. The insights of the Carnegie-Mellon group were significant, but they stopped short of advocating behavioral theory as an alternative to normative models. In fact, the Carnegie-Mellon group carefully specified that the purpose of behavioral theory was to describe human problem-solving processes, not to prescribe how choices should be made in order to maximize. There was no conflict and thus no contradiction.

The nonrational formulations of Lindblom and Quinn are another story. Muddling through and logical incrementalism are offered not just as descriptive models but as prescriptive theories as well. Therein lies the danger of nonrational models of decision making. There is no disputing that rationality is impossible. And since the decision maker cannot enjoy perfect knowledge, nonrationality becomes a necessity. It is only when this necessity becomes a virtue and the quest for better knowledge and information in decision making ceases that the stage is set for disaster.

CHAPTER 6

What Managers Really Do

Rational and Nonrational Views

Who can imagine developing a theory of the functioning of the human body without first observing a real body? The theorist would at least be expected to examine an occasional cadaver. Yet the earliest theories of what managers do developed with no observations of real managers aside from the personal, limited experiences of the manager proposing the theory. In fact, formal theories of manager behavior were quite advanced before observations of managers became a focus of research. Well into the decade of the 1960s what we knew about administrative behavior and what managers actually do was based more on commonsense impressions and mythology than on empirical facts (Sheriff, 1969).

The fact that academic management researchers paid little attention to how real managers behave is alarming but not surprising. Management is an applied art, and the emphasis has traditionally been on developing guidelines and recommendations to aid in accomplishing better management. The goal of management research and theory has never been to understand administrative behavior. As a result, most of the early attention in the field was directed toward the results hoped for, not the daily activities of managers.

Andrew Grove, president of Intel, illustrates the point. According to him, one problem in understanding managerial behavior is the distinction that must be drawn between the activities and outcomes of management. Activities are what managers do, while outcomes are what managers achieve. The latter seem significant while the former appear trivial. Of course, the same is true of surgery. When we see such outcomes as cured patients and lives changed for the better through successful operations, the importance of the healing art is obvious. The significance of "less important" activities such as scrubbing and suturing is more difficult to appreciate (Grove, 1985). In the same sense, the existence of a strategic plan for the company or a new and innovative organization structure appears significant when compared to the answering of telephones, business lunches, and frequent staff meetings that constitute much, perhaps most, of a manager's day. Yet, these activities are not unimportant, because, as Stewart (1984) notes, "we need to understand what it is that managers do before we can decide what managers should know and how they can best acquire this knowledge" (p. 323).

Before we begin this chapter, a word of caution is required. This discussion will differ a little from the format used in previous chapters because most of the systematic research on what managers do is of such a recent origin. With the exception of Fayol, we will not be able to point to a long tradition of concern over this vital issue. Therefore, we will be forced to concentrate much of our attention on more recent literature. However, even at the risk of deviating from the overall design, this issue is too important to ignore.

Management: A Functional View

Although the emphasis on analyzing the activities of managers, or what managers do, is of fairly recent origin, it would not be accurate to infer that concern about the outcomes of management action has been equally novel. In fact, Henri Fayol, whose concern for theory was discussed in Chapter Four, developed a comprehensive picture of managers as planners, organizers, coordinators, and controllers that has become known as the *functional* view.

Industry or business, in his way of thinking, consists of six types of activities:

1. Technical activities, including manufacturing and production.
2. Commercial activities, such as buying, selling, and exchanging.
3. Financial activities, including the search for the best sources of capital.
4. Security activities to guard against fire, theft, floods, and social disorder.
5. Accounting activities, involving data gathering and the presentation of financial statements and statistics.
6. Managerial activities, which include forecasting, organizing, commanding, coordinating, and controlling. More specifically, Fayol stated that "to manage is to forecast, and plan, to organize, to command, to coordinate, and to control" (1949, p. 6).

Good technical, commercial, and financial operations build the resources that require protection and safeguarding. This makes the last three types of activities necessary.

Although Fayol was concerned with the development of guidelines for improving management practice and assisting in the understanding of management as a process, his more fundamental goal was to develop a theory of management. He was particularly concerned about the fact that there were no schools where people could go to learn management. Such schools did not exist, according to him, because there was no general theory that could be taught within their walls. Without a theory, no teaching of management was possible.

His presentation of principles and concepts was part of his strategy to build a theory of management that would make possible the training and development of current and aspiring managers. This training was the responsibility of schools, businesses, the family, and the state. If the family would emphasize the principles and procedures of home life, management concepts would "penetrate naturally" the child's mind and form the foundation for later learning in school. Even though postsecondary education, in Fayol's view, should be general in the sense of providing exposure to the liberal arts and sciences, it should also offer courses on management. Organizations should offer workshops and encourage all types of management study by employees, and the state should set a good example by adding management to the curriculum in state schools.

In the first part of *General and Industrial Management* (1949), Fayol sought to establish the case for the necessity of teaching management. In the last part he tried to indicate what the teaching should include. Management historians regret that Fayol's book represents only half of what was to be an integrated four-part work that could not be completed before his death. As it stands, however, the book provides an unequaled argument for the importance of management education and training (Carter, 1986).

Managers as Reflective Calculators. The view of managerial action presented by Fayol is consistent with the classical economic theories and scientific approaches to decision making discussed in the previous chapter. If we are to scientifically approach any problem, we should first define it, develop an action plan, itemize, analyze, and select the best approach, and then follow up to ensure that the goal is properly accomplished. Fayol believed that management should be approached in the same way, and he carefully outlined the steps involved in a systematic technique of administration and management. These steps were logical and straightforward. Under the heading of administrative operations Fayol included planning, organizing, coordinating, commanding, and controlling.

To plan is to study the future and arrange a way of dealing with it. Actually, Fayol proposed a unique concept by stating that planning should be considered only one part of a broader function called *prevoyance*. Prevoyance consists of forecasting or foreseeing the future, but it is more. It includes preparing systematically for the future that is discovered in the process of forecasting. In the scheme presented by Fayol the result of planning is more than a formal plan. The output from the process of prevoyance includes ways of accomplishing the plan. In contemporary terms we would think of the outcome as a series of goal statements as well as the strategies for goal accomplishment. Prevoyance is an action-oriented approach to planning.

To organize involves developing a design for the business that will effectively relate human and nonhuman resources. Organizing means developing a structure to assist in goal accomplishment. *To coordinate* is to unite all activities taking place in the organization. Through coordination things in organizations are given their proper proportion, and means are adapted to the ends they are intended to accomplish. Coordination and organization allow the manager to orchestrate the resources of an organization toward goal accomplishment.

To command is the function that ensures the organization will operate as it was intended to operate. Command activities are those that make the organization operate properly. In the most general sense command includes attempts to motivate employee action toward organizational goals and leadership.

Finally, *to control* involves ensuring that everything is carried out in accordance with the plan "that has been adopted, the orders that have been given, and the principles that have been laid down" (Urwick, 1937, p. 119). When all these functions are properly conducted, the reflective calculating manager achieves a unity within the organization that allows for efficient and effective operations.

Building Unity Through Management. Fayol's review of each of the functions in the final chapter of *General and Industrial Management* leaves no doubt as to how he viewed the unity of the management process. He saw managers as logical, well-informed people who have a goal, a plan, and a will to ensure that results are achieved. This is possible when the manager approaches problems in the following manner.

First, successful organizations must have foresight, and it is the responsibility of management to provide the futuristic view through planning. Plans should be unified vertically, with those at the bottom levels of the organization flowing logically from those at the top. In other words, the goals of the departments should be directly reinforcing to overall organizational objectives, and work-group goals should be reinforcing to those of the departments. Horizontal unity is also essential if groups are to be properly coordinated. All the goals of production units and marketing departments should be closely related. At the same time, financial plans and objectives in purchasing and credit departments should facilitate rather than hinder the accomplishment of goals in line departments such as production and sales. This point underlines the importance of interdepartmental communication and coordination. Plans should be precise enough to provide direction but flexible enough to allow for changing conditions. The best plans, in Fayol's thinking, evolve from experience and stress unity.

Ideally, organizing a business results in providing it "with everything useful to its functioning: raw materials, tools, capital, and personnel" (p. 53). Fayol directed a great deal of his attention toward the human organization, using the military analogy of the chain of command and quoting Taylor when arguing that many people have the potential for success in management and should be given the opportunity to manage through decentralization of the organization structure. On the matter of organization, however, Fayol stopped short of endorsing Taylor's functional foremanship because of his fear that the "Taylor System," as he called it, negates the unity-of-command principle. As a manager and a theorist, Fayol appeared unable to recommend an organizational system in which employees simultaneously report to more than a single boss.

The calculating manager, having planned and organized effectively, must now get things moving. At this point command enters the picture. The manager's command goal is to get the greatest return possible from all the workers under her or his supervision. This is to be done under the watchful eye of the supervisor, but Fayol cautioned that initiative will develop and be maintained only if employees have the freedom to make mistakes.

Harmonization of all aspects of the organization is achieved through coordination. Well-coordinated businesses build units that operate in harmony, and weekly meetings of department heads are useful in building this relationship. Finally, control verifies that everything conforms to the plan. Control of commercial activities requires checks on quantities, qualities, and prices. Control of technical operations involves operational progress, and financial controls are directed toward cash and other assets through financial records and reports.

Advocates of Fayol's work extended the logic of his view of management behavior and gave us two concepts that are supported by many and rejected by others: (1) the universality of management functions and (2) the transferability of management skills.

Since Fayol argued that all the functions he itemized apply to the governing of organizations in all industries, support grew for the idea of the universality of management functions. All managers, including the president of General Motors, generals in the army, chancellors of universities, and even the pope, plan, organize, coordinate, command, and control. Thus, the functions of management are universal.

Second, as the person moves higher in the organization to more purely managerial jobs, he or she performs fewer technical functions, so that the job becomes predominantly managerial. In view of this situation, Fayol suggested that the person performing strictly managerial functions should be able to transfer those talents to other industries and even different careers. The business executive might transfer managerial expertise and become a successful hospital administrator or dean of a business school. The general in the army, because the job is essentially managerial, should find success in civilian jobs at similar organization levels. Dwight Eisenhower's service as general of the army, president of Columbia University, and president of the United States provide some support for this argument, as does Robert McNamara's success in the Office of Strategic Services and as a Ford Motor Company "whiz kid," president of Ford, secretary of defense, and president of the World Bank.

Of course, not everyone agrees with either of these logical extensions. Many people continue to insist that health care management and public administration are fundamentally different from the management of business firms. Yet when we look for evidence of people who have found success in more than a single industry or company, the examples are not hard to find.

The image of managerial work created by Fayol is demanding and requires unusually qualified people to measure up to the task. The reflective calculating manager is one who has

> all the requisite knowledge for settling managerial, technical, commercial, and financial questions before him and also has sufficient physical and mental vigor and capacity for work to be able to melt all of the weight of business contracts [p. 71].

Is it really possible in our increasingly complex organizational world to be a reflective calculating manager? For that matter, was it ever possible? Should we think of Fayol's image of management as fact or folklore? In the words of Simon, do managers really have the "wits" to be reflective calculators?

Changing Stereotypes of Management Behavior

Is the reflective calculating manager folklore or fact (Mintzberg, 1975)? Attempts have been made to study managers and thereby gain insights into what managers actually do. One of the most comprehensive attempts to summarize these findings is that of C. P. Hales (1986). In his review, he confronts head on several of the issues that seem to be avoided by other writers. For example, he does not treat managerial behavior and managerial work as synonymous or assume that mere observations of managers are a sufficient basis for dealing with the complex question of what managers do. Also, he addresses the effectiveness question—that is, to what extent does what managers do match what managers ought to do in order to maximize organizational performance? Hales's study is particularly comprehensive because he attempts to look not just at the activities managers perform but to "shed light on five major areas . . . about managerial work" (p. 90). These areas are:

1. The *elements* of managerial work (what managers do).
2. The distribution of a manager's *time* between work elements (how managers work).

3. *Interactions* of managers (with whom managers work).
4. *Informal* elements of managerial work (what else managers do).
5. *Themes* that pervade managerial work (what qualities managerial work has).

After reviewing many studies on the subject, Hales summarized the following "body of facts" on managerial work. First, it combines managerial elements with specialty and professional elements. Managers almost always perform some nonmanagerial functions in the course of doing their jobs. Second, the substantive elements of management work entail providing liaisons, managing human behavior, and taking responsibility for getting work done. Next, the nature of a manager's work varies in duration, time span, and unexpectedness. It is difficult, perhaps impossible, to predict the variety of a manager's work tasks during a given period. Managers spend a great deal of every day troubleshooting and solving ad hoc problems.

The communication patterns managers employ vary according to what the communication is about and with whom it is taking place. Managers do a lot of persuading and engaging in brief face-to-face encounters. As a result, they have little time to spend on any particular activity or in the formulation of systematic plans. A great deal of the manager's time is spent accounting for and explaining what he or she does and in informal "politicking." Managerial activities are also frequently concerned with conflict resolution. Finally, managers are able to exercise considerable choice in terms of what is done and how it is accomplished.

These generalizations summarize much of the research on managerial behavior and work. However, one of the most popular sources on the subject suggests a different way of looking at what managers do (Mintzberg, 1973).

Roles Managers Perform. Mintzberg views the manager's job as a series of roles assumed throughout the process of achieving organizational goals. In presenting his argument, he identifies three major categories of roles: interpersonal, informational, and decisional. Each has a series of subcategories.

The *interpersonal roles*, as the name implies, involve the

manager in developing relationships with other people and groups. These roles directly influence the status and the authority of the manager.

Frequently, a manager is called on to perform as a *figurehead* and to render ceremonial and symbolic acts. During the restructuring and rebuilding at Chrysler, for example, it was necessary for Lee Iacocca himself to get out to the company's production facilities and talk to employees. This was a means of building confidence in his leadership and maintaining morale. Managers, in their interpersonal relations, are also expected to function as *leaders* and to motivate others, as well as provide for effective staffing and training activities. Iacocca's success as a leader is illustrated by the chants of "Lee! Lee! Lee!" by rank-and-file union members when he came to Chrysler's Sterling Heights, Michigan, assembly plant to launch a new line of sports sedans. The manager also needs to fill a *liaison* role in forming communication links with individuals and groups outside the organization who are likely to provide favors. Even though it was important for Iacocca to get into the plant and talk to employees, it was essential that he fly back and forth to Washington when Chrysler was attempting to convince Congress to bail the company out with government loans.

The *informational roles* of managers involve receiving and transmitting information. Sometimes the manager is seen as the *monitor* or nerve center of information flow in the organization. In this role the manager is a dispatcher and routes information to various internal and external groups. Sometimes the role is more that of the *disseminator* of information. Once the manager receives the information it must be selectively shared with people in the organization, and choices must be made about who will most directly benefit from the sharing of information. In *High Output Management* (1985) Grove provides a diary of a day in his life as president of a major high-technology corporation. He spent one two-hour block of time lecturing in the employee orientation program. This program was designed to allow senior managers an opportunity to provide new professional employees with information on company objectives, history, and expectations.

A final information role is that of *spokesperson.* Managers are regularly asked to represent the organization to various out-side groups. Sometimes this role requires nothing more than giving the standard "canned" speech to a local civic club. At other times it may entail an extremely stressful interview before live television cameras at the scene of a serious industrial accident. One of the more interesting developments relative to the spokes-person role is the manner in which chief executives such as Victor Kiam of Remington Products, Frank Borman of Eastern Airlines, and Iacocca have taken to the airwaves to promote their own products and services. In general, they have done quite well, it seems, with some consumers placing more trust in what the "president" has to say (Poindexter, 1983).

The *decisional roles* are diverse and far ranging. They can include everything from scheduling one's own time to negotiating with labor unions. When the manager acts as an *entrepreneur,* she or he searches the environment for new and challenging opportunities. The entrepreneurial role involves taking the risks necessary to succeed in a competitive industry. The role of *disturbance handler* is assumed when the manager attempts to correct or fine-tune the organization's progress toward goals when things knock the operations off course. Frequently, managers are expected to function as *resource allocators* and make decisions concerning whether to commit organizational resources to alternative uses. In Grove's documented day, he made a decision not to grant a manager a pay increase that would have placed him outside the normal range of salary for such a job. This was a resource-allocating decision. Finally, managers fill the role of *negotiator* when they bargain with employees, with their bosses, or with outside groups such as labor unions.

A Different Image of Managerial Work. Mintzberg (1975) notes that there are four myths about managerial work that do not hold under careful examination. The first is the view of the manager as a reflective calculator, as pictured by Fayol. According to actual research, the manager seldom spends more than nine minutes on any task, and in Mintzberg's sample of five CEOs only 10 percent of the activities of these high-level executives required more than an hour to complete. Studies of foremen show that they engage in as many as 583 activities in an eight-hour shift. That is an average of one activity every forty-eight seconds (Guest, 1956). Rather than being the careful planner depicted by Fayol, the real-life manager jumps from issue to issue, continually responding to the demands of the moment with little apparent concern for the future.

The second myth is the image of the manager as one who has properly planned and delegated and can therefore concentrate on exceptions while efficiently spending most of his or her time doing the important things required by the organization. Again, the classical stereotype does not hold. In addition to handling exceptions, most managers feel an obligation to engage in ritualistic and ceremonial duties and information-processing activities. This occurs even in high-level government positions. When Cyrus Vance was secretary of state, for example, he arrived at work before 7:00 A.M., and more than forty meetings and telephone calls later, he arrived back home after 7:00 P.M. While much of his work was important, some was insignificant or even foolish. At the top level of organizations and in high-level political positions, power and influence have as much to do with symbols and appearances as with substance and reality (Adams, 1979). Managers such as politicians and public servants feel an obligation to do those things required of their position even if at times these actions are unbecoming.

The third myth is that managers need and use information that is systematic and well documented. This kind of information is most often supplied by management information systems. In reality, managers prefer verbal media or information that is obtained fast, usually by telephone calls and meetings. Mintzberg's research found that most managers consider mail a burden, a pain in the neck. One of the CEOs he observed came in on Saturday and processed over 140 pieces of mail in three hours. The sample of five CEOs responded to only two of the forty routine reports they received during the period of the study, and in twenty-five days of observation the managers initiated (excluding responses to other correspondence) only twenty-five pieces of mail.

The final myth, in terms of this and the preceding chapter, may be one of the most damaging and disappointing of all if we believe what Mintzberg tells us about managerial behavior and work. This myth is that management is rapidly becoming a science and a profession. Yet all the evidence points to the fact that most of what managers do remains locked deep inside their brains. Intuition and judgment have more to do with management than objective data, hard facts, and precise science. Although today's managers are competent by any standard, Mintzberg voices surprise that the way managers act is "fundamentally indistinguishable" from the way their counterparts acted a hundred or a thousand years ago. In his words:

> The information they need differs, but they seek it in the same way—by word of mouth. Their decisions concern modern technology, but the procedures they use to make them are the same as the procedures of the nineteenth-century manager. Even the computer . . . has apparently had no influence on the work procedures of general managers [Mintzberg, 1975, p. 54].

Controversies seldom answer questions such as "Who is right, Fayol or Mintzberg?" Instead they cause additional questions to be asked and more research to be conducted, and eventually we at least understand more about the phenomenon under consideration. This pattern holds true with regard to managerial work and behavior.

Additional Attempts to Understand Managers

One of the more widely discussed attempts to study management behavior was developed by J. P. Kotter (1982). He studied fifteen general managers using interviews, questionnaires, archival records, and more than 500 hours of direct observation. General managers (GMs) for purposes of this study were defined as individuals who hold positions with multifunctional responsibilities for a business.

The general managers who participated in this study displayed twelve similar patterns of behavior:

1. They spent most of their time with other people. About the only time they spent alone was on airplanes or when commuting to work. Most spent about 70 percent of their time with other people, and some spent as much as 90 percent.
2. Time was spent with many people other than the manager's direct boss and subordinate. Some of the time was spent with the subordinate's subordinates, the boss's boss, customers, and suppliers. The formal chain of command was frequently violated.
3. An extremely wide range of topics were discussed with other people. Virtually everything that remotely related to their business or industry was discussed.
4. When interacting with others, general managers asked a lot of questions. Literally hundreds of questions could be asked in a short conversation.
5. Big decisions were rarely made in the course of these conversations.
6. The interactions and conversations with others contained a considerable amount of joking, kidding, and nonwork-related issues.
7. In a large number of cases the substantive issues discussed were recognized as unimportant to the business or the organization. These general managers regularly engaged in activities that "even they regarded as a waste of time."
8. General managers seldom gave orders or told people what to do in these encounters.
9. In spite of this, general managers frequently attempted to influence others. Instead of telling people what to do, however, they tended to request, persuade, and intimidate.
10. In allocating their time, the participants tended to behave in a "reactive mode," with few of the encounters being planned.
11. Most of the time spent with others was consumed by short and disjointed conversations.
12. All the general managers worked long hours.

Kotter's view of successful management behavior has more in common with Mintzberg's than with Fayol's. The effective managers he studied did not approach their jobs by planning, organizing, motivating, and controlling in a formal sense. They relied on continuous, informal, and more subtle methods in approaching the complex demands of the management task.

In the course of their work these managers produced agendas and networks rather than long-range plans and organization charts. The agendas they developed were not in conflict with formal plans but were less numerical, covered a wider time frame, dealt with more people-oriented issues, and were, in general, "less rigorous, rational, logical, linear" than one would expect of formal planning. Similarly, the networks the general managers built were not in conflict with the formal structure of their organizations, but they did include more people inside and outside the firm. The cooperative relationships developed went far beyond the regular formal roles required by the organization. Grove (1985) indicated that early in the morning on the day he chronicled he received a call from a competitor that was "ostensibly about a meeting of an industry-wide society" (p. 45). In reality, the competitor was feeling him out on business conditions, and Grove "did the same." This is the nature of the network the general managers built and relied on for valuable information that could be gathered quickly and might not be readily available within their own organization.

Admittedly, this type of managerial behavior appears quite "unmanaged." Kotter (1982) objects to this conclusion, however, and argues that efficiency strangely results from this apparent inefficiency. The agendas allowed managers to react efficiently and opportunistically to the flow of events around them while knowing that they were doing so within a larger, more rational framework. The network allowed for "terse and efficient" conversations. Together the agendas and networks made it possible for the managers to achieve efficiency and cope with the extreme demands of their jobs. These demands, by the way, consistently resulted in work weeks that averaged fifty-nine hours.

Research on larger samples of managers in more diversified industrial settings has confirmed many of Kotter's observations. Luthans, Rosenkrantz, and Hennessey (1985) observed and recorded the behaviors of fifty-two managers in a state department of revenue, a medium-size manufacturing plant, and a campus police department. This study confirmed that networking activities such as interacting with outsiders and internally oriented socializing and politicking were positively associated with success in management.

Importantly, this study did suggest that successful and less successful managers behave differently. The researchers found that even though Mintzberg's roles were all observed they did not occur with equal frequency and that the successful managers were more likely to engage in activities similar to the planning and coordinating functions described by Fayol. Stewart (1984) came to a similar conclusion when she noted that variations among the activities of managers in similar jobs raise questions about the existence of a common core of management activities found in all firms and industries.

An Integrative View of Management

One popular and long-lasting description of management was provided by Katz (1955), who based his model on the skills managers need for success. *Skills* are abilities that can be developed and that are actually manifested in performance. They are not necessarily inborn, nor do they lie dormant. Instead, they are used to aid in accomplishing the goals of the person who possesses them. Katz argued that there are three types of skills that are important to managers:

1. *Technical skills*, which involve specialized or professional knowledge. Technical skills in areas such as engineering and accounting require analytical abilities, and some, as in the field of medicine, require the use of the techniques of the specialty.
2. *Human skills*, which enable a person to work as a member of a group and to build cooperative effort that can be directed toward efficiently accomplishing common goals.
3. *Conceptual skills*, which involve the ability to see the big picture. This type of skill enables a person to see the inter-

dependencies among various parts of an organization and how changes in one part will influence changes in other parts. Skills of this nature are the kind needed to appreciate the relationships between business and its publics in different economic, political, and social environments.

All three types of skills are important to managers. However, we can imagine that the relative importance of these skills changes with the level of the organization.

To illustrate, consider the foreman in a manufacturing plant, the sales supervisor, or any other type of first-line supervisor. Each must continue to use many technical skills required in former nonmanagerial jobs. The foreman spends time in actual production operations, and the sales supervisor makes a number of sales throughout the day. Both are required to develop human skills and to use them in motivating their employees to perform well, communicating effectively what is expected, and providing the kind of leadership required by the organization. Their technical skills enable them to work with things, while their human skills help them deal with people. As supervisors they are also expected to learn certain conceptual skills and see how their area of responsibility relates to and is dependent upon other areas in the organization. Not much of their time and energy, however, is consumed by such lofty concerns.

When foremen or sales supervisors are promoted into middle-level management, they do not exercise their technical skills as often as they did as first-line supervisors. Their human skills are no less important at this level, because middle managers spend a great deal of time leading, motivating, and communicating. The organization now demands greater development of their conceptual skills. The success of middle managers demands that they be able to work successfully with heads of other functional units. At this level there can be no excuse for a lack of proper appreciation for a picture larger than that outlined by one's own department.

Finally, when the manager arrives at the top of the hierarchy, his or her technical skills are seldom used. The general manager who is trained as an engineer will do little engineering, and the head accountant will seldom function as a true accountant. These upper-level executives will continue to require human skills, which will be no less important than they were the day the person first became a manager. At this level, however, the tremendous challenge relates to the use of conceptual skills. The interdependency of all units is the primary factor that demands much of the chief executive's time. It is this manager's job to ensure that the efforts of production, sales, finance, and personnel are mutually reinforcing and work toward the same goal. Also, it is up to the top executive levels to ensure that the organization interacts favorably with the larger social, political, and economic systems.

Can We Reconcile the Diversity?

In this relatively brief chapter we have presented four different views of management work. Is it possible to reconcile them in a manner that will help us in understanding what management work is really like to those who do it every day?

Thanks to a framework like that provided by Katz, it is possible to relate the various schemes. Initially, we can dispense with the technical skills by stating that all the models and findings on management work we have reviewed concede that managers do need technical skills and use them on occasion. Kotter (1982) provides a little more emphasis on this aspect in his discussion of management success, where he observes that the managers in his sample thought of themselves as general managers and as capable of managing almost anything well, yet each was also highly specialized in many ways, and each specialized set of interests, skills, knowledge, and relationships allowed each manager to behave in ways that fit the demands of the specific situation.

Human skills represent no problem of reconciliation. All observers of management behavior recognize the importance of this type of skill. Mintzberg chose interpersonal roles as one of his major categories; Fayol's functions of coordination and command particularly relate to human factors; and Kotter emphasized how much time managers spend with others, communicate inside and outside the organization, and seek information from those around them.

In the area of conceptual skills there is also reasonable agreement. Managers must conceptualize situations if they are to be effective planners. Certainly when we include the action orientation that was such a critical part of Fayol's view of planning, conceptual skills are critical. From the perspective of Mintzberg, the behaviors required to fulfill certain informational and decisional roles require an ability to conceptualize. Monitors and disseminators of information must understand interdependencies within an organization if their dispatching and routing of information is to aid in achieving organizational effectiveness. Entrepreneurial and negotiating roles require a similar type of understanding of the broader environment. The behavior of Kotter's sample of executives indicated an equal emphasis on conceptual abilities. Even though the general managers were not observed making "big" decisions, they were constantly gathering information, asking questions, and holding brief encounters designed to increase their knowledge of relevant circumstances. However, the agendas these managers constructed contained ideas that involved commitments far into the uncertain future and were complex in the sense that they required the coordination of different units to succeed. The networks of the general managers also extended beyond their immediate subordinates and bosses—even far outside the boundaries of their own organizations.

It is not essential that managers study the research on managerial work to be successful managers. In fact, as we have observed, it might be better if they remain unaware of the "unsystematic" nature of much of their work. The important point for managers to remember is that they are responsible for doing certain things that others in their organizations cannot do. Managers must *plan* and thereby provide a sense of direction and offset uncertainty. The goals that are so important to good planning become the standards used in control. Managers must also *organize* and *coordinate* diverse organizational units and ensure each makes its unique contribution to the organizational mission.

Managers must also *control* operations and ensure that things are working as they should. The activities they use to accomplish these tasks are called *functions* or *roles*. The label is not important, but it is imperative for managers to realize that they alone are responsible for these tasks and must ensure that all are accomplished.

Implications and Conclusions

When researchers better understand what managers do, they can help managers by providing them with the kind of information that will be most relevant and useful in completing their tasks. When managers obtain a better understanding of what they actually do, it will be easier to compare actual behavior with the behavior required of managers if their organizations are to function effectively and efficiently.

The research to date on administrative behavior is compelling in the sense that it acknowledges that management is not a rational process and managers are not the reflective calculators envisioned by Fayol. On the other hand, a degree of efficiency can and often does result from what appears on the surface to be a highly inefficient process of jumping from one problem and topic to another. It is true that managers seldom have time for leisurely planning, but they do develop agendas. Neither do managers normally have either the time or the resources to build the type of organization necessary to monitor the environment for signs of change and to muster all the internal resources necessary to operate at maximum efficiency. However, they do build networks, and these informal linkages reach into areas and make contact with people who could never be reached through formal channels. Managers are pragmatists with demanding jobs and long working hours. They do what they need to do to keep things operating under the conditions that exist. By and large, they do it well. If observations of managers prove anything, they confirm that managers work hard, build relationships, and negotiate with numerous people in the process of acquiring success for their organizations.

PART THREE

Managing Purposeful Systems

If we are to manage, we must have a goal. One of the first things early writers on management recognized is that management presumes the existence of a goal or objective. Otherwise, we cannot tell if management has taken place.

Goal-oriented organizations are purposeful systems; that is, they are created for a purpose. In this part of the book we look at two major issues. The first is goal setting and task management; this is the subject of Chapter Seven. The idea of the task or the proposed objective was a part of the theories of the early scientific management writers. Taylor talked about it. So did the Gilbreths, Emerson, and Gantt. The writers during the human relations period also made frequent references to the significance of goals and task management.

The importance of this theme has continued to modern times. Management-by-objectives, as the name implies, is a management technique (some say philosophy) based on clearly established goals and appraisal on the basis of results. The contemporary emphasis on strategic management always includes discussions of mission statements and the need to carefully formulate and communicate the purpose of the organization. Recent interest in goal setting by behavioral scientists also emphasizes the importance of stating goals, allowing participation in their formulation, and providing timely and regular feedback relative to goal accomplishment.

Chapter Eight examines another topic that has been recurring in management thought and that relates directly to the purposefulness of organizational systems: the responsibility of management. Some believe this topic has only come to the forefront in recent years. In reality it has been a regularly recurring theme in the literature over the past century.

CHAPTER 7

Setting Goals and Managing Tasks

Creating Purpose in Organizations

The starting point of formal organization and of the coordination of operations that organizations are designed to ensure is a goal—the organization's raison d'être. Krupp (1961) says it well by stating that the attainment of goals is possible only within the constraints imposed by the environment, and the process of management involves decision making, the selection of alternative strategies, and the evaluation of outcomes in terms of preconceived goals. This is one of the most fundamental precepts of traditional (and modern) management, for without clear, concise, and communicated goals, no management is possible. How, for example, can managers provide direction, offset uncertainty, and evaluate accomplishments if they do not have goals to use as standards of performance?

Goals are defined as "conceptions of desired end states." Managers think of them primarily as projections of what they hope to accomplish (Bolman and Deal, 1984). However, if goals are to be useful, they must be more than good intentions. They must "degenerate into work" (Drucker, 1973). There are many kinds of goals, and the terms used to describe them are numerous; *objectives*, *ends*, and *outcomes* are the most frequently used. In this chapter no precise distinction will be made between objectives, ends, and goals. In fact, the terms will be used interchangeably to describe an organization's targets, performance standards, or desired future states.

Although objections have been raised (Georgiou, 1973) to the "classical goal paradigm," or the view that organizations are essentially instruments of goal accomplishment, the logic of this view is compelling. Dissenters say that because decision makers are not always sure of their goals (à la muddling through and logical incrementalism) or have so many they cannot pursue one to the exclusion of others, the classical goal paradigm is too restrictive. The lack of rationality on the part of decision makers does not, however, alter the fact that organizations are purposeful, goal-directed phenomena. People create them specifically because they cannot accomplish their goals acting alone (Barnard, 1938).

From the Task to the Grand Purpose

Most of the interest in goal setting today centers on planning and the development of grand strategies for organizations. Strategic management is often thought of as more exciting than the day-to-day battles managers fight in the trenches. This has not always been the case. In the earliest days of scientific management the idea of the *task* related to the most basic elements of work and was a fundamental part of the systems proposed by Taylor, the Gilbreths, and others.

Task Management. Taylor (1914) stated that the "most prominent single element in modern scientific management is the task idea" (p. 39). This idea involved fully planning the work of every employee at least a day in advance and issuing complete written instructions describing in detail the task to be accomplished and the means for accomplishing it. Among other things, the task was used as the standard for determining the bonus that would be earned when work was judged meritorious. Some writers, specifically Locke (1982) and Wren (1987), believe that the task idea provided much of the practical foundation for widely used techniques such as management-by-objectives (to be discussed later in this chapter). While we might debate the similarity of management-by-objectives and task management, there is no arguing the fact that early discussions of the "task" revealed the supreme importance placed on goal setting.

Taylor's idea concerning the task was endorsed and expanded by Lillian Gilbreth ([1914] 1973). Whereas Taylor presented the importance of the task, she described, in detail, the nature of the concept. Unlike most scientific management writers, Lillian Gilbreth was trained as a psychologist. In fact, she earned a Ph.D. in psychology despite tangible barriers to women entering psychology or any other profession at the beginning of the twentieth century.

It is impossible to say whether her interest in task management resulted from her knowledge of engineering and psychology or from the fact that she was the mother of twelve children. For those who have read *Cheaper by the Dozen*, written by her son and daughter, the importance of goal setting, organization, and control to the efficient management of such a large household becomes quite clear.

The task, in Gilbreth's way of thinking, is a goal to be sure, but it is not one that was casually or theoretically determined. It results from an elaborate process of measurement and synthesis. Recall from Chapter Four, Gilbreth ([1914] 1973) believed that under scientific management a task is determined through a complex process of analysis and synthesis. Analysis involves the "separation" of anything that is complex "into its constituent elements . . . and the explanation of the principles upon which the division is made" (p. 123). Synthesis, by contrast, is the process of putting things back together or of combining separate elements into a whole system. By now, the relevance of analysis and synthesis to goal setting should be becoming clear.

According to Gilbreth, the result of synthesis, which presupposes analysis, should be assembling of the various elements of a job into a task. However, when we view the task in this manner, the standard for work is not some abstract or "blue sky" objective that is determined in a theoretical manner. Rather, it is the standard for a particular kind of work based on what "has actually been done and what can be expected to be repeated" (p. 130). The task is not an imaginary ideal or an im-

possible dream of what we hope can be expected. It is the "sum
of observed and timed operations, plus a definite and sufficient
percentage . . . for overcoming fatigue" (p. 131).

The resistance of managers and workers to the task idea
was impossible for Lillian Gilbreth to understand. This resistance
was caused primarily, she believed, by an ignorance of the idea
of *task*. Although she did not like the term because it has connotations that are inherently objectionable, she could think of
no better label for it. However, she clearly recognized that the
accomplishment of goals involves a "means-ends relationship"
when she stated that everyone in the organization should have a
defined task to perform and that organizations should also have
tasks. The individual and organizational tasks should be related
in such a manner that the accomplishment of the former leads
to achievement of the goals of the latter. This was an advanced
and sophisticated recognition of a complex process—especially
in the early days of scientific management. This thinking is, for
example, the basis for the theory of mutual reinforcement and
the managerial logic upon which management-by-objectives is
founded.

The task idea that developed early in the history of management illustrates the important role of established goals in the
conduct of management. We should recognize that the task is a
goal in the purest sense of the term. However, it is very different from the connotation applied to modern meanings of *goal*.
In contemporary discussions, goals are thought of as aspirations
or things to be achieved if we "really get our acts together" and
work as hard as we can over the next year. In Gilbreth's view,
and the view of writers such as Taylor and Gantt, the task is a
demonstrated, empirical reality. That is, the task or performance goal of a given job, department, or organization is the
level of accomplishment possible when (1) tools and conditions
of work have been standardized, (2) the method by which the
work is to be done has been prescribed, (3) the time the work
should take has been scientifically determined, (4) an allowance
has been made for fatigue, and (5) the quality of output has
been stated (p. 133).

From Task Management to Organizational Purpose. One
day when you feel especially brave, walk up and down the halls

of your office and ask a random sample of employees to tell you the mission of the organization. Do not be surprised if you fail to receive a single correct response. Most employees do not have any idea what the mission of the organization is, and those who venture a guess will probably state it in such general terms as to be meaningless. If you have any courage left, ask your boss to discuss the mission of the organization with you. Be prepared for a response something to the effect of "I am doing the best I can to keep this organization operating one day to another. I do not have time to talk about obvious things like the company's mission." Obvious things? The mission must not be too obvious if none of the employees you talk to know what it is. In fact, if someone gives a good answer, are you really sure *you* know the mission well enough to evaluate it?

The case for a well-conceived and communicated organizational mission statement is as strong as, or stronger than, the argument favoring well-defined and understood task instructions. The purpose of the business is a fundamental question that must be seriously addressed by all managers. It is not enough to simply and jokingly "cop out" like some are inclined to do by making statements like "Everyone knows what we are all about—if we don't make a profit we all lose our jobs" or "The purpose of the corporation is to make money. Everyone here knows that." Of course, every informed manager and employee knows a business must make money if it is to continue operations. But that is not really addressing the organization's purpose. This issue is much more complicated.

Barnard (1938) itemized three elements of an organization: (1) communication, (2) willingness to serve, and (3) a common purpose. Cooperative systems require a purpose that is generally accepted by the members of the organization. One must know what the purpose is before it can be accepted. The inculcation of the "belief in the real existence of a common purpose is an essential executive function" (p. 87). In Barnard's view, the organizational purpose is distinct from individual motives, but the two are closely linked and necessarily reinforcing if satisfaction on the part of the individual and the organization is to result (Grundstein, 1981). However, Barnard added another important element to the organizational purpose. He believed the purpose is essential to add meaning to the environment. If an organization's environment is to make sense, it must be looked at from some perspective. "A mere mass of things" outside the organization does not have meaning to the manager. The mass must be reduced, organized, and structured according to some basis of discrimination (that is, a purpose). The purpose transforms the "mere mass of things" into something "significant, relevant, interesting" (pp. 195–196).

Consider, for example, the differences in the way environment is perceived by large private corporations in the United States and by state-owned enterprises in countries such as Brazil, Germany, or Canada. The private American corporation has as its purpose a reasonable return on the capital invested by stockholders. Management's job is to scan the environment and focus on opportunities for investment and gain. The state-owned enterprise may scan the same environment and ignore opportunities for profit because of the excessive risk that must be assumed in a time when the national economic plan calls for a reduction in risky investments (Aharoni, 1986). The environment is thus interpreted in different ways by organizations with different purposes.

In more recent times the discussion of mission statements is an indication of the continued concern for the purpose of organizations. Drucker (1954) placed a great deal of attention on the development and communication of organizational purpose. He contended that many businesses fail simply because they do not ask themselves the elementary question "What is our business?" The answer, it is important to note, is determined more by the customer than by any other single person or group.

The mission statement of an organization precisely answers the critical question asked by Drucker. It defines the unique purpose that sets an organization apart from all others and identifies the scope of the firm's operations in terms of products and markets (Cochran, David, and Gibson, 1985). When properly developed, the mission statement of an organization is a comprehensive planning tool that enables managers to focus on the present and future opportunities facing the firm. They can do so because the statement targets the company's customers, defines its principal products or services, limits its geographical domain, identifies core technologies, prioritizes the organization's values or goals, and provides insights into the firm's philosophy. Studies have shown that firms with more comprehensive mission statements are higher performers in financial terms. Research has also indicated that of all the elements that could be included in mission statements, components relating to corporate philosophy, self-concept, and public image are the most important (Pearce and David, 1987).

This overview illustrates how the emphasis on goal setting has changed from the scientific management writers' concern for the task to modern writers' emphasis on strategic management, organizational missions, and goals. The role of planning as a management function and the specific nature and purpose of goal setting have changed, but each period of management thought has included goals as an important element in the theory of organization. However, few writers appreciated the importance of goals as coordinating devices to the extent of those who were preoccupied with the classical concepts of organizational design.

Goal Setting and Administrative Organization

Mary Parker Follett was born in 1868 and educated in the United States, England, and France. She was trained in political science and spent time in her youth as a social worker in Boston. Later she became a consultant to many large corporations. Although her best-known contributions relate to conflict management, as we will discuss later, Follett understood the importance of obtaining unity in organizations and the place of goal setting in this process. She argued that the test of any business is whether or not all its units move together (are coordinated). This functional whole, or "integrative unity" as she called it, is similar to what Lillian Gilbreth called synthesis. Integrating has as its goal making a whole of the organization, with each of the interrelated parts efficiently pursuing the common goals (Follett, 1924).

One of the most damaging criticisms any employee can make of management is that the company operates like four or five different organizations rather than four or five departments within a single organization. No synergism, no cumulative effect is being achieved by the organization because of the lack of a common goal. Teamwork, in the most general sense, is missing and the organization is suffering.

Purpose, Objectives, and Teamwork. Urwick (1952) discussed many principles of organization and drew freely from the work of Fayol and Follett. When discussing goal setting and organizational purpose, he was to the point and left no room for misunderstanding. According to him, "unless we have a purpose, there is no reason why individuals should try to coordinate together at all or why anyone should try to organize them" (pp. 18–19). Under the discussion of organization and coordination, Urwick presented the principle of the objective, which insists that all parts of an organization lead to the accomplishment of an objective. The objective provides the basis for coordinating the efforts of the various departments and individuals in the organization. Objectives flow logically from the purpose, and every organization must be an expression of the purpose it is created to accomplish. Urwick, like Drucker, noted that even though we may say the purpose of a business is to make a profit or provide a service, in fact, the purpose of all business firms is to make or distribute some product or service that customers need.

At a more practical and behavioral level, Henry Dennison (1931) pointed out that teamwork, an essential ingredient in the success of any business, relies on the existence of understood goals. Teamwork at the level of individuals can be thought of in much the same way as interdepartmental relations within the organization. If individual efforts are to be synergistic and are to accomplish more than each individual would when acting alone, the individuals must have knowledge of a common purpose. The goal must be definite and specific rather than vague and general. Moreover, if the maximum benefit is to be achieved, the individuals must genuinely desire to have a common purpose. Teamwork, according to Dennison, does not require leadership as long as the objective or goal to be accomplished does not change. The desire for and knowledge of the common purpose are sufficient as long as the end remains the same. This approach to examining the importance of goal setting illustrates the concern Dennison had for individual and interpersonal relations and eventually how it led him to view all social relationships (Duncan and Gullett, 1974).

Objectives and Coordination. One of the most interesting examinations of the importance of goals or objectives in administrative organization was given by Mooney and Reiley in *Onward Industry* (1931, 1932). Although A. C. Reiley is given credit in the 1931 edition as having done most of the research, Mooney has been remembered as the primary driving force behind the ideas presented in the book.

J. D. Mooney was born in 1884 in Cleveland, Ohio. He received a degree in business from New York University and completed his doctorate in engineering at the Case Institute of Technology. He held important positions at Willys Overland Motors and Eversharp and rose to the position of vice-president of General Motors. He was highly trained as an engineer and experienced as an executive.

Much of the writing of Mooney and Reiley is devoted to the *coordinative principle.* Although they concede that organizations begin when two or more people combine their efforts in pursuit of a given purpose, they quickly point out that this combination alone does not constitute organization. The first principle of organization is that the efforts of the combining parties must be coordinated. They must, in other words, act together. For this reason, most writers carefully and accurately point out that the theme of these writings is coordination. That, however, is not the whole story.

Coordination implies an objective. Even though every member of the organization does not carry a "deep consciousness" of the purpose, it is expected that understanding is better as one moves up the organization and is less precise at lower levels. In fact, one of the responsibilities of top management is to ensure that an understanding of purpose "sweeps down" through the organization, since the more the rank and file are permeated with the purpose, the greater will be the coordinated effort. This is the identical point made by Barnard about the executive's responsibility to "inculcate" the belief in employees that a common purpose exists. At this point, Mooney and Reiley provide an extremely informative argument that relates organizational objectives to the concept of *doctrine.*

"Doctrine in its primary sense means simply the definition of the objective" (p. 27). Because doctrine captures the idea of credo, philosophy, and so on, it becomes almost synonymous with the objective. However, the doctrine also deals with the procedures for accomplishing the objective. Mooney and Reiley state that it is essential that the doctrine (objective) be both desirable and legitimate. For example, the objective of the business organization to obtain profits through service is both desirable to employees and legitimate in a social sense. If these conditions are met, managers can effectively lead organizational members in "feeling" and "absorbing" the objective and making it the norm upon which individual actions are based. When the foundation of desirability and legitimacy is established, it can be translated into the unity of spirit that ensures coordinated efficiency. It is this type of coordinated effort that leads us to the concept of teamwork and illustrates the critical character of common purpose and coordination that is essential for organizational efficiency and effectiveness. Again we see Dennison's idea of teamwork and the relationship it has to objectives and coordination.

From task management to organizational purposes and mission statements is a direct route that traces much of management thought over the past seventy-five years. However, there are other developments in the area of goal setting that are even more familiar to managers and employees, especially the "philosophy" known as management-by-objectives, or MBO.

Management-by-Objectives

Since we are talking about goal setting, we cannot ignore the significance of management-by-objectives. A reading of the literature of management will confuse even the seasoned executive with regard to this concept. MBO is at the same time one of the most loved and one of the most hated terms in management. Some praise it as a philosophy, others call it a fad, and still others condemn it as another form of snake oil or even worse. The magnitude of this love-hate relationship, however, suggests that we should not dismiss MBO too quickly.

Origins of MBO. If we accept the classical goal paradigm introduced at the beginning of this chapter, we can say with confidence that MBO is nothing new. In fact, all management, by definition, is management-by-objectives. If we cannot manage without goals or objectives, then it follows that all management is some form of MBO. In a sense this is true. However, not everyone who talks about MBO is talking about the same thing. For example, McConkey (1983) says that 40 percent of the *Fortune* 500 companies have employed some form of MBO, yet a close examination will reveal significant differences in the mechanics of these MBO programs. Obviously, not all MBO programs are the same, and certain aspects of MBO can be traced to the early days of scientific management.

Earlier we noted that some writers believe that the task idea developed by Taylor and expanded by Lillian Gilbreth was a forerunner of MBO. Perhaps so. However, most specialists in management attribute the beginning of MBO to Peter Drucker (1954). That is, while no one argues that elements of MBO have existed from the earliest days of human cooperation, the synthesis, to use Gilbreth's term, was accomplished by Drucker. He was the one who brought all the elements together into the philosophy of management known as MBO.

Drucker was born in Austria in 1909 and educated at the University of Frankfort. As the Nazi party came to power in the 1930s, he left for England and later for the United States. Drucker's career has extended over many years and numerous jobs, ranging from journalist to economist to consultant to college professor. He has served as a professor of management at New York University and other colleges and universities and is currently Clark Professor of Social Science at the Claremont Graduate School in California. He has written textbooks, novels, and even an autobiography. However, the book that is most often identified as the beginning of MBO is *The Practice of Management* (1954).

Elements of MBO. The common characteristics of MBO can be itemized in a short list. The three essential elements of true MBO programs are:

1. The establishment of clear, concise, and communicated goals
2. Participation in the goal-setting process by those who will be expected to work under the system
3. Performance evaluation based on results

Theoretically, the purpose of MBO programs is to provide employees with targets or quantitative milestones to accomplish, to allow them an opportunity to offer input into what the targets should be, and to permit evaluation based on the results achieved relative to the established goals. MBO, as the name implies, is a goal-oriented or objectives-based management system.

There are as many types of MBO programs as there are organizations that employ the technique, but certain well-known implementations deserve some special attention. General Electric developed a form of MBO called *work planning and review* (WPR). The General Electric program evolved from some experiments performed in the company on goal setting. Under the WPR system, employers were said to develop better job attitudes, managers began working more directly and closely with those responsible to them, and organization members became more receptive to new ideas (Meyer, Kay, and French, 1965).

The experience of Purex with a version of MBO known as *goals and controls* was equally favorable. Raia (1974) indicated that productivity improved even though participation was limited. The performance improvements apparently lasted a relatively long time in spite of the facts that managers complained of excessive paperwork and employees felt that measurable, quantitative goals were overemphasized, to the exclusion of more qualitative aspects of their jobs.

One of the more comprehensive reports of an implementation of MBO was given by Carroll and Tosi (1973), who described the experience of Black and Decker. These writers reported that more difficult goals resulted in favorable attitudes toward the program and in improved relations between employees and managers. Frequency of feedback was found to be positively related to attitudes, performance, and employee-manager relations. Praise was found to be more valuable than criticism.

When Drucker first put it all together with respect to management-by-objectives, great excitement was generated for the success of this emerging philosophy. MBO offered a practical way of managing as it should be done—by investing time in planning so as to reduce the time required for control. MBO could be an aid to planning because it forced managers to think seriously about goals. Explicit goals assisted in improving communication, and the opportunity to participate held the promise of increasing the level of employee motivation. Moreover, if the planning was done properly, much of the threat associated with performance evaluation and control could be eliminated. Everyone was in favor of improving the process of performance evaluation. Unfortunately, something happened to the philosophy of MBO. Lee (1980) states that when MBO slipped from a philosophy to a program it became a fad and merely a fashion to be followed. The philosophy could not be "implanted in announcements accompanied by a set of forms and procedures and a few training sessions" (p. 279).

Although we can point to reported successes at companies like Black and Decker, Purex, and General Electric, we must admit that MBO, as currently conceived, has received mixed receptions in real organizations. Comprehensive evaluations such as that of Ivancevich (1972) consistently entertain reservations about the success of this widely used management technique.

The skepticism and mistrust evident about management-by-objectives are understandable given the number of cases where failure, or at least some degree of disappointment, has been the outcome. However, the improper use, premature implementations, and related difficulties should not obscure the fact that MBO as a philosophy is logically sound and pragmatically useful. In this approach to management, the emphasis is properly placed on goal setting. MBO gives employees opportunities to interact with managers and provide input into the standards against which their performance will be evaluated. It also provides a predictable means of obtaining feedback on how well goals are being accomplished. When we compare the philosophy of MBO with the recommendations of early writers such as Taylor, Gilbreth, and Mooney and Reiley, we find that the potential for improved performance clearly exists.

After all, what is it that goal setting is supposed to accomplish? Perceptive managers recognize that most employees want and need three things from a job. First, they need to know what is expected. It is impossible to produce at or near one's potential if the task is not understood. In every case the scientific management writers recognized this critical point. Let the workers know what is expected. In the case of task management let them know a day in advance and provide instructions and training in the most efficient ways of accomplishing the task. Second, employees need to feel they have a part in establishing the standards of performance. Finally, and equally important with knowing what is expected, employees need regular feedback on how they are actually doing. No manager does an employee a favor by withholding feedback on performance. Bad news is not the worst news. At least when the feedback is negative workers can focus their energies on improving performance. The worst news by far is no news. Lack of feedback merely perpetuates unsatisfactory performance and causes bad relations when radical corrective action is initiated.

What about the future of MBO? No one can say with any degree of confidence. Although the principles are sound, the popularity of the concept seems to be declining. The primary reason for this reduction of popularity results from the paradox pointed out by Kerr (1973): It works best for employees who need it least (helpful managers and honest, mature employees) and it works best in situations where it is least needed (stable, mechanistic environments).

Thus we have the example of a philosophy of management founded on goal setting that is only marginally successful according to the best available information. This brings us to the final major topic of this chapter: What is going on now in the area of goal setting?

Goal Setting: A Modern Behavioral Perspective

If goal setting is as important as we say, and if the tradition that began with task management and continued through management-by-objectives to the current emphasis on mission statements and strategic planning is well established in organization theory and management practice, we would expect research to focus on the importance of this phenomenon. In other words, if the promise of goal setting is so great, we would expect researchers to investigate this facet of management in an attempt to know all they can about this critical element. If we find no interest in the literature on the subject, we will be tempted to conclude that goal setting is not as important as Taylor, Lillian Gilbreth, Drucker, and others believe it is.

Goal Setting and Performance Improvement. Management researchers and managers are interested in the influence that new management concepts and theories ultimately have on performance. Locke, Shaw, Saari, and Latham (1981) provided a startling review of the motivational potential of goal setting. They illustrated, for example, that of more than 100 studies on goal setting, 90 percent found that it significantly increased performance. No other motivational technique known to date can come close to duplicating that record.

The research confirms what earlier writers suspected: that goal setting increases productivity. Yet to the manager, research evidence is not always enough. If the director of human resources or some other executive is to invest thousands of dollars and hundreds of hours in a comprehensive goal-setting program, it has to make intuitive as well as scientific sense. Therefore, at the level of intuition, we should ask, what is there about the existence of goals that makes people more productive? Three reasons can be offered for such improvements (Locke and Latham, 1984):

1. Goals focus the attention of employees and managers on relevant and important factors.
2. Goals regulate how hard a person actually works. Energy is spent in proportion to the difficulty of the goals accepted by the managers and the employees.
3. Difficult goals increase an individual's resolve, and persistence is "directed effort that is exerted over time."

This intuitive view of goal setting makes sense to managers and researchers. No one can accomplish all there is to do. Energy, like money, is subject to the economic law of scarcity. All of us have more we would like to do than our energy or time will allow. Goals define for us those things that are most relevant and direct our behavior toward the accomplishment of a few important outcomes.

It is also clear that we work harder to accomplish those goals that demand our best. Peters and Austin (1985) talk about "making a difference at the margin." They focus on the key term *excellence*, and illustrate how performing an extra act of courtesy to a customer here or doing something a little better there can make a difference in the overall effectiveness and profitability of an organization. This is a good example of how demanding goals can motivate the extra type of performance that can make a big difference in an organization.

At this point a word of caution is needed. Even though goals should be demanding and difficult, they should not be impossible. When goals are thought to be impossible to obtain, they are not meaningful to employees and the motivational effect is lost. This is where experience is critical for the manager who uses goal setting as a motivational technique—one must know the difference between the demanding and the impossible.

Finally, when employees accept the legitimacy of goals, they are more persistent in pursuing them. They not only work harder, they work longer. The key words here are *accept* and *legitimate*. Goals, if they are to be motivational, must be accepted, and often the opportunity to participate in goal setting will increase the acceptance of the chosen objectives. This issue of acceptance and the closely related topic of performance feedback are perhaps the unique contributions of advocates of goal setting since the introduction of the concept during the scientific management era and the refinement of the process by the administrative organization writers.

We will conclude this analysis of goal setting by looking in some detail at how managers can encourage the acceptance of goals and what actions they might take to ensure the maximum motivational impact.

Participative Goal Setting. One of the key elements of MBO, as we noted earlier, is that goals should be set in a participative manner. This is one way to increase acceptance. In fact, earlier theories of management, particularly those of Taylor, are often criticized because they had little or no apparent appreciation for participation on the part of workers. Recent research on this issue has provided some interesting results.

To the surprise of many, the research of Meyer, Kay, and French (1965) at General Electric suggested that the way goals are set is less important than the fact that they exist to provide direction. More important to the ultimate acceptance of goals are such things as an explanation of why and how goals are assigned, instructions on how to complete the tasks so as to maximize the likelihood of goal attainment, and selection of employees who are capable of performing the work that will be required to attain the goals.

The reason this is so interesting when we put it in proper perspective is that all of the elements that are really critical in goal acceptance were integral parts of the task management concept of scientific management. To illustrate, the task, as explained by Lillian Gilbreth, was not an abstract, impossible goal that could be achieved only through superhuman or heroic performance. Instead, it was a level of work that was demonstrated as "achievable" under specific, reasonable conditions. Workers could willingly accept the possibility of the task because they could see it accomplished.

Taylor, by the same token, recognized that tasks could be made demanding only when people were "constitutionally" suited to perform the job. He included as one of the main duties of managers the responsibility to "scientifically select, train, teach, and develop workmen." Finally, one important writer (in fact a psychologist) of the scientific management period who has not yet been mentioned is Hugo Munsterberg. Munsterberg is sometimes called the father of industrial psychology because so much of his work was devoted to developing scientific ways to select the right employee for the right job. His pioneering work on the scientific selection of streetcar drivers, and extensions of his research into the selection and training of soldiers in World War I, was the beginning of the use of scientific approaches to vocational guidance and selection (Munsterberg, 1913).

Lillian Gilbreth emphasized the practicality of the task concept. Taylor recognized the futility of expecting tasks to be accomplished if those responsible for accomplishing them were constitutionally unable to perform the job. Munsterberg provided a scientific means of matching individuals with jobs. These three people did much to help us understand the importance of and the process for achieving goal acceptance and task commitment.

While no one would suggest that participation reduces the benefits of goal setting, and, all other things being equal, there may be very good reasons why allowing employees a say in the goals that will be used to evaluate their performance is a good idea, the failure of the early writers to focus on participation is not as dysfunctional as some modern critics contend. Acceptance and perceived legitimacy of goals are the key elements in employee commitment. The scientific management writers accurately focused on demonstrated achievability, instruction and training, and scientific selection of workers as the most critical success factors in the area of goal setting.

Goal Setting and Feedback. One of the fundamental requirements of MBO is evaluation based on results. This implies that the manager will, at predictable intervals, provide information to employees on how their performance is measuring up to the standards. Feedback appears to be an essential element in the successful use of goal setting to improve performance. Giving employees information on how their performance is measuring up to the established goal provides an opportunity to "stroke" those who are on target and to offer encouragement and assistance to those who are not. Those who are on target are reassured that their current pace of work is appropriate and that to continue will result in satisfactory or better evaluations. Those who are performing below expectations can take corrective actions by working harder or obtaining assistance and can "salvage" success rather than being "doomed" to failure (Matsui, Okada, and Inoshita, 1983).

To be effective, feedback should be provided according to some basic principles. First, feedback should be given on as many aspects of the work as possible. In customer service settings, for example, if only the number of claims is stressed in the evaluation, the quality dimension may be underemphasized. Employees may respond by dealing with as many customers as possible while allowing the quality of each encounter to suffer. Next, feedback should be given at predictable intervals and as fast as possible. One of the reasons that computerized teaching machines are so effective is that they give almost immediate feedback. The recency of the performance information has a significant influence on performance and motivation. Another reason for the success of teaching machines is that the feedback goes directly to the performer. Ivancevich and McMahon (1982) demonstrated how information on performance of engineers generated by the engineers themselves was more effective in improving performance than information that came to the engineer through a supervisor. Finally, it is important to provide feedback only in the quantities that can be dealt with and acted on by the employee. If the feedback cannot be managed in a way that allows employees to digest the information in a relatively easy manner, it is not likely to have a positive impact on performance.

Goal-setting theory and practice have much to say to modern managers. What Taylor and the Gilbreths observed about goals at the turn of the century is equally true today. Goals motivate higher performance.

While participation in goal setting is desirable and builds commitment, the existence of goals, regardless of their origin, and the use of regular feedback on performance are more important. Knowledge of goals and performance data consistently improves motivation.

Perhaps, however, there is another reason that goals should be established and feedback regularly provided. It is the right thing for managers to do. This adds an ethical dimension to goal setting. Making sure that employees understand what they are expected to do increases the likelihood that they will do it. Making employees aware of how they are doing provides an opportunity to overcome failures and build a successful future. Managers who provide employees with opportunities to succeed can rest knowing they are providing tangible improvements in the quality of life at work.

Implications and Conclusions

Most managers should spend more time setting goals and communicating them to employees. In the hectic, day-to-day world of crises only the most courageous managers will have the nerve and the will to take time to develop and communicate goals. An investment of time in serious goal setting, however, can pay large and tangible benefits. These goals will provide employees with a sense of direction that is necessary for coordination of diverse functions. Goals also offset a great deal of uncertainty on the part of everyone, and they provide a standard or basis for evaluating the results achieved.

One important lesson from this chapter is that participation is good but the existence of goals is better. Research shows that employees are more concerned with the attainability of goals than with participation. They are even more interested in the nature of the feedback that is instrumental in determining the types of rewards they will receive. Although participation does not directly improve performance, it is probably a good idea to obtain as much input as possible from those who know about the particular task for which goals are being set. The opportunity to participate can be very helpful in establishing the legitimacy of the goals.

The temptation to "put out fires"—and there are always plenty of these in organizations—is ever present. However, the perceptive and successful manager will find time to set goals and develop appropriate plans. Without them, the organization is simply a ship floating aimlessly into an environment that is merely a disorganized mass of flotsam and jetsam. Success in today's competitive business environment requires substantially more. Plans must be well conceived, communicated, and implemented. The structure of the firm must be appropriate in view of the predetermined goals. Finally, controls must be established in a manner that focuses on performance rather than on things that are only remotely related to the real mission of the organization. The environment currently facing managers in large and small organizations is one that is confusing to many experienced executives. There was a time when working hard and efficiently ensured success. But working hard today is not enough—successful managers must be smart as well. Part of this "smartness" is anticipating the future, setting goals that are ambitious yet obtainable, communicating expectations, and carefully following up on goal accomplishment. Goal setting may seem to be a diversion from more important things. In reality, however, it is one of the most important things managers do.

CHAPTER 8

Managerial Responsibility

Balancing Accountability, Obligations, and Values

It seems that times never really change. Just when it appears widely accepted that business has a responsibility to society, scandals develop. Ivan Boesky admitted guilt in an insider trading scheme; Jacob Butcher was convicted of bank fraud; Aldo Gucci pleaded guilty to tax evasion, as did Albert Nipon and Victor Posner; and Paul Thayer of LTV Corporation served time in prison for insider trading. The scandals have been so frequent that a writer in *Time* ("Having It All . . . ," 1987) stated that "what began as the decade of the entrepreneur is becoming the age of the pinstriped outlaw." This, we hope, is an overstatement. Yet all agree that the question of the responsibilities and values of managers is as critical today as it was in the years of the environmental crisis and other social issues.

The factory system, and the methods of mass production it made possible, has served us well economically. Even the most utopian reformer is likely to concede this point. When Babbage looked at the engines that drove the Industrial Revolution, he saw the music of prosperity. And even though Ure recognized evil lurking in the factories, he believed it was the doing of the slubbers, not the industrialists. Yet the very same factories that increased wealth and improved efficiency were the economic prisons of the working class. Heilbroner (1953) describes, in all

too vivid terms, the horrors of mid-eighteenth-century England.
In the mines of Northumberland, for example, he talks of men
and women working together

> stripped to the waist, and sometimes reduced from
> pure fatigue to a whimpering half-human state . . .
> sexual appetites aroused at a glance were gratified
> down some deserted shaftway; children of seven or
> ten who never saw daylight during winter months
> were used and abused and paid a pittance and . . .
> pregnant women drew coal cars like horses and
> even gave birth in the dark black caverns [p. 29].

The Business of Business Is . . . ?

The idea that managers have a responsibility to groups
other than owners is not new. Sometimes we are tempted to
believe that things are simpler and fairer when we leave market
forces alone to allocate resources, even if the process works to
the disadvantage of a large segment of society. Babbage did not
divert his energies to such philosophy, Ure was too busy defend-
ing an exploding industrial society, and classical economists
were determined to make their models of reality analytically
simple, even if it meant making assumptions about maximizing
behavior that were empirically false. Fortunately, the negative
by-products of industrialization did not escape the attention of
everyone.

The Making of a Welfare Capitalist. Robert Owen, a contemporary of Babbage and Ure, was born in 1771 and, by his
own admission, was a "manufacturer for pecuniary profit"
(Owen, 1825). Whereas Babbage was a technologist and Ure was
someone who tended to see things as he wished them to be,
Owen was impossible to stereotype. He sought profit, yet he
disliked private property. In fact, his contempt for private property led him to advocate the formation of a "village of cooperation," which was, in reality, a commune where children were to
be taken from parents and "educated" to ensure they were
taught the "proper values." The government in the village was

expected to play an active role in economic and industrial planning.

Where Babbage and Ure saw magic in the machines, Owen saw suffering. His concern became so great that he had little option except to purchase a manufacturing facility and do his best to improve the plight of the workers. This he did in New Lanark, an industrial oasis in the wilds of Scotland. New Lanark became a tribute to a man who has since been labeled a welfare capitalist and a utopian socialist. In New Lanark the abuse of children was prohibited, child labor laws were passed and enforced, and "the company" built public schools and streets.

Owen, from all available evidence, was concerned about workers. Heilbroner (1953) finds this and the radical difference between Owen's ideas and those of Babbage and Ure surprising. Actually the discrepancy is not hard to understand at all. Babbage and Ure were born into prosperous, if not wealthy, families. Owen enjoyed no such accident of birth. He was born in Wales, the son of poor parents, and at the age of nine left school to become an apprentice draper. There was no university, no travel, and very little happiness in his childhood. Such a reality makes for a different perspective on machines and factories. The view from the inside out is different from that of the outside in. Babbage and Ure were the benefactors of factories; Owen, at least in his childhood, was their victim.

Through acts of fate and sensible investments, Owen became a successful businessman and even managed to purchase a textile mill. Immediately he went to work making his factories more tolerable places to work. In fact, the entire village of New Lanark was a pleasing place thanks to Robert Owen. Children received schooling rather than strappings, and workers were treated kindly, even if the kindness was paternalistic.

Owen advocated devoting more time and attention to the human being or, as he called it, the "living machine." The person should be kept neat and clean, treated with kindness, and supplied with all the necessities of life. Regulated hours of work for all, child labor laws, public education, company-furnished meals at work, and industrial involvement in community projects were all part of Owen's plan. His mistake was that of many zealots—the belief that everyone would agree if only they knew the truth about injustice. In the final analysis, Owen not only was naive but also did not understand human behavior nearly as much as he wished to improve it.

His enthusiasm about the success of New Lanark persuaded him to pursue reforms through legislation. Needless to say, he was not successful. In fact, his reforms were so firmly rejected that he decided to travel to the "New World" of America, where people desired freedom and cared about their fellow men and women. In New Harmony, Indiana, he attempted to replicate and improve the New Lanark experiment. Again, he misjudged the character (or lack of character) of his fellow men and women. New Harmony ended in failure, and Owen returned to England, where he became involved in the organization of a national workers' union—which was found no more acceptable than his village of cooperation. What a strange combination was Robert Owen—capitalist and socialist, manufacturer and organizer of unions, profit seeker and reformer.

Owen is not remembered in management history for his successes. They were few indeed. Rather, he is remembered for his courage and his commitment to reducing the suffering of the working class. He is remembered most as the first person to seriously address the ultimate obligation of management—not just as an institution but as individuals responsible for using human and nonhuman resources in the accomplishment of corporate goals. The tradition he started remains today in questions asked about the ultimate responsibility of management and managers.

From Owen to Gantt. In Chapter Three and other places we have mentioned Henry L. Gantt, perhaps the most influential of Taylor's associates. A close examination of Gantt's writings reveals the tremendous influence Taylor had on his ideas and theories. However, there was a uniqueness to Gantt that in some ways went beyond the ideas of his tutor. This is particularly true when it comes to the responsibilities Gantt believed managers have to workers and society. In short, Gantt appeared considerably more enlightened than Taylor on issues relating to individual and social welfare.

There is no doubt that a person's experiences fashion, to

a great extent, his or her philosophies. We noted earlier that Gantt, like Owen, was not favored on matters of birth. The Civil War turned the fortunes of the Gantt family from prosperity to privation. In the process, Gantt came to understand an aspect of work that Taylor never seemed to recognize or appreciate—the perspective of the worker. Gantt seemed always to better understand the person doing the work, and for that reason he concentrated more on such processes as motivation, leadership, and training.

Gantt respected democracy in government and on the job. He was influenced, to the great surprise of many, by the goals of the government of Russia. Much of his writing took place around the time of the Russian Revolution, and as a consequence he was familiar with the economic and social philosophy that led to the overthrow of the czar. His affection for the socialist cause, it might be noted, did not endear him in business circles, but it did enable him to operate in a different manner than Taylor.

For example, one of Gantt's accomplishments was the use of beneficial aspects of Taylor's system along with elements of "welfare work" at firms such as Bancroft and Sons, where he served as a consultant. The responsiveness of Gantt to the wishes of the Quaker owners resulted in strained relationships with Taylor, who believed his associate was giving in too much to the desires of the proprietors (Nelson and Campbell, 1972). That, however, did not deter Gantt from proceeding in his own way and accomplishing some impressive results.

Gantt's philosophy regarding the payment of workers also differed from Taylor's. For example, he developed a task-and-bonus system in which workers were paid a bonus in addition to their regular day's pay when they followed instructions and accomplished all their work within the time required. Foremen also shared in the bonuses of their workers, and rewards were given for suggestions that resulted in increased efficiency. This task-and-bonus system exhibited more concern for workers than did Taylor's system. One of Gantt's papers, "Training Workmen in Habit of Industry and Cooperation," has been praised by several writers as a unique insight into the humanistic dimension of management and labor (Alford, 1934).

As important as Gantt's views about the worker were, his ideas concerning the social responsibility of business and management were even more significant. As his writings developed, Gantt became increasingly convinced that management should concentrate on its "broad obligations" to society. In his last book, *Organizing for Work* (1919), he talked of a "parting of the ways" that he feared would take place if America's free enterprise system did not find some means of reconciling the quest for profits with the welfare of society. Gantt clearly viewed business firms as institutions existing for the good of society. If, at any time, society deemed the costs of corporations excessive compared to the benefits received, the sanctions could be withdrawn. One gets the impression from Gantt's writings that he considered such actions possible if not probable.

In the midst of the social and economic upheavals in Europe, Gantt could see analogies to the United States. In fact, he believed that all industrial societies had to ensure the equitable distribution of returns to all the factors of production, with special emphasis on labor. Capital was entitled only to the return it rightfully earned. Anything more amounted to excess profits. He was greatly concerned about the apparent desire on the part of business to emphasize profits over community service. If business did not accept its social responsibility and devote itself to service, Gantt believed the community would "ultimately make the attempt to take it over in order to operate it in its own interest" (Gantt, 1919, p. 15).

Gantt had a special fear of big business. He was convinced that small enterprises, because of their competitive situation, must concentrate on service to the customer and society if they are to survive. In his view, as businesses become larger and control more of the market (develop monopolistic power), they become less responsive to customers and pursue excess profits through higher prices.

With Gantt we see the continuity of the concern for social responsibility that emerged in the midst of scientific management. The theme continued in Barnard and others. Gantt, however, perhaps because of his fascination with the Russian Revolution or because of the loss of his family's wealth, possessed a zealousness that reminds one of Owen. This zealousness did not emerge again until a less well known but highly significant contributor to the field of management appeared on the scene. His name was Ordway Tead, and his ideas were as revolutionary as those Gantt admired in Russia.

Ordway Tead: Conscience of a Developing Art

Tead was born in Massachusetts in 1891. At the time of his birth, Gantt was busy perfecting his task-and-bonus system at Midvale Steel. Tead had planned to become a minister but was disillusioned by the amount of hypocrisy in religion and chose business instead. He held a variety of jobs and even worked as a management consultant before finding his true calling in 1920 when he was hired by McGraw-Hill Book Company in the area of business publishing. Within five years he had become the editor for social science and economics books at Harper and Brothers. This position provided him with a base or forum for developing and expanding his ideas on business, economics, and social issues. Tead was more a reformer in the tradition of Owen than an observer like Gantt.

Emergence of a Theme. In his first book, *Instincts in Industry* (1918), Tead introduced some of the more important instincts he thought existed in all human beings. The themes of psychology and leadership continued in his writings for the next two decades (Tead, 1929, 1935). For our purposes in this chapter, however, Tead made his most important statement on management and social philosophy in *The Art of Administration* (1951). This book, according to the foreword by Lawrence Appley, took advantage of all of Tead's previous writing, experience, and exposure to other authors and combined everything into an attempt to deal with the inequalities and injustice he saw in his day. In a real sense, the book is the magnum opus of Ordway Tead.

Tead began his analysis of social philosophy and management at the level of the individual worker. He believed there is no necessary contradiction between organizational efficiency and employee happiness and welfare. Yet many people express discontent with work. Something is missing. This missing ingredient, according to Tead, is the "glory of inner confidence, zest,

and a sense of significance" (p. x). He saw participative management as the best means of hammering out a political, industrial,
and economic order in which all people could live and work
with dignity and self-respect, and he saw management as a critical factor in ensuring that this future become a reality.

Management, Tead believed, is a "grave social liability"
unless the human being is taken into account. Human beings
should never be reduced to the level of a machine or made victims of a "soulless business world bent on mere profits" (p. 4).
Imagine the response these ideas received in 1951. Social responsibility was not an established doctrine. Moreover, private
enterprise advocates of that day, as today, saw no relationship
whatsoever between business's quest for profits and the exploi-
tation of the human resource. In fact, such advocates were likely to envision profit seeking as the ultimate defender of the
rights of workers.

Tead Builds His Argument. The starting point for any
serious argument regarding social responsibility must be the goals
of the organization. The goals, after all, are the factors that
most directly provide us insights into what a business values and
the priorities it places on each value. Tead believed there are
several legitimate corporate aims. The more important are legal,
technical, profit making, personal, and public. Successful managers must consider all these aims if they propose to build an
effective organization. Most of us assume that profit making is
the primary driving force that controls all business operations.
It is not. Tead stressed that without accomplishing important
secondary goals, the primary goals stated in the corporate charter and the quest for profits can never be realized.

In Tead's view, it is important—in fact, it is essential—to
prioritize goals. This is one of the most effective ways to communicate what is most important to employees. If managers do
not make corporate goals appealing to employees in a "sustained
way," they cannot obtain more than a nominal, grudging, indif-
ferent response from their efforts to motivate workers. Tead
stated:

> Managers have to be experts in the clarifying, artic-
> ulating, and purifying of aims, in assuring the rela-

tive appeal of the several prevailing or possible
goals, in bringing about their pervasive communication, and in supplying the supporting conditions
which make acceptance of them likely throughout
the organization [1951, p. 23].

Tead, like many social critics, thought that worker satisfaction, loyalty, and productivity can be best obtained when
employees have a stake in the final outcome of business activity.
For this reason, he advocated profit sharing as a way to provide
workers with such a stake. Profit sharing would be instrumental
in building a "partnership attitude" between workers and managers. Otherwise, rank-and-file employees would be involved
only in creating profits and never allowed to share in the fruits
of their labor.

Making workers stakeholders, however, does not ensure
cooperation and hard work. The association between ownership
and productivity is not automatic. Some businesses have been
generous but paternalistic, and employees have rejected such a
philosophy of rewards. Paternalistic approaches sooner or later
are rejected because they are regarded as "a substitute for au-
tonomous and self-respecting participation by employees in affairs they eventually realize to be their own" (p. 36).

Tead believed that society was more complicated in 1951
than in 1900. By implication, we can infer he would think the
1980s are more complex than the 1950s. He perceived society
as characterized by big corporations, big schools, big cities, and
big governments. Because of the bigness and a substantial degree
of mobility, people seemed less in agreement about how to
achieve democracy, equality, and justice than when the economy was less urban, less industrialized, and less concentrated.

In a time of significant activism, Tead proposed that managers become proactive and "spell out in some detail what the
nature and aims of a democratic society are" (p. 82). At this
point an almost radical activism can be sensed in Tead the social critic. However, it was his conviction that when people are
working together to achieve worthy goals and when people's
creative expression and meaningfulness of life are enhanced,
their "rightful democratic claims" are being satisfied. Could it

be that Tead was suggesting that management and managers become agents of social change? Indeed he was, because of his belief that corporate aims cannot be viewed apart from democratic aims. There is no escaping the conclusion that he saw helping organizations operate democratically as an "intrinsic" purpose of management. He stated the argument as follows:

> Democracy as a moral aspiration with its concomitant institutional expressions is an influence extended into the lives of all and in all areas of our activity. And good administration has a major role in helping to translate this intrinsic American aspiration into processes and procedures which promise well for the growth of robust personalities [p. 91].

Tead was idealistic but not unrealistic. He recognized the dangers of democracy. He even quoted Chester Barnard and observed that the freedoms of action, thought, and speech necessary to democratic processes require a greater sense of responsibility, initiative, and adaptability on the part of individuals.

Tead anticipated many contemporary issues and ideas, such as the quality of work life that he called *collective cooperation*. In this system workers and managers strive in harmony for the "progressive improvement of any and all phases of operation looking to the increasing productivity of the entire enterprise" (p. 166). The prerequisites for such cooperation are familiar: job security for workers, quality work standards, criteria for promotions, guidelines for laborsaving modernization, employee grievance procedures, job classifications and wage and salary administration, and provision for the workers' old age, safety, and death.

Tead believed that when corporations provide these conditions, employees are more likely to believe that the company and its managers care about them, and they, in turn, will care more about the organization. Collective cooperation can best, perhaps only, be accomplished through coordination, which includes all managerial efforts to formulate, adopt, transmit, give effect to, interpret, and oversee organizational policies. Managers, according to Tead, should ask themselves, "Do we all know what we are up to now, and are we all relating our efforts to this end in the best possible way?"

Above all, Tead believed there is a need for greater appreciation of the social and moral significance of management and its role in business and society. To him, the most profound meaning of management is "a more participative, more dynamic type of managing where organized administrative relations are democratically proposed, are mindful of the whole man [person], and are ethically sensitive" (p. 207).

Ordway Tead is rarely discussed in the history of management thought. Claude S. George (1972) refers to him as a "minor" writer and Daniel Wren (1987) devotes little attention to him. Significance is, of course, a matter of judgment. Certainly, Tead does not deserve the recognition of Taylor or Barnard. He was, however, one of the first management writers of modern times to courageously advocate the social responsibility doctrine. His personal philosophy, particularly his concern for social injustice, was applied to real management issues. His implicit, and sometimes explicit, view of the role of business in solving social ills was at least two decades before its time. In 1950, it was unusual to suggest that business had any stake in correcting social problems, much less taking the proactive role of actually defining social problems.

Management was to hear more about social issues with the passage of time. In the 1960s, civil rights and the evils of racial discrimination were to focus on the question of employment and promotion equity. In the 1970s the environmental crisis and the role of business in protecting the ecology of "spaceship Earth" came to the forefront. The 1980s brought even more issues. We are fortunate to have the wisdom of Tead, Gantt, and others to guide us through these turbulent times.

Social Responsibility and Management

Steel mills emitted smoke and particulate matter into the atmosphere for years and automobile exhaust fumes filled the lungs of millions of people, yet only a few complained until relatively recently. What is it that has increased the interest in the social impact of business in recent years? There are at least three reasons for the growing social consciousness.

First, people have become more affluent and their needs have changed. At the turn of the twentieth century the majority of people were concerned about having jobs and ensuring that their economic and security needs be met. The same steel mills that emitted smoke provided jobs, and employment was a more basic need than health status—especially when adverse health effects did not show up until twenty years later and were not readily connected to the mill emissions. Things are different as we draw near the last decade of the century. Employment is important, but all of us are more aware of the ill effects of a polluted environment. We are more prosperous and less willing to sacrifice our future health for job security today. We have become more aware of the psychological and physiological aspects of earning a living.

Second, the corporate form of organization has effectively separated ownership and management. It has become common for the managers of firms not to be the owners and vice versa. The identity between managerial effectiveness and profits has been distorted as additional criteria of performance have been applied to the work of the professional manager (Chandler, 1977). Professional (nonowner) managers are often evaluated on the basis of labor relations, turnover rates, absenteeism, and sometimes the number of employees and the size of the budgets they oversee.

Third, the simple truth is that managers are becoming more socially conscious. A survey of 513 executives by the Opinion Research Corporation, reported in *USA Today* (May 23, 1984), provided support for this point. The sample of executives thought that high ethical standards are important components of corporate responsibility, but less than 40 percent thought companies are doing a "first-rate job" in the area of ethics. The executives also believed companies should take the responsibility of working for a pollution-free environment, but only 32 percent thought corporations are doing a good job of preventing pollution. Finally, only 25 percent of the executives thought corporations are making socially responsible decisions.

Drawing the Lines in the Controversy. In recent years,

the social responsibility controversy has been debated according to two somewhat extreme positions. The first is the familiar
profit-maximizing argument. Theodore Levitt (1958) stated
that "welfare and society are not the corporation's business. Its
business is to make money" (p. 44). Milton Friedman (1970)
more directly stated that professional managers are agents of
the owner, and their social responsibility is to increase profits.

The alternative position maintains that business is a social
institution and should consider the impact of its decisions on
the larger social system. The corporation that hires thousands of
people and affects millions with a single decision cannot, according to this argument, disregard the social impact of its
operations. Robert D. Kilpatrick, chairman of the board of
CIGNA Corporation, has stated that CIGNA is part of the
communities in which it operates and "shares with these communities a bond of interest and obligation" (CIGNA Corporation, 1985). Perhaps a more familiar example is that of William
Marriott, head of the Marriott Corporation, who applies the
principles of the Mormon faith to his business life. His involvement, through the Boy Scouts of America, in fighting teenage
drinking could adversely affect his business interests; however,
he maintains that business firms must sometimes "give up short-
term business interests for long-term social gains" ("Marriott
. . . ," 1985).

Another example is Philippe Villers, the mastermind behind Computervision and Automatix. Villers is a high-tech capitalist who is sometimes referred to as the "social conscience of
Route 128." He is a corporate executive who has personally
talked to the prime minister of Greece about halting the arms
race, has publicly criticized the Reagan policies in El Salvador,
and spends a great deal of his time working for Amnesty International and the American Civil Liberties Union. He has even
established his own foundation to assist the elderly ("Philippe
Villers . . . ," 1985).

Some Issues and Responses. The responsibility of business firms and managers is regularly questioned on television
and in the press. In this section we will briefly review a few of
the issues that have been the focus of a significant amount of

investigation and criticism on the part of writers, politicians, and other individuals concerned with the role of business in modern society.

In the early 1980s labor unions and business economists began to focus on a strange phenomenon—the salaries of top executives in the United States. We cannot be sure why this issue became so popular. It might have been the fact that executives were asking labor unions to grant wage concessions in the interest of job security while they pocketed extremely large "total salaries" and worked busily preparing "golden parachutes" (rich compensation packages given to executives when they leave their firm) to ensure their own future welfare. It could have been because the Japanese were beating us competitively with executives who earn considerably less than their American counterparts. No doubt some of the bad press resulted from the fact that, in general, there was no correlation between what an executive made and the performance of the company he or she managed.

Drucker (1986) refers to trends in executive compensation as the "greed effect" and philosophically dismisses it as a scandal but not an entirely important one, because only a few people are affected. Besides, he argues, the unions and the Internal Revenue Service are sure to rectify the situation in the not too distant future.

The magnitude of the problem is illustrated by the fact that in 1985 Victor Posner of DWG had a total income package of over $12 million, while Lee Iacocca of Chrysler was paid almost $12 million—and that figure increased to $20 million in 1986. T. Boone Pickens, the famous corporate raider, made over $8 million while contributing very little, some would argue, to the welfare of corporations or society. At the same time, a golden parachute of $35 million was obtained by Michel Bergerac of Revlon in the Pantry Pride takeover. Parachutes of more than $5 million are commonplace.

From the social perspective the question, of course, is how such large sums can be justified. Unions complain that executives make too much compared to rank-and-file employees. Stockholders wonder whether managers are really their agents or independent contractors working for themselves. The greed effect certainly operates, but there are legitimate defenses for the compensation packages. Perhaps the best defense relates to the comparisons executives like Iacocca make to professional athletes and rock stars. Who, one should ask, really deserves the most pay: the chief executive of a *Fortune* 500 corporation that employs thousands of people and possesses assets greater than most states, or the rock star, bonus baby, or free agent? The market, to a great extent, determines the economic value of all services, and surely the talents of the leaders of industries must be among the most scarce and valuable of all resources. In spite of the fact that all these salaries may be scandalous, most would cast their lot with corporate executives rather than entertainers or athletes.

Another current ethical issue is product liability. Almost fifteen years after A. H. Robbins Company stopped selling the Dalkon Shield intrauterine device, it must regularly defend itself from claims involving product liability in courts across the nation. To date it has paid over $179 million in damages and court costs. Ford Motor Company continues to insist that the transmission it installed in almost 25 million cars between 1968 and 1980 does not slip out of park when the motor is left running. The Center for Auto Safety, however, estimates that such slips have accounted for over 200 deaths and thousands of injuries. The Center estimates that Ford may experience a liability of over $500 million when all cases are settled. Similarly, Firestone Tire and Rubber faces substantial liability for alleged defects in its Firestone 500 tire. Firestone says it has been involved in over 8,000 lawsuits related to the tire and that costs of recall and related measures have totaled over $180 million.

Debate continues about the most appropriate manner to prosecute product liability cases. The diversity of individual state laws is one reason given for the need for federal legislation. Proponents of new legislation also contend that punitive damages should be limited.

The social problem presented by product liability cases centers on the very heart of the private enterprise system. Critics argue that in a system of free enterprise the corporation must always see to the welfare of the customer. Never should chances be taken with the health and safety of those who trust the corporation by purchasing products or services. The temptation to "cheat" in the system comes when decisions are made to not report adverse effects in the testing of drugs and other health products or to withhold vital engineering information that might suggest the unsafe nature of such products as airplane or automobile braking systems. Such dishonesty, when it occurs, supports premature entry into a market for purposes of making a profit. Withholding or misuse of information can usually be exposed as irresponsible and unethical behavior (Duncan, 1986). It can never be defended. It is illegal, is socially irresponsible, and can never be justified as anything other than a shortsighted approach to decision making.

Business firms are often criticized and seldom praised— even when they actively pursue programs that aim to improve social problems. For example, ALCOA recognized that aluminum cans were rapidly becoming an environmental problem. In response the company instituted a recycling program. Recently, ALCOA has set up "issue centers" to consider problems of the environment, health, and energy. The goal of the centers is to clarify, analyze, prioritize, and recommend policies for overcoming current and anticipated problems.

Procter & Gamble's leadership in refusing to sponsor television shows that feature excessive sex and violence inspired other firms, including Quaker Oats and General Foods, to establish similar policies. In 1981 Procter & Gamble, the largest purchaser of television advertising time, canceled its support for fifty television programs it found unsuitable (Work and Hamilton, 1983).

Question and Response

That business firms have been the focus of criticisms relating to social responsibility is probably not surprising. But how have firms responded to the critics?

Organizations respond in many different ways to the social needs that are perceived around them. Sometimes responses are defensive, as has frequently been the case in incidents involving product liability. In 1980, Levi Strauss, for example, settled out of court a number of claims resulting from accusations that the company had engaged in price fixing with its dealers. The settlement amounted to $12 million, but Levi Strauss insisted the settlement did not constitute an admission of guilt. Although this type of defensive response costs the organization a great deal of money, it is not unusual to equate the amount of the resources committed to the sincerity of the response. For example, consider the following.

Firms usually begin responding to social issues in ways that many would classify as tokenism. At times tokenism is merely a way of avoiding coming to grips with the real issue. At other times it may be a low-risk way of attempting to deal with social concerns. For example, Atlantic Richfield (ARCO) has been an industry leader in a relatively low-cost response known as *constituency building.* The various stakeholders in the organization (stockholders, employees, managers, and so on) are encouraged to become informed about and participate in the development of public policies that may affect the company. Another example is given by the National Association of Manufacturers, which states that there are now 200 to 250 board-level committees focusing on public policy issues likely to affect business firms, whereas there were only about 20 such committees in 1975. The concern, if not the commitment, for social issues is growing.

Sometimes important social services can be performed by businesses without tremendous commitments of financial resources. In 1984 Trailways Corporation announced the inauguration of Operation Home Free, in which the bus company provided a free ride home for runaways. The company distributed 250,000 posters and sponsored public service announcements. In the first month of the program about 200 youths received free rides back home. In Philadelphia CIGNA Corporation developed the Nonstandard Investment Program, designed to selectively commit resources and capital to community investments that promised "overriding positive social value for higher risk and/or lower return than would normally be expected"

(CIGNA Corporation, 1985). To date it has provided, among other things, low-cost rental units for the elderly, housing for low-income families, and low-cost alternative health care for the Hispanic population of the city.

Perhaps one of the most widely discussed and debated situations in recent years is that of General Motors's involvement in South Africa. GM's dilemma can best be appreciated by recognizing that the company has operated continuously in the Republic of South Africa since 1926. Throughout this time apartheid, or the systematic separation of the native blacks and the white population, has been the official policy of the government. As repeated unsuccessful attempts have been made to convince South Africa's leadership to relax this policy, activists in the United States and throughout the world have suggested that economic sanctions and commercial withdrawal are the only means to effect desired changes. For a number of years GM resisted the persistent calls for its withdrawal. The justifications used for the company's continued presence were:

1. All foreign companies, including GM, operate in South Africa as guests of the country, and the options available to influence social change are limited. GM tried, according to its statements, to influence the policy of apartheid through positive pressure on government policies. Much of this pressure was applied through organizations such as the Associated South Africa Chamber of Commerce, the Federated Chamber of Industries, and the American Chamber of Commerce.

2. In response to the partial embargo imposed on South Africa by the U.S. government in 1978, GM discontinued any sale to the police and military of vehicles specially adapted for their use. The company continued to sell regularly equipped vehicles to private individuals, however, because it believed that such a restriction of sales would effectively force it out of the South African market, because of the bad press such an action would entail.

3. GM engaged in a number of internal actions to reduce its participation in apartheid. Racial discrimination in hiring

and promotion was reduced; all company facilities, including eating and comfort areas, were desegregated; and attempts were made to provide training that would allow the promotion of more blacks into managerial positions.

Finally, GM resisted disinvestment and withdrawal because of the belief that if all U.S. firms left South Africa, the American leadership role in the area would be significantly reduced. Many corporate officials even held that such a move would hurt the black population because of the jobs it would eliminate.

Hypothetical issues of this nature are difficult to discuss and almost impossible to solve. Withdrawal of American firms would certainly cause loss of jobs and suffering. The American presence and leadership would be reduced as well. At the same time, such an action might cause a "crisis of conscience" in South Africa's white government. No one could say for sure what the ultimate outcome would be. That is why socially responsible decisions are so complex and multidimensional and why many managers attempt to avoid making them. Such decisions, however, must be made. The real issue is whether business or government will be the ultimate decision maker. In the case of GM, it eventually became apparent that disinvestment and withdrawal would be the only action that would satisfy the demands of the public. Other firms have reluctantly reached decisions that they would have preferred to postpone or ignore entirely. However, society expects more. Business, many believe, is too large and important to abstain.

Business decisions have never been easy. Nothing leads us to believe they will be any easier in the future.

The concern about management's responsibility is not new. There have been significant champions of socially responsible business for centuries. The concern is real, proper, and at least a little ironic. While we should never justify irresponsible decision making, we cannot help but wonder whether business morality can be expected to exceed that of the larger society. We live in a time when political figures are forced from high because of misconduct. Even religious leaders are not free from criticism. To the extent that irresponsible acts occur in business, we must wonder whether business can be rightfully expected to rise above the moral climate in general.

Ultimately, we must opt for higher standards of conduct for politicians and bureaucrats as well as for business executives. Society deserves more and, as Gantt warned, may very well demand it.

Implications and Conclusions

The social responsibility of management was not discussed very much at the turn of the century. Robert Owen had his say, but most people chose not to accept his views. Gantt was beginning to illustrate that social consciousness and hard-nosed management are not mutually exclusive alternatives. With the aid of these individuals, and particularly Ordway Tead, the social responsibility controversy has become more focused.

Several things appear evident today. First, although there are some diehards, at least for the present most vocal business managers believe that organizations have obligations to society as well as to the owners of the firm. Second, knowing what is right to do relative to social concerns is never easy. All actions have reactions, and care must be taken to consider both the costs and benefits of social consciousness. The case of South Africa is a good example. If all American firms were to disinvest and withdraw, adverse social consequences would result. For one thing, the influence of the United States in that country would be greatly reduced. Withdrawal and disinvestment would also mean unemployment to many who can barely survive with a regular paycheck. Yet to do nothing could be interpreted as an act of condoning apartheid. Almost no one would respect a firm that explicitly or implicitly accepted such a policy. The stakes are great in socially responsible decision making, and the right and wrong answers are never easy to find.

Third, managers need to recognize that such dilemmas are not new. The precedent for thinking about social responsibility dates back to the eighteenth century, and such thinking has been an obligation of management since its early beginning. There is no escaping it—if one is to manage, one must address the question of social responsibility; but the answer will never be simple. Decision making at its best is complicated. Strategic decision making is even more complex, and when social issues are involved the complexity is multiplied. Executive decision making is a tough and thankless task. When executives make decisions that have a social dimension to them, and most do, the job is even tougher and more thankless. However, there is consolation. As Drucker (1986) notes, nobody in America is important except "people who don't really matter." That is one of our safeguards against tyranny. "We save our adulation for people who never become a menace—for baseball players and rock stars and movie idols who are completely innocuous" (p. 13). Decision makers should take heart. The fact that they are criticized is the best evidence that what they do is important.

PART FOUR

Managing the Human Factor

For most of the first quarter of the twentieth century, management held tightly to the principles of scientific management. The names of Taylor, the Gilbreths, Emerson, and Gantt were associated, even identified, with the developing science of management. A few mentions might have been made of Fayol, perhaps from European travelers. Scientific management, however, was the rule of the day.

At some point in the early 1920s managers at Western Electric's Hawthorne Works outside Chicago proposed a study of working conditions and productivity. As Chapter Nine will illustrate, the intent was not altogether altruistic. The research started innocently enough—actually, as a fairly typical scientific management problem. But before the studies at Hawthorne were over, they represented a major counterpoint in management thought.

By modern behavioral science standards, the Hawthorne studies were not impressive. The hard-line behavioral scientists today would probably consider them worthless. Researchers Mayo and Roethlisberger would only reluctantly be accepted into their fraternity if at all. Regardless of the studies' scientific merits or limitations, the fact remains that management has not been the same since the Hawthorne researchers published their findings. The studies, in fact, ushered in the human relations school of management thought. Social scientists were suddenly interested in the problems of industry, and such issues as motivation, communication, and leadership became legitimate topics for management research along with time and motion studies, planning, organizing, and controlling.

In Part Four, the issues of motivation and leadership are explored. Chapter Nine examines motivation from Taylor to Skinner, and Chapter Ten illustrates how leadership developed as an "Americanized" discipline in itself.

CHAPTER 9

Work and Motivation

Exploring Different Assumptions About Human Nature

If we choose to despair at the lack of change with regard to the social responsibility of management as we did in Chapter Seven, our hopes might be elevated with regard to motivation. The fact is that even if philosophies remain the same, times change in management as in society. Nowhere are the changes more evident than in the views of management pioneers regarding human nature and motivation. Some of these views, by today's standards, are shocking. Taylor, for example, surprises even the most insensitive reader by stating that successful pig iron handlers were so "stupid and so phlegmatic" they more closely resembled in their "mental make-up the ox than any other type" of animal (Taylor, 1914, p. 59). Skinner (1953) similarly tries to make us believe that human behavior is really no more complicated than that of his experimental pigeons. Yet the majority of contemporary management writers are emphatic in their belief that human beings are unique.

Notwithstanding the counterinfluence of Skinner, the predominant view of the worker has evolved from that of a simple, economic creature to a more complex psychosociological human being who is an individual yet greatly influenced by fellow workers and the work environment. In fact, the image of human beings at work changes so drastically from the writings of

Taylor to the need theories of Maslow that one cannot help but wonder whether humans are really the object of both theories. The ox in Taylor's steel mill becomes the social creature at Hawthorne and perhaps even an angel or some similar almost divine being in Maslow's humanistic view. Our task in this chapter is to reconcile these various views and make some sense of motivation theory and practice as presented in selected theories from human relations and behavioral science applied to management.

Counterpoint at Hawthorne

What can one say about the Hawthorne studies that has not been said many times before? Perhaps nothing; certainly very little. Yet beginning in the late 1920s something was going on at the Hawthorne, Illinois, works of Western Electric that would, in time, radically influence management thought regarding human motivation. The most comprehensive report of these events is provided by Roethlisberger and Dickson (1939). However, the roots of the events can be traced as far back as 1910 and involve such seemingly unrelated organizations as General Electric, Commonwealth Edison, trade associations, the National Electric Light Association, and the National Research Council.

Apparently it all began with General Electric's desire to sell more light bulbs. Of course, more light bulbs meant more electricity, and that interested Commonwealth Edison. Because the National Research Council relied on influential executives from firms like Commonwealth Edison and General Electric for advice and assistance, it suddenly became interested in light bulbs and electricity. Some small-scale studies suggested that a relationship existed between worker productivity and illumination, but a careful scientific inquiry was needed to prove the association and true science demanded the "noncommercial" image that could be provided by the National Research Council. The council was persuaded to form a committee on industrial lighting by its honorary chair, who happened to be Thomas Edison himself, and one of its members who worked for AT&T

quickly volunteered the Hawthorne Works as a test site (Greenwood and Wrege, 1986). The Hawthorne Works, located outside Chicago in Hawthorne, Illinois, belonged to Western Electric Company and assembled telephones for AT&T. The components of a "noncommercial, scientific study" suddenly fell together. For some interesting and generally unknown details about the Hawthorne studies, one should refer to Bolton, Toftoy, and Chipman (1987) and Greenwood, Bolton, and Greenwood (1983).

Brief Details of the Studies. The studies at Hawthorne progressed through four stages and involved more than 20,000 workers before they were completed (Cass and Zimmer, 1975). Relay assembly experiments, involving five telephone assemblers, were designed to analyze the effects of working hours on productivity. The experiments controlled for shorter working hours, rest periods, and so on. Even a wage incentive program was introduced.

Mica splitting experiments were conducted to investigate the effects of rest periods and length of working hours on performance. A large-scale interviewing program was designed to probe deeper into worker attitudes. While all the experiments are important and interesting, space limitations prevent a comprehensive examination of the details. However, it was probably in the bank wiring observation room that the radical change in motivational philosophy began to emerge. Experiments here focused on many aspects of the informal organization. The researchers gradually came to recognize that work is more than earning a living, even in hard times. Employees also receive important social benefits from work. In fact, the work group is a social unit that can restrict the output of the individual, develop its own standard of a good day's work, and even effectively use its influence to ensure that rewards do not go to people in direct proportion to the quantity and quality of work performed.

People Behind the Studies. A retrospective view of the Hawthorne studies immediately brings two names to mind: Elton Mayo and Fritz Roethlisberger. George Elton Mayo was born in 1880 in Australia, where he was educated in ethics, logic, and philosophy. He even went to medical school but did not graduate. Mayo came to the United States in the early 1920s to conduct research for the Rockefeller Foundation before joining the department of industrial research at Harvard in 1926. His two most important books for our purposes are *The Human Problems of an Industrial Society* (1933) and *The Social Problems of an Industrial Society* (1945).

Fritz J. Roethlisberger, born in New York in 1898, was a gifted child fascinated with geometry, chemistry, and physics. He attended Columbia and M.I.T. and received degrees from both even though he became disillusioned with schools and retired to Greenwich Village to dream of becoming a writer (Roethlisberger, 1977). Fortunately, he decided to give education one last try and enrolled at Harvard, where he was "taken in" by a young Australian professor who was none other than Elton Mayo. This chance meeting eventually did much to change the course of management history.

How Hawthorne Influenced Motivation Concepts. Taylor's comment about pig iron loaders illustrates how little progress motivation theory and practice had made during the scientific management era. All this changed with the publications of Mayo and Roethlisberger. In *Management and the Worker* (1939), Roethlisberger and W. J. Dickson (an executive at Western Electric) promised not to just report the Hawthorne research but to provide accounts of the "trials and tribulations" they encountered along the way. Because of the social nature of work, the authors recommended that organizations introduce the "explicit skill" of diagnosing human situations. This focus on interpersonal relations should be a philosophy of the organization and should extend to all people in management and supervisory positions. To simply have a few highly trained individuals capable of counseling is not enough. Such skills leave when the individual retires or makes a job change. Instead, it is important to involve many people and create an organizational climate that emphasizes interpersonal relations. Managers should commit themselves and their organizations to the conscious process of studying human situations and should conduct business on the basis of what is learned.

The insights into human nature gained by Roethlisberger

at Hawthorne developed quickly in his writings. In *Management and Morale* (1941) he stated boldly that people are motivated more by sentiments than by money and that groups influence the behavior of individuals in such significant ways as to make it essential that managers recognize that business firms are more than mere economic institutions—they are social organizations composed of human beings and should be managed accordingly. *Man-in-Organizations* (1968) demonstrates the breadth of Roethlisberger's thinking.

The relationship between the worker and the efficiency expert or engineer (that is, the *technologist*) is an illustration of the types of insights of which Roethlisberger was capable. The technologist, according to him, operates on the basis of the "logic of efficiency" and views technology, specialization, and automation as ways of reducing fatigue. Recall how all the engineers in scientific management argued that specialization and automation would free the worker from heavy work. Workers, however, view the same factors in terms of the reduction in skills required for the job and the consequent reduction in the perceived importance of the individual. What begins as a source of help in the language of efficiency becomes a source of grievance in the language of sentiments.

Roethlisberger was one of the first to recognize the unique position of the first-line supervisor as the go-between or person in the middle. He was an advocate of supervisory training but believed that only those people with the appropriate attitudes should be placed in such training programs, that supervisors should be prepared for lifetime learning, and that supervisory training should aid prospective managers in asking better questions, becoming better observers (à la management by walking around), and making better decisions.

Mayo's View of Human Nature and Motivation. One might expect the pupil's (Roethlisberger's) ideas to mirror those of the mentor (Mayo). To some extent they did. To a greater extent they did not. There is a distinctiveness in Mayo's writing that is not always evident in Roethlisberger's. Mayo began *The Human Problems of an Industrial Society* with a caution, stating that "in industry, as in medicine, the inquirer who seeks a single remedy for all ailments is doomed to failure" (p. vi). In management there are never simple answers or quick fixes, and woe to the manager who looks for one. If one is found, it is probably wrong!

Mayo addressed a number of industrial problems, including fatigue, monotony, and motivation. In his study of a mule-spinning department of a textile mill near Philadelphia, he noted how the job fit all criteria of the "monotony model." The semi-automatic process required enough of the worker's attention to be irritating but not enough to totally absorb his mental abilities. The department never produced to standard, and workers were pessimistic about all aspects of life. The turnover rate was 250 percent. Mayo's interventions, including rest pauses and pay for output, resulted in a stabilization of turnover at 5 or 6 percent. The department became the standard for all other units in the mill. In his discussion of this study, Mayo presented one of the fundamental principles of all human relations theories, the maxim of *individual differences:* "All individuals are different. What bores one may stimulate another" (p. 32). Workers are individuals, and any theory of work that tempts managers to treat everyone the same will fail. The successful manager and the effective organization always recognize the uniqueness of each person. This maxim sounds simple but it is complex; it sounds trite yet is profound. A worker may not like a particular incentive program and may even resist all types of change, but everyone likes to be recognized and treated as an individual.

Mayo defended the sociopsychological explanation of productivity improvements at Hawthorne. Production increased, he believed, because working conditions were made more pleasant and greater freedom was provided to workers. In fact, his interests became progressively social and political. (He published a third book in his "trilogy," *The Political Problems of an Industrial Society* [1947], which never attained the recognition of the first two publications.)

Mayo pointed out that all societies have two primary goals. The first is to ensure the material and economic survival of its members. The second is to maintain "spontaneous cooperation" throughout the entire structure. The challenge was to develop ways of accomplishing these objectives. The *rabble hypothesis* or "invisible hand" of classical economic theory seemed no longer capable of achieving voluntary cooperation. Management had to be proactive if coordination was to be achieved. Chandler's (1977) "visible hand" was not only a reality to Mayo, it was a necessity for economic survival and cooperation. In summary, we can say that Mayo, and to an extent Roethlisberger, provided several guidelines that are as useful as they are practical:

1. Individuals are different, with unique wants, needs, goals, and motives. Successful motivation demands that workers be treated as individuals.
2. Human problems are never simple.
3. A worker's personal or family problems may adversely influence performance at work.
4. Communication is important, and effective communication is critical. Few managers, in Mayo's opinion, were prepared educationally or practically for the human, social, and political problems of an industrial society.

Need Theories and the Humanization of Work

Mayo and Roethlisberger moved motivation theory away from the economic view of scientific management. They introduced ideas that were influential in their time and set the stage for new contributions by others. Discussions of sentiments, motives, and individual differences made the movement to theories of human needs less difficult.

Abraham Maslow and the Theory of Human Needs. Ask any junior business, education, or arts and sciences student what he or she remembers about introductory psychology and likely as not the student will mention Maslow's needs hierarchy. This is not surprising, since this hierarchy has probably been discussed in more than a fourth of all the courses he or she has taken at the university. However, the mere fact that the need hierarchy is familiar makes it no less profound.

Abraham Maslow was born in Brooklyn in 1908 and received his doctorate in psychology at the University of Wisconsin. Although the years immediately following the completion of his education were tragic in the sense that he was a victim of anti-Semitic prejudice, he managed to get a job at Columbia University working as a research assistant to the famous psychologist E. L. Thorndike. Even though jobs were almost impossible to obtain for Jewish scholars, it is said that Maslow resigned his position because Thorndike gave him the assignment of determining how much of behavior was caused by heredity and how much was the result of environment. Maslow sent a note to Thorndike saying the assignment was "silly" and "not worth doing" (Wilson, 1972).

Fortunately, neither religious prejudice nor silly assignments discouraged Maslow from becoming one of the most widely known and recognized psychologists of the twentieth century. He eventually became chairman of the psychology department at Brandeis University and a founder of humanistic psychology. Many of his writings made significant contributions, although our attention here will be directed primarily toward his best-known book, *Motivation and Personality* (1954, 1970).

Maslow defined motivation as the "study of ultimate human goals" (p. 66). Although all human beings have essentially the same goals, different cultures influence the ways in which goals are accomplished. It is an essential part of Maslow's theory that human beings never fully attain their objectives. When one need is satisfied or one goal is accomplished, others replace it.

Maslow made three basic assumptions about human nature that provide the foundation for his theory: (1) human beings are wanting animals whose needs are never satisfied; (2) it is the state of dissatisfaction or unsatisfied needs that motivates human action (according to Maslow, "the best way to send someone searching for love is to deny them love"); and (3) needs are arranged in a hierarchy, with the basic, lower-level needs at the bottom and the higher-level needs at the top.

Maslow's Hierarchy of Needs. At the base of the need hierarchy are the *physiological needs* for food, water, clothing, and shelter. These are survival needs—without them we die. They are with us at birth. As the physiological needs are satisfied *safety* or *social needs* appear. Human beings need protection from danger and the uncertainty of the future. Food may no longer be a problem for most people in industrialized nations, but they have a pressing need for protection against income loss in old age, catastrophic illness, and other dangers in the uncertain future.

Not all needs relate to the individual's personal security and survival. Human beings also need companionship and a sense of belongingness. Thus, the third level in the hierarchy is *belongingness needs*. People need to be accepted by others and to feel a part of groups. Next, the *esteem needs* appear, because all of us desire self-respect. We need to believe what we do is important and that we are honest, fair, and accepted as friends and respected colleagues. When we are assured of such acceptance, our esteem needs become satisfied. At the very top of the hierarchy is the *need for self-actualization*—making all we can of the talents and skills we have developed. While other needs are often satisfied, few "normal" people ever become self-actualized. Self-actualization is a quest, a goal, not a defined accomplishment. There are always jobs to be done, relationships to mend, and opportunities to pursue.

At one point Maslow classified the needs in the hierarchy into two major categories. *Deficiency needs* encompass the needs at the lower levels, including physiological, safety, and belongingness needs. *Growth-motivated* or *developmental needs* are the esteem needs and self-actualization. Note that the deficiency needs are satisfied by factors somewhat external to the individual like food, a safe environment, friends, and loved ones, whereas growth needs are more intrinsic or internal to the individual. This realization will appear again in our discussion of job enrichment.

Maslow illustrated the importance of maintaining favorable working conditions in his discussion of the "theory of threat." The general public at large and employees in an organization can experience severe psychological problems when faced with threats. When an individual confronts deprivation of a life goal, conflict results. Consider the case of *threatening conflicts* in which an employee is forced to choose between two important yet mutually exclusive goals. For example, the sales manager who holds a political office in her local community is required to relocate in order to advance in her organization. The move, however, will require her to resign from the elected office. How does she choose between organizational success and loyalty to the voters?

Another, more serious threat is *catastrophic conflict*. In this case the employee is faced with only threatening options. At least in the relocation example the manager can either receive a promotion or retain a highly valued political office. But the employee who has been "offered" early retirement may perceive his only options as leaving his life's work and sitting in a rocking chair the rest of his days or remaining in an organization where he is not wanted. This is catastrophic conflict. In the extreme, it can lead to such violent outcomes as suicide.

Unlike many, perhaps most, psychologists Maslow provided insights into the healthy rather than the pathological human being. A major portion of *Motivation and Personality* is devoted to the self-actualized personality. Maslow's subjects for his theory were friends, acquaintances, and students that he believed were motivated to self-actualize. The first important difference in the self-actualizing personality is the individual's attitude toward life. Self-actualizing people "live more in the real world of nature than in the man-made mass of concepts, abstractions, expectations, beliefs, and stereotypes that most people confuse with the real world" (p. 25). Self-actualizing people perceive what is real rather than what they wish or hope to be real. They are unselfish and concerned with the welfare of others.

Even though self-actualizing personalities care about the welfare of others, they are problem centered and are often thought to be cold and aloof. However, this type of person desires an ever closer relationship with the person they love most. A more complete knowledge of this "relevant other" is a constant goal. The partner's needs become the needs of the self-actualizing person, and caring is an essential part of the love relationship. The picture provided of this exceedingly healthy person is one who needs privacy yet intensely loves and cares for others. The self-actualizing individual sets goals and works to accomplish them yet is guided by a set of principles and a code of ethics that sometimes makes him or her appear so "good" that others may even come to dislike someone who so clearly provides a role model for the more "normal" people in the organization.

Revision of the Need Hierarchy. While the hierarchy of needs as presented by Maslow is popular, it is not without limitations. One of the most obvious is the inability of ordinary people to distinguish among the various levels in the hierarchy. If these levels cannot be identified and isolated, it is difficult, perhaps impossible, for managers to individualize and customize motivational programs.

In response to this criticism, Clayton Alderfer (1972) proposed his *existence, relatedness, and growth theory* (ERG). In this theory, human needs are divided into three categories: existence, relatedness, and growth. Existence needs correspond to Maslow's physiological and safety needs; relatedness needs are similar to belongingness and internal esteem needs; and growth needs compare to external esteem and self-actualization needs.

Even though ERG theory has gained in popularity because of its relative simplicity, it is similar in most ways to Maslow's theory. Both schemes recognize the existence of several types of needs and propose a relationship among them that can be useful in motivating and rewarding individual behavior in organizations. However, Alderfer does not conceptualize needs in a hierarchical arrangement and suggests that all needs can be active at any given time. Some, such as growth needs, may actually increase in intensity the more they are satisfied (Mitchell, 1984). Even though actual research data on human needs tend to "fit" Alderfer's theory better, it has received limited research support. There is certainly little reason to look upon ERG theory at this time as a radical alternative to Maslow's popular and familiar need hierarchy.

Focusing on a Single Need: McClelland's Achievement Motive. If you find need hierarchies, even simple ones like Alderfer's, unrealistic and confusing, McClelland's motivation theory is for you. This theory focuses on a single need: the need to achieve. McClelland has also done a great deal of research on the need for power, but his most significant contribution remains the achievement motive, which will be the subject of this discussion.

David McClelland was born in Mt. Vernon, New York, in 1917. He studied languages at MacMurray College and graduated from Wesleyan University in 1938. He received his doctorate in psychology from Yale and joined the department of social relations at Harvard in 1956.

When one reads the work of McClelland (1961) and McClelland and Winter (1969), it is impossible not to be impressed with the brilliance of the research designs. For example, in studies of economic growth and the achievement motive, McClelland artfully examined the relationship between the *need to achieve* (n Ach) evident in children's stories in one time period and the consumption of electrical power at a later time (consumption of electrical power being used as a "surrogate" measure of economic development). The underlying theme of McClelland's research was that the achievement motive is at least partially responsible for economic growth. More specifically, the research was directed toward discovering whether a relationship exists between the need to achieve and the performance levels of individuals, organizations, and societies. Once he found such a relationship, McClelland developed a training program designed to increase the need to achieve in managers, owners of small businesses, and other groups.

To illustrate the practical significance of all this, one of McClelland's studies indicated that small-business owners "trained" to possess higher achievement needs were more active in community affairs, invested more money in expanding their businesses, and employed twice as many people as a similar group who did not receive the training (McClelland, 1978).

There are many possible implications of McClelland's research. However, one of the more important relates to the motivation of entrepreneurial talent in a society at large. McClelland argued that societies with higher achievement motives produce more energetic entrepreneurs and that these entrepreneurs, in turn, produce more rapid economic growth. Entrepreneurs must take risks, and the willingness to assume moderate degrees of risk is associated with higher n Ach. Moreover, the data show that people with higher achievement motives believe they have a greater likelihood of success than those with low n Ach believe. People with higher achievement motives are generally more energetic, creative, and hardworking. Finally, these people receive greater satisfaction from the knowledge that they are successful than from public recognition and praise.

McClelland also addressed the issue of how high achievement motives are, and can be, developed. First, it is important that parents and managers set high standards of excellence and respond warmly and promptly when children and employees perform consistently with the desired behavior standards. For countries that desire to use these findings to accelerate economic growth it is necessary to (1) break orientations toward tradition and increase the "other-directedness" of the citizens; (2) increase the n Ach by initiating such actions as insisting on excellence and setting high performance standards; and (3) provide for better allocation of existing achievement-oriented resources by channeling the most appropriate human talents into areas where they can have the greatest impact on organizational and social performance and by recognizing and rewarding the achievement-oriented people in the firm and nation.

To this point we have examined several motivation theories. All share one thing in common—they focus on how the individual's needs are aroused and how this aroused energy can be directed toward higher performance. Now we will shift the orientation, from the individual to the nature of work. The individual will be no less important than before. However, the importance of work and what it means to the worker should be a constant concern to all success-oriented managers.

From the Individual to the Job:
Herzberg's Two-Factor Theory of Motivation

Not too far from the location of Maslow's and McClelland's research in the mid1950s, a group at Psychological Services of Pittsburgh found existing theory incomplete. The result of their dissatisfaction was the publication of *Job Attitudes: Review of Research and Opinion* (1957), a book by Frederick Herzberg and others.

Herzberg was born in Lynn, Massachusetts, in 1923. He received his doctorate from the University of Pittsburgh, where he also earned a master's degree in public health. It was during his tenure as the research director at Psychological Services of Pittsburgh that he and his associates published his first of a series of books on motivation. Later he was the Douglas McGregor Professor of Psychology at Case Western Reserve University, and today he is Distinguished Professor of Management at the University of Utah. After reviewing several thousand articles on the subject of motivation, Herzberg concluded that much confusion existed in the field and that a "fresh approach" was needed. He then set out to provide this fresh approach.

A Fresh Approach to Motivation. In *The Motivation to Work* (1959) Herzberg, Mausner, and Snyderman took an entirely different approach than that used in *Job Attitudes.* The earlier review of the literature had convinced the authors that the major failure of prior work was that it was fragmentary. Research that examined the factors affecting workers' attitudes toward work rarely looked at the effects of these attitudes. Studies of the effects of attitudes about work, on the other hand, almost never included anything about the origin of the attitudes. What was needed, according to Herzberg, was an investigation of job attitudes "in toto," or a study that would simultaneously examine factors, attitudes, and effects. This was called the *factors-attitude-effect* (F-A-E) complex or unit.

Armed with this need for a fresh approach, Herzberg and his associates collected data from professional employees (such as accountants and engineers) in nine dissimilar plants in the general area of Pittsburgh. The respondents were interviewed and asked to relate incidents about times when they were either extremely satisfied or extremely dissatisfied with their work. Analysis of the results indicated something that motivation researchers had not recognized in the past—that the factors leading to job satisfaction were different from the things that led to job dissatisfaction. In other words, managers could not look at a single factor such as working conditions and assume that if employees were dissatisfied with the conditions a little expenditure on painting the facilities, providing more rest periods, and contracting with a background music company would solve the motivational problems of the company. To the contrary, it was determined that certain factors operate to increase job satisfaction while other factors only decrease it. The factors that could increase satisfaction were labeled *motivators*, while those that could only decrease it were called *hygiene* factors.

What All This Means to Managers. The results of Herzberg's initial research in *The Motivation to Work* stirred a great deal of executive interest because the implications were profound. Herzberg had illustrated that certain aspects of a job (he called them hygiene factors no doubt because of his public health orientation) are the "necessary but not sufficient conditions for motivation." Factors such as company policies and administration, supervision, interpersonal relations with bosses and peers, and general working conditions provide only the basic conditions of work. Just as public drinking water systems make no one "well" but merely prevent people from becoming "ill," these hygiene factors cannot motivate people. They can only keep people from being dissatisfied. The worker expects safe surroundings, reasonable company policies, and pleasant relations with the boss and peers. If these conditions are not present, employees will be dissatisfied, but if they are present employees will not be motivated to higher performance.

The motivating factors, on the other hand, include such things as an opportunity for achievement, recognition for a job well done, a chance to assume greater responsibility, advancement, and the nature of the work itself. These factors address the need for a job to be a source of self-actualization and personal growth.

The manager should note that the factors that only have the power to increase dissatisfaction if not present are all external, or *extrinsic*, to the job. They relate to the surroundings, fellow workers, and company policies. The motivators, on the other hand, are internal, or *intrinsic*, to the work itself. The key to motivation, in Herzberg's view, is simple. If you as a manager want to motivate employees or other managers, give them meaningful work that provides an opportunity for achievement, advancement, and recognition. This recommendation clearly established the idea of *job enrichment* that has been so much a part of recent motivation theory and practice.

The third book in Herzberg's "trilogy" was *Work and the Nature of Man* (1966). Here the author elaborated on techniques used in prior studies and provided citations of evidence that the theory works in a variety of settings. To a great extent the book is a defense of the earlier research, which had received a great deal of criticism regarding its relatively small sample of professional employees in the general vicinity of Pittsburgh.

Perhaps the greatest contribution of Herzberg's work is that it gives managers something tangible to work on when addressing the motivation problem. This, of course, is the job itself. Advocates of job enrichment argue that work must be made more meaningful. It is not enough to merely enlarge tasks or rotate them to keep people from becoming excessively bored. Work should be fundamentally designed to provide meaning for the one performing the task.

One company that adopted many of Herzberg's ideas was American Telephone & Telegraph (Ford, 1973). The AT&T approach was based on three basic principles:

1. Defining jobs so that employees would have natural areas of responsibility and logical tasks. This is called *horizontal loading*, or ensuring that the job is structured in a way that is logical and sensible to the one who must accomplish it. In and of itself, however, horizontal loading results in little more than job enlargement, not enrichment.

2. Providing employees with more control and responsibility over the job. This involves *vertical loading* and actually provides the employee with some managerial aspects of his or her own job.

3. Giving frequent performance feedback to the employee to provide a sense of responsibility, achievement, and recognition. Again, this involves vertical loading, since performance feedback and evaluation were traditionally considered a managerial role.

The AT&T experience with job enrichment, although there were isolated failures, was overwhelmingly favorable.

The important thing to remember is that Herzberg's theory focuses on the task and on ways to make work more meaningful. Taylor, Gantt, and Gilbreth were obsessed with defining and measuring the task; Mayo, Roethlisberger, Maslow, and other human relations writers insisted on recognizing that tasks have to be accomplished in a social setting; Herzberg, however, convincingly argued that the task must have meaning. To define and measure is fine; so is positioning work in the social arena. However, if the task does not have meaning in and of itself, it is not likely to motivate workers to high levels of excellence.

We have seen that Taylor was inclined to view human nature in somewhat primitive terms. Mayo, Maslow, and now Herzberg presented a view of human beings as highly unique and "chosen" demigods. That changes, however, as the loop is closed with some of the more popular motivation theories discussed today. The image of the human being is once again radically altered. We are not returned to the level of oxen, nor are we allowed to continue on the plane of angels. The final two theories we will discuss are classified by Mitchell (1984) as *intended choice* motivation theories.

Motivation and Human Choice

Intended choice theories of motivation, which according to one writer have occupied 80 percent of recent motivation research, "involve current situations or informational factors that influence an individual's intention to choose one action over another" (Mitchell, 1984, p. 19). The first theory to be briefly discussed relates to the employee's perceptions of the outcomes that will result from various behaviors when the goal is simply to maximize the payoff. The individual is viewed as a rational actor in search of the greatest benefit from a limited expenditure of energy.

Expectancy Theory. Expectancy theory was first introduced by Victor Vroom (1964). To understand this theory you need to know a few important terms. The first is *expectancy*, which, according to Vroom, is "a momentary belief concerning the likelihood that a particular act will be followed by a particular outcome" (p. 17). *Valence* is the attractiveness or perceived value attached to the particular outcome by the individual. The magnitude of the valence is determined, in turn, by how *instrumental* the outcome is in obtaining something of value. To illustrate, an employee may choose to work hard because she believes that hard work will lead to higher earnings (high expectancy). The valence of the higher earnings is determined by how instrumental the money is perceived to be in purchasing the new car that is needed by the employee and her family. Therefore, the motivational *force* on a person to perform a particular act or choose a particular alternative is equal to the perceived likelihood (expectancy) that the act will lead to a desired outcome times the perceived value (valence) of that outcome. In more practical terms, the essence of Vroom's theory is summarized by Pecotich and Churchill (1981) as follows:

> [A] person's motivation to expend effort on any task depends upon: (1) expectancy—the person's perception of the probability that expending a given amount of effort on that task will lead to improved performance; (2) instrumentality—the person's perceptions of the relationship between improved performance and the receipt of certain outcomes such as more pay, a promotion, and so on; and (3) valence—the person's perception of the desirability of receiving these outcomes or rewards [p. 214].

Vroom's expectancy theory is complex and difficult to understand. A reading of his *Work and Motivation* (1964) will do little to clarify the points, since the mathematical properties of the various measurements are frequently highlighted. However, we can itemize four important implications and guidelines for managers from Vroom's work.

First, it is important to recognize that the anticipation of the reward is more important than is often considered. People make choices on the basis of what they think will happen in the future rather than on the basis of what happened in the past.

Second, rewards should be closely and explicitly tied to actions that are considered desirable by the organization. The behaviors that are considered valuable should be rewarded openly, frequently, and generously. Third, people value different rewards (Mayo's maxim of individual differences), so some attempt should be made to match organizational outcomes with the desires of individual employees (Mitchell, 1984). Finally, rewards should be equitable in terms of the effort required to accomplish the task.

Expectancy theory is not easy to apply. It is abstract and complicated in one sense but general and easy to relate to in another. All of us understand the importance of the expected outcome in determining our behavior. Expectancy theory provides an opportunity to apply what we know about ourselves to the motivation of those with whom we work.

If we characterize the implicit assumption made by expectancy theory about human nature, we must describe it in one word: rational. Human beings are viewed as calculators; even with limited information, they calculate the wisdom of a behavior now in terms of its likely outcomes in the future. The image of human beings provided by our final theory of motivation, Skinner's operant conditioning approach, is less complimentary. The basic orientation of Skinner's theory was introduced in the discussion on science and management in Chapter Four. In the remainder of this chapter we will look at the implications of this scientific orientation to the study of motivation.

Operant Conditioning and B. F. Skinner. B. F. Skinner was born in Susquehanna, Pennsylvania, in 1904 and was attracted to psychology by reading the experiments of the Russian physiologist Ivan Pavlov. In 1931 Skinner received his doctorate from Harvard University, and after a period of postdoctoral research he moved to the University of Minnesota and later to Indiana University. He returned to Harvard in 1948. Actually, none of Skinner's books deal with management, and virtually all of his original research was done on pigeons rather than people. Nevertheless, the findings of his studies have been applied to the field of management, which is why we must concern ourselves with his views on motivation and learning.

Skinner believes that motivation theorists place too much

attention on the "inner being" along with related factors like needs, motives, and desires (Hart and Scott, 1972). By contrast, his theory concentrates solely on observable phenomena—stimuli and responses.

Skinner's theory of operant conditioning is one type of learning theory. *Learning* is defined by psychologists as any relatively permanent change is an established relationship between a stimulus and a response. Learning can occur in two ways: by classical conditioning or by operant conditioning. In *classical conditioning* the stimulus precedes the response, as in the famous Pavlovian experiments with salivation in dogs. In *operant conditioning*, the response takes place prior to and in anticipation of the stimulus. This is the basis of Skinner's theory.

While we cannot explain Skinner's theory in its entirety, a few elements must necessarily be discussed. Skinner states that operant conditioning is the process by which behavior is altered and learning takes place. The process is facilitated by *positive reinforcement* of desired behaviors. A positive reinforcer is anything that increases the frequency of the desired response when it is present. A monetary payment for a job well done is a positive reinforcer. The key to understanding Skinner's theory lies, however, in the manner in which reinforcement takes place, or the schedule of reinforcement.

To this point there is really nothing unique about operant conditioning theory. Even Frederick Taylor recognized the potential motivational impact of positive reinforcement. The problem with Taylor's differential piece rate was that, in Skinner's terms, this reward system amounted to *continuous reinforcement.* Every time the worker produced a unit at or below standard, the same payment was made. Even when the standard was exceeded the reward was paid continuously—only the rate of payment varied. Such continuous reinforcement is familiar to all of us. Every time we complete a week or month at work we receive our pay, and the amount is based more on a contractual agreement than on performance.

If we use O to represent the operant behavior (production of another unit of a widget or completion of another day at work) and C to represent the consequence (receipt of the day rate or salary), we can illustrate what is meant by a continuous reinforcement schedule in the following manner:

$$O-C, O-C, O-C, O-C$$

Each time the behavior takes place, the consequence or payment is received. This type of reinforcement schedule encourages steady yet unenthusiastic behavior. The primary incentive is to complete the interval of time necessary for receipt of the weekly paycheck or to produce enough to keep your job.

In addition to continuous reinforcement, the manager may choose some form of *partial reinforcement.* As the name implies, the desired consequence does not follow every iteration of the behavior; instead the reinforcement comes after either a fixed or variable interval or ratio. We will deal only with ratios, although the principles are the same when applied to intervals.

With the *fixed ratio* schedule the consequence occurs at predictable points. It may, for example, take three or four iterations of a task before one receives positive reinforcement. Symbolically, this can be presented as

$$O-O-O-C, O-O-O-C$$

Every three times the task is completed, the reward or consequence follows. For example, a manager might hire a consultant and indicate that partial payments will be made when the project is 30, 50, and 100 percent complete. The incentive is to complete the project as fast as possible in order to receive a paycheck. While this is likely to result in harder and faster work, potential problems exist. What, for example, is there to discourage the consultant from working so fast that the quality of the work suffers?

With *variable ratio reinforcement,* one cannot predict the exact iteration that will result in the desired consequence. Symbolically, this might appear as

$$O-C, O-O-O-O-O-C, O-O-C$$

The best illustration of this schedule is the game of chance. No one can predict exactly when the winning poker hand will be dealt or which pull on the "one-armed bandit" will result in the payoff. The excitement of this type of reinforcement schedule is what makes the work of the laboratory researcher rewarding. Who knows whether the next iteration of an experiment will result in a finding of great scientific significance. This type of schedule is considered one of the most motivating forms of reinforcement. The problem is, how can this be applied to management? Obviously, no labor union or employee is going to allow employers to pay according to a random schedule. There are, however, many examples of how operant conditioning concepts have been applied in organizations.

For one innovative alternative, consider the way the *Denver Post* used a variable ratio reinforcement schedule to stimulate advertisement sales. The management of the *Post* became aware of a "slot machine" developed with a microcomputer that could be programmed to pay off according to different specifications. Employees who sold advertising space were given one chance to play the machine each time they sold a classified ad. Each play provided an opportunity to win up to $50.00, although the average payoff was $.12. Obviously, the average payoff would not provide a substantial monetary incentive to work hard. However, the possibility of winning $50.00 for each sale and the excitement that accompanied playing the machine resulted in a tremendous increase in classified ad sales after only a few months of operation (Higgins, 1983). Additional impressive results have been reported when operant conditioning principles have been applied in small businesses such as grocery stores and video game parlors (Komaki, Waddell, and Pearce, 1977).

Much has been written about management and motivation. In fact, so much has been written that managers are often confused by the volume and conflicting prescriptions of motivation theories. How is the manager to make sense out of a field that even the researchers cannot agree on?

Managers need to focus on the underlying similarities rather than worrying about the differences. Even though Skinner might object, one cannot go wrong by carefully examining the fact that people are different—they have different experiences, they aspire to different goals, and they are motivated by different needs. Of course, even the most sensitive manager cannot design a motivation program for each employee. If she could, the organization would probably not allow it. Managers, however, need to think of employees as individuals. They need to appreciate that the people who work with and for them all have unique talents and potentials to contribute to organizational goals.

Implications and Conclusions

This chapter has provided far-ranging insights into the nature of several important theories of human motivation. The work of human relation theorists like Mayo, Roethlisberger, and Maslow has been contrasted with the more naive views of scientific management. The more contemporary behavioral views of McClelland, Herzberg, Vroom, and Skinner have also been examined. Even though the theories differ with respect to their focus and complexity, all have important lessons for present and future managers.

One of the most important things to be gained from this discussion is how the writers make different assumptions about human nature. To a great extent what they conclude is determined by what they assume. Taylor looked at pig iron loaders, especially good ones, as strong, not particularly smart, oxen. The controls and procedures he developed were testimonies to his mechanistic view of human nature. Opposite assumptions by Maslow led, logically, to opposite conclusions. The results of Skinner's assumptions are equally predictable.

In the next chapter we will look at leadership and begin at precisely the place where this chapter ends—with the assumptions the manager makes about the employees who are responsible for performing important tasks.

CHAPTER 10

Leadership

Art, Style, or Science?

"Jazz is not the only native American contribution to world culture. Leadership as a body of theory and research is distinctly an American creation" (Stogdill, 1974). What a claim! If it had been made by anyone other than Ralph Stogdill, himself an institution in leadership research, we would not take it seriously. Leadership is an important topic to every civilization and, as civilizations go, America is far too young to fancy itself the originator of such an important field. Of course, Stogdill's point is not that leadership originated in America but that leadership theory and research did.

Regardless of its origin, it is no wonder that leadership has received so much attention. Nations have been founded, impossible military victories achieved, powerful corporations created, and mighty labor unions built because of the vision and leadership of a few people. While it is true that not all leaders are managers, it is difficult to imagine a successful manager who is not a reasonably good leader. An area as complex and diverse as leadership provides particular challenges to one looking for evolutionary threads, for historical triggers. Yet, threads and triggers can be found, or at least imagined, if we look closely enough. For example, leadership research began with a focus on the relatively few "great" people who live in every society, populate every organization, and appear to possess certain "traits" that are not universally or equally distributed throughout society. This is where our search and survey must begin.

By the middle of the twentieth century, leadership researchers faced a dilemma. The trait approach, which sought to identify the qualities of great leaders, was not working. There were too many exceptions to almost every trait identified. Inconsistency in theory leads to inadequate practice.

The focus changed to leader behavior and ushered in concern for what is involved in being a leader, the proper way to lead, the influence of the leader's assumptions about followers, and other issues. Ultimately, many believe, the elusive key to prediction in the area of leadership must lie in a complex "match" of the situation faced by a leader with the manner in which the leader responds. This situational or contingency view dominates most of contemporary leadership research.

The plan in this chapter is to steer a course that will allow a view of one, or in some cases two, popular illustrations of each of the phases of leadership theory and research. Our "specimens" will be carefully selected in terms of how well they illustrate the particular orientation to leadership under review.

The Art of Leadership

Stogdill (1974) indicated that the earliest systematic research on leadership was directed toward identifying the *traits*, or characteristics, of great leaders. This is not surprising. All of us have marveled at the accomplishments of great people. History is rich with examples of personalities who soared to greatness or, as Shakespeare put it, "had greatness thrust upon them." It was only a matter of time until enterprising researchers looked for predictors of how individuals achieve greatness.

An example of this tradition is the view advanced by Ordway Tead, who was introduced in Chapter Eight. Long before he wrote *The Art of Administration,* he published a book on leadership. The title was, you guessed it, *The Art of Leadership* (1935). He defined leadership as the "activity of influencing people to cooperate toward some goal which they come to find desirable." Tead believed that most people want to belong to goal-oriented (purposeful) groups like business firms, churches, synagogues, and civic clubs. Since only a few can lead, most people, it can be inferred, desire to be led and are comfortable as followers. A few, however, invariably emerge as leaders, and these individuals are of particular interest.

People can be led in many ways. Suggestions can be used and are instrumental in building good relations. Leaders sometimes intimidate, but exhortations or pep talks are more successful. Tead even gave consideration to the usefulness of persuasive, thorough, logical arguments. However, it was his occasional hint about the situational nature of leadership that was most unusual in his writings. Even though he focused primarily on the traits of the leader, Tead was aware that leaders use the "logic of events" in arriving at the proper time to exercise their influence. Sometimes prospective leaders even create problem situations to which they can uniquely respond. Perhaps that is why we remember the leaders best who have set forth worthy and challenging goals and then responded to them. Lyndon Johnson was known for his idea of the "Great Society," John F. Kennedy for his goal of "putting a man on the moon before the end of the decade," and General Douglas MacArthur for his pledge to return to the Philippines.

The goals that give leaders power must be definite, must be appealing, and must be ones with which followers can enthusiastically identify. The "law of the situation," as discussed by Follett (1949), implies that the situation is given and the leader merely responds in a unique way. Tead made a similar point but took a different direction by observing that the situation may be created by the perceptive leader, and history testifies that this often is the case.

What It Takes to Be a Leader. Like most early leadership writers and in spite of the "logic of events" and the "law of the situation," Tead believed successful leaders possess certain identifiable traits, with the most important being:

1. Physical and nervous energy. Leadership is hard work, so the leader must have more than the average amount of energy.

2. Sense of purpose or direction. The leader must have goals and inspire others to pursue them.
3. Enthusiasm. Good leaders often feel themselves "commanded by power." Their enthusiasm is somehow converted into command or influence.
4. Friendliness and affection. Tead did not believe it is better for a leader to be feared than loved. To the contrary, leaders need to be liked by followers if they are to exercise the necessary influence over them.
5. Integrity. True to his conscience, Tead believed leaders have to be trustworthy.

People want leaders who are decisive and who create confidence among followers. Followers need to believe that matters are in good hands. Leaders have to take the heat when bad decisions are made and overcome the temptation to blame others for their failures. Harry Truman's attitude that the "buck stops here" gained him respect and gave citizens the confidence that someone would address serious problems eventually, even if it was the president. Good leaders need to be effective communicators, have a sense of humor, and, perhaps above all, be good teachers. After all, the leader is the only teacher many employees ever have.

How Leaders Lead. The effective leader communicates expectations to employees and defines the boundaries of followers' discretion. As we mentioned before, Tead was idealistic but he understood human nature and was a realist concerning it. He even admitted that power has a corrupting influence and can lead to vanity. A cursory reading of history will verify this generalization. We should, therefore, be on the lookout for hazards of leadership. For example, Tead knew that leaders often have more desire for self-enhancement than the population at large. Sometimes leaders insist on having their own way and take things personally when others disagree. Often they identify so closely with their goals that any disagreement is considered an act of disloyalty. Remember Frederick Taylor's bizarre behavior in the Eastern rate case. It is exciting to read of the accomplishments of the great people of history, but it is depressing to read of the equally, if not greater, weaknesses of these same people who eventually failed in their response to the "logic of events."

When we consider Tead's social conscience, as we did in Chapter Eight, it is not altogether surprising that he even dared, in 1935, to deal with the important question of female leaders. He stated that sometimes women are "severely critical" of female leaders because women bosses set higher performance standards for female followers than their male counterparts do. He believed that the most successful women leaders are those who remain themselves, who are proud of themselves as women, and "who have added to their stature and insight through pride in the integrity of their own essential femininity" (p. 256). How women leaders might interpret this concern today is open to question, but knowing what we know about Tead, we can only assume the concern was genuine and sincere.

In one of his most profound statements on leadership, Tead states that "good leading depends on good following. The leader points the way but the followers must decide that the way is good" (p. 298). This statement is profound because it begins to hint at an idea in leadership that was to emerge much later in the development of the field. This important idea was that leadership depends on more than the personality of the leader.

Getting Away from Traits

Much of the early leadership research was sponsored by the military, for obvious reasons—the military always needs "a few good leaders." If the traits of good leaders could be isolated, future leaders could be identified. But, alas, the list of essential leadership traits became exceedingly long, and the conflicting findings concerning the traits were impossible to reconcile. Frustration led some researchers to simply deny any relationship between personality traits and leadership. Others continued the research, and still others were confident that personality had a relationship to leadership but that the association was more complicated than originally imagined. The search expanded to look for the other factors that would somehow complete the puzzle.

This pilgrimage led leadership researchers through many productive and unproductive mazes of data and information. Along the way the complexity of the problem of leadership began to surface. It became increasingly clear that the leader's personality, the style of leadership, and the general situation were all important determinants of leadership effectiveness.

Search for a Theory Begins. Tead's ideas on leadership were intuitive and originated primarily from his personal experiences. It was only one short decade after the publication of *The Art of Leadership,* however, that some extraordinarily important studies of leadership were conducted at Ohio State University.

Shartle (1979) notes that even though the multidisciplinary program of leadership research at Ohio State actually started in 1945, the roots of the studies were established in the occupational research sponsored by the U.S. Department of Labor and the War Manpower Commission that began in 1934. One of the early pioneers of this research was Ralph M. Stogdill.

Stogdill was born in 1905 and served a long and distinguished career as professor of management science and psychology at Ohio State, where he had earned his doctorate. He worked for the Ohio Bureau of Juvenile Research and was an officer in the U.S. Maritime Services. In 1946 he became associate director of the Ohio State Leadership Studies. He is the author of numerous books and articles on leadership and continues to be recognized as one of the great contributors to the field (Van Fleet, 1979).

The Ohio State Leadership Studies were significant for several reasons (Schriesheim and Bird, 1979). Many believe they represent an important counterpoint to the way leadership was traditionally viewed. Prior to the 1950s the traitist view was dominant. Stogdill (1974) changed this with his massive review of leadership research and his argument that while some traits are found across leaders, leadership is best "considered in terms of the interactions of variables which are in constant flux and change" (p. 64). This argument was enough to alter the dominant view of leadership as a set of traits to leadership as an activity. The importance of studying leader behavior rather than leader characteristics became the order of the day.

The most familiar aspect of the Ohio State studies was the identification of two factors or dimensions of leadership: consideration and initiating structure. *Consideration* includes support of followers' behavior, friendliness, and recognition of individual contributions to group goals; *initiating structure* relates more to task-oriented aspects such as directing followers, evaluating performance, scheduling, and so on. Unlike later theorists, the Ohio State researchers did not present these dimensions as conflicting or mutually exclusive. In fact, effective leaders could actually rank high on both dimensions. Consideration and initiating structure were thought of more as complementary than conflicting aspects of leader behavior. But even though this complementarity carried over into later approaches like that of Blake and Mouton (1964), research into leadership behavior and the way in which leadership is exercised began to converge on mutually exclusive, at least by implication, leadership assumptions and styles.

Leadership Assumptions and Styles. Although consideration and initiating structure were recognized by the Ohio State researchers as parallel, much of the subsequent leadership research has compared various mutually exclusive styles of leadership. Perhaps dichotomies between task-oriented and employee-oriented, autocratic and democratic, and so on were theoretical conveniences that allowed managers some freedom in isolating various types of leader behavior. Or, perhaps those who proposed the mutually exclusive options really believed that different styles can be more effective ways of leading. In any event the dichotomy is firmly established in the literature of management.

Consider the dichotomy we face when looking at the assumptions that leaders make about followers. This has been conveniently "packaged" for us by Douglas McGregor (1960), who believed that the way managers were behaving less than three decades ago placed them in the position of "facing the past while backing into the future." They were basing their actions on assumptions about employees that may have been true in the past but were certainly not descriptive of contemporary reality.

Douglas McGregor was born in Detroit, Michigan, in 1906. He earned his doctorate from Harvard in 1935 and served as an instructor there until he became a staff member in the industrial relations section at the Massachusetts Institute of Technology in 1937. Later he directed that section. He was president of Antioch College from 1948 to 1954, after which he returned to M.I.T. to serve as professor of industrial management until his death in 1964.

McGregor's most influential book was *The Human Side of Enterprise* (1960). In this book he proposed the best-known dichotomy of management: Theory X and Theory Y. McGregor called Theory X the "traditional view of direction and control." When this view is adopted, the leader makes several assumptions about the people under her or his leadership:

1. The average human being has an inherent dislike for work and will avoid it if possible.
2. Because human beings dislike work, they must be coerced, controlled, directed, and threatened with punishment if they are to put forth adequate effort toward the achievement of organizational goals.
3. The average human being prefers direction, wishes to avoid responsibility, and has relatively little ambition. Most of all, security is desired.

The leader who adopts Theory Y, which McGregor refers to as a means of "integrating individual and organizational goals," on the other hand, assumes something quite different about followers:

1. The expenditure of physical and mental effort in work is as natural as play and rest.
2. The threat of punishment and external control are not the only means available for increasing effort toward the ac-

complishment of organizational goals. Humans are quite capable of exercising self-direction and self-control in the service of objectives to which they are committed.

3.   Commitment to objectives is a function of the rewards associated with their attainment.

4.   The average human being learns, under proper conditions, not only to accept but to seek responsibility.

5.   The capacity to exercise a high degree of imagination, ingenuity, and creativity in the solution of organizational problems is widely, not narrowly, distributed in the population.

6.   Under conditions of modern industrial life the intellectual potential of the average human being is rarely utilized.

According to McGregor, the principle that derived from Theory X was that of direction and control through the exercise of authority. Theory Y, by contrast, was based on the principle of integration, or the creation of conditions such that the members of the organization achieve their goals best by aiming their energies toward the success of the enterprise. This principle of integration literally creates the conditions whereby individuals achieve their personal goals in the process of contributing to the objective of the organization—the process of mutual reinforcement.

The assumptions of a leader are important, according to McGregor, because what one believes to be true causes one to behave in a certain way. This behavior, in turn, causes others to behave exactly as one expected. This is the way people create *self-fulfilling prophecies.* If a leader assumes that followers are lazy, are irresponsible, and must be forced to work hard, it is likely that a system of incentives and appraisal will be set up that guarantees followers will behave in precisely this manner. Precise rules and regulations will be developed, and managers will closely supervise workers to ensure that work is not only completed but also accomplished in the precise manner that the leader desires. Workers will soon find ways of getting around the system and will eventually behave irresponsibly—just as Theory X predicts.

On the other hand, if followers are assumed to be responsible and mature, a system of incentives and appraisal will be set up that encourages them to behave in a mature and responsible way. Opportunities for professional and personal growth will be provided, supervision will be relaxed, and workers will respond with more mature behavior.

Interestingly, McGregor has been criticized for thinking of leadership only in terms of either Theory X or Theory Y when, in reality, followers possess some characteristics described by both theories. In fact, McGregor apparently recognized the danger of thinking in terms of such extremes and indicated early that leaders should engage in *selective adaptation* with respect to their assumptions. The amount of control exercised by the leader or manager should be selectively adapted to the maturity and dependency of the followers. Immature and dependent employees require a great deal of control. Perhaps they meet most of the assumptions of Theory X. Mature and independent followers require little control and are best described by the assumptions of Theory Y.

Other criticisms of McGregor are more legitimate. His so-called theory was really a nontheory and was based more on hopes than it was on evidence of any substantive nature (Lee, 1980). *The Human Side of Enterprise* is a classic of the field not because of its scientific sophistication but because of its clarity and its focus on a "soft" although important part of leadership—what the leader assumes about followers does in fact affect leader behavior. Like the legendary Greek sculptor Pygmalion, managers often "create" the type of employee behavior they encounter. However, to believe that managerial assumptions are the only or even primary source of laziness and irresponsibility on the part of employees cannot be justified intuitively, and this idea has not been investigated enough to allow for such a sweeping generalization.

The importance of managerial assumptions led managers and management writers to consider the relative merits of different styles of leadership and management. Soon, the primary question in leadership research became, what is the best way to lead?

Likert and the System Four Organization

Many researchers have focused on styles in leadership because the switch to a focus on leadership behavior was immediately directed toward this important issue. We will look at the work of Rensis Likert (1961, 1967) as an illustration of this research direction. Likert's work accurately represents the types of issues to be considered when thinking about appropriate and inappropriate leadership styles, and it is based on more and better data than most of the other research in this area.

Rensis Likert was born in Cheyenne, Wyoming, and received his doctorate at Columbia University. He worked at New York University and the Life Insurance Sales Research Bureau before he became director of the Institute for Social Research at the University of Michigan.

Organizations: From One to Four. Likert published the foundations of his theory of leadership in 1961. In *New Patterns of Management*, two ideas appear particularly significant for managers. First, the most effective leaders/managers are those who form a *linking* function with people above and below them in the organization. In other words, the leader who functions as a "linking pin" keeps employees aware of what higher management is up to and keeps higher management aware of what is going on among the workers. Second, Likert proposed his famous *principle of supporting relationships*, which stated that leaders should ensure "a maximum probability" that all interactions in an organization be viewed as supportive and designed to build and maintain a sense of personal worth and importance. Likert contrasted various types of organizations on the basis of the type of leadership style used. Other factors he used to classify different organizational systems were the nature of the motivational forces employed, the character of the communication processed, the interaction-influence process, the character of decision making, how goals are set and prioritized, and the manner in which control is exercised. His resulting four organization types are (Likert, 1967):

1. System One organizations. Likert applied the label *exploitive authoritative* to this type of organization. Man-

agers or leaders do not trust followers. Motivation is based on fear, threats, and occasional rewards. Communication flows down from the top and the little that flows up tends to be inaccurate and distorted. Goals are imposed from on high, where all important decisions are made.

2.   System Two organizations. This type of organization is called *benevolent authoritative*. Leaders and followers exhibit a "master-servant" relationship. There is some involvement of followers, at least more than in System One. There are also more rewards and upward communication is better. The relationship between leaders and followers is best described as paternalistic.

3.   System Three organizations. Likert called this a *consultative* form of organization because leaders are clearly in control but followers are consulted before decisions are actually made. Upward communication is cautious and unpleasant and information is not freely offered.

4.   System Four organizations. Likert described this type of organization as *participative*. Leaders trust followers and believe employees seriously work toward accomplishing organizational goals. Communication is accurate and flows vertically and horizontally. Goals are formulated in a participative manner by people who will be directly involved in decision making and in accomplishing the objectives.

Most leaders develop System Two or System Three organizations, and the move to System Four, which Likert recommended as most preferred, requires significant changes in leadership philosophies. Moreover, one should not expect changes to take place immediately. When new programs are established in large, complex organizations, the manager should expect as much as a year to pass before many employees will recognize that changes are actually taking place, and even more time is required before tangible results can be expected (Likert, 1967). Perhaps this is why attempts to build a System Four organization sometimes fail—it takes time. It is difficult to keep the confidence and enthusiasm of top management long enough to effect the type of changes required by the participative system. However, results of research presented by Likert indicate that it is worth the time and energy spent to move from a System One or Two organization to System Four.

System Four and Organizational Effectiveness. Managers using Systems One and Two generate less group loyalty and lower performance goals and experience greater conflict, less cooperation, less favorable attitudes toward management, and less motivated employees. The result is an organization with lower sales volume, higher sales costs, and lower earnings on the part of everyone. The System Four organization, with its focus on supportive relationships, group decision making and supervision, and high performance goals, attains higher sales and earnings with lower costs.

Likert's human relations orientation is evident throughout *New Patterns of Management* (1961) and *The Human Organization* (1967). The "linking pin" concept is a fundamental aspect of Likert's theory because of its importance in ensuring the successful overlapping of different groups in the organization. While it is crucial that the successful manager function as a conduit for vertical communication, the linking pin also facilitates horizontal relationships. When communication is designed according to the linking-pin concept, a manager such as the production superintendent actually becomes a member, for purposes of communication, of two or more groups on the same organizational level. Membership in these overlapping groups creates more team spirit and encourages open, free, and direct communication. This results in higher levels of mutual trust, shared responsibility, and intergroup commitment to organizational goals.

In summary, Likert's ideas are consistent with those of McGregor. Both argue that the type of climate management establishes in an organization influences the performance of employees. While both writers recognized that situational variables can radically affect leader behavior, the theme is clear: greater focus on the human factor will lead to higher levels of individual and organization performance. Moreover, even though Likert and McGregor would not deny the importance of situational factors, there is little doubt from their writings that both believed the human relations orientation of Theory Y and the System Four organization to be preferable to other styles of leadership. This, however, is less than a universally accepted proposition in contemporary leadership research. In recent times the "logic of events" and the "law of the situation" have assumed much greater importance as factors in leadership effectiveness.

A Theory of Leadership Effectiveness

Not everyone agrees that a particular style of leadership will result in the most effective form of organizational behavior. Although there are many dissenters, it was Fred Fiedler who first put the argument together and supported it with research data.

Fiedler was born in Vienna, Austria, in 1922 and received his doctorate in psychology from the University of Chicago in 1949. Although he is currently a professor of psychology at the University of Washington, he was at the University of Illinois when he published his most influential book, *A Theory of Leadership Effectiveness* (1967). This book reported the results of extensive research and eventually made a significant impact on the way managers think about leadership.

Leadership Under Different Conditions. In developing his view of leadership effectiveness, Fiedler studied a number of different types of groups. In characterizing different group situations, he used three criteria:

1. The leader's position power. The relationship of the leader to the group members is determined to a large extent by the power she or he exercises over the followers. Some positions, like that of army general, have high power because the position itself enables the person to require group members to comply with orders or directions. Who would dare ignore an order from a highway patrolman with a badge on his chest and a pistol at his side? However, position power alone does not directly affect performance, even though a strong position does make the leader's job easier to perform.
2. The nature of the task. Tasks in organizations may be structured or unstructured. The structured task is laid out step

by step, is easily predicted, and in many cases can be programmed in advance. The press operator on an assembly line has a highly structured task. Other tasks, like that of the heart surgeon, are unstructured and cannot be programmed. Leaders of groups with structured tasks have an easier job and require less position power because the leader's power can be inferred to a great extent by the instructions for the job.

3.   Leader-follower relations. The relationship between leaders and followers "appears to be the most important single element in determining the leader's influence in the small group" (p. 29). When leaders are highly regarded by followers, no signs of rank are needed to get followers to work hard.

Using these three aspects, Fiedler classified leadership situations in terms of their favorableness or unfavorableness for leaders. To illustrate, by arranging the three dimensions of the task (power position, task structure, and leader-follower relations) in all possible combinations, he arrived at eight unique combinations, or *octants*. Octant I is the most favorable situation facing a leader: position power is strong, the task is highly structured, and leader-follower relations are good. An example would be a popular squad leader in the army. Octant VIII is the least favorable: the leader's power position is weak, the task is unstructured, and leader-follower relations are poor. An example would be an unpopular project leader working with a group of engineers on a complex technical problem.

A Matter of Style. To determine the most effective leadership style for each of the octants, Fiedler classified the styles of group leaders on the basis of how they responded to their "least preferred co-worker" (LPC). Without going into an excessive amount of detail, a leader's LPC score was determined by how the leader reacted to the person with whom she or he would least like to work. If a leader scored the least preferred co-worker high, he or she was getting past personalities and still believed the co-worker to be nice, intelligent, hardworking, and perhaps competent, despite the lack of preference to work with him. The leader who is able to separate the person from his works and who derives satisfaction from building and maintaining satisfactory personal relationships is called a *relationship-motivated leader.* Leaders who described the LPC in negative terms, thereby linking the individual's poor performance with undesirable personality traits, received a low LPC score. The low-LPC leader derives his major satisfaction from accomplishing the task and for this reason is called a *task-motivated leader.*

In developing his argument, Fiedler studied a number of groups, ranging from surveying teams composed of civil engineering students to bomber crews. His findings indicated a significant interaction between the personality of the leader and the situation in which leadership takes place. Because situations vary, different leadership styles will be required in different situations. Fiedler's research has been labeled the *contingency theory* of leadership because of this emphasis on situational differences.

The basic finding of Fiedler's research was that task-motivated leaders generally perform best either in highly favorable situations where they have strong position power, structured tasks, and good leader-follower relations or in highly unfavorable situations. Relationship-motivated leaders, by contrast, tend to perform best in intermediate or moderately favorable/unfavorable situations (Fiedler, 1974). This finding has implications for management that go far beyond those possible with traditional theory.

Implications of Contingency Theory. Situational theories are realistic. We all know that disparate strategies work in different situations. Unfortunately, when we admit to the possibility of situational factors, things become very complicated. It is much simpler when we can have confidence in the "one best way" to lead and manage. Recruitment of new managers and their placement is relatively easy when situations do not have to be considered. You find a person who wants to be a manager, who appears to possess certain desired traits, and who is "trainable," and you promote her. The problem is, of course, that sometimes this approach does not work. Fiedler's theory helps us understand why.

Imagine the frustration of the manager of human resources who finally convinces top management that the company's supervisors could benefit from a good course in human relations. The course is presented and paid for and the performance of some supervisors improves, but the performance of at least as many others decreases. Contingency theory has an answer. Perhaps those task-motivated managers who, by accident, had been placed in charge of groups with favorable or unfavorable leadership situations have had their "styles" altered enough to make them more relationship-motivated, just as the seminar proposed. Now their style no longer properly matches the reality of their group situation, so performance drops. Those whose effectiveness has improved were probably "mismatched" from the beginning. They might have been originally task-motivated and placed in group situations that were moderately favorable, where a relations-motivated leader would have been most effective. The seminar, by helping them focus more on human relations, would be expected to improve their performance.

This example illustrates the importance of matching the leader's style with the group situation. Rather than spending a lot of money on human relations seminars, a company might invest its limited funds in recruitment and placement activities to ensure that the styles of prospective managers are properly diagnosed, as are the leadership situations in various groups.

The style and circumstance can be effectively matched. Unfortunately, group situations and even leadership styles may change over time. The relationship-motivated leader who is charged with the responsibility of building a new project team might find his style effective during the formation of the group when the situation is only moderately favorable. As the project matures and is functioning smoothly, the work becomes more structured, the power position of the leader more defined, and the leader-follower relations improved to the point where a task-motivated style would be more appropriate. Then, as the project begins to wind down, the relationship-motivated style may once again be more effective as the situation evolves again to only moderately favorable.

The relationship between the trait and the situational

views of leadership is admittedly complex, and attempts to reconcile the two are often inadequate. However, Bavelas (1960) provided a useful summary and partial resolution to the apparent conflict with the following proposal:

1. Similarities between organizations make it possible to say useful things about the type of person who is likely to emerge as a leader.
2. Uniquenesses of any particular organization make it necessary to consider the situational factors that influence who is likely to lead.
3. When situations vary from organization to organization, we cannot say what traits will facilitate the emergence of leadership.

Some Prospects for the Future

The dynamic nature of leadership and the fascination the subject has held for managers and society at large will ensure the continued improvement of our understanding of the field. Today, in addition to the work being done in contingency theory, significant theoretical advances are taking place. Some of these, like Victor Vroom's work in leadership and decision making, represent an extension of the more familiar leadership-style research to other aspects of leader and management behavior.

Leadership and Decision Making. The Vroom and Yetton (1973) model, as it is called, conceives of the leader's role as controlling the process by which decisions are made in that part of the organization for which the leader is responsible. This model makes a particularly important contribution by illustrating how different leadership and problem-solving styles, such as autocratic, consultative, and group-oriented, can be effectively used for different types of problems. Moreover, this approach makes the direct implication that the effective leader may, and should, display different styles of leadership and problem solving depending on the type of problem faced at a particular time. For some problems, like those for which time is of the essence and successful implementation is not dependent on acceptance of the solution by the followers, the leader might be highly autocratic. Other situations will require more consultative and group-oriented approaches. The challenge to the leader is to appropriately determine the style that is most likely to be successful for the problem at hand.

Vroom and Jago (1974) have attempted to take this "theory" one additional step by developing a leadership training program. According to these authors, the critical skill of all leaders is the ability to adapt their behavior to the demands of the situation. An important aspect of this adaptability is the skill to select the appropriate decision-making process for each problem. In this sense, Vroom's approach is similar to the situational view of Fiedler, although it requires considerably more individual adaptability and is applicable to a more limited range of leader behavior (that is, decision making).

Path, Goals, and Leadership. The final developing trend in leadership research that must be briefly reviewed is *path-goal theory.* The primary thrust of path-goal theory is concerned with how the leader's actions influence followers' perceptions of their work goals, their personal goals, and the "paths" to achieving them (House and Mitchell, 1974).

Many of the details of path-goal theory will be familiar because it is based on expectancy theory, which we discussed in Chapter Nine. Thus, the idea that leadership effectiveness is related to the leader's ability to make rewards available to followers and to distribute these rewards contingent on the performance of various tasks or the accomplishment of specific goals is in line with prior discussions.

In path-goal theory, leader behavior is acceptable to followers if they believe such behavior will be immediately satisfying or will satisfy some need in the future. Thus, leader behavior will be motivational to followers if it makes the satisfaction of followers' needs contingent on effective performance and improves the environment of the followers by providing the support and rewards necessary for effective performance.

As a practical matter, path-goal theory suggests several ways in which leaders can provide the types of actions that will motivate higher performance on the part of followers. For example (House and Mitchell, 1974):

1.   The leader can increase motivation by recognizing and arousing followers' needs for outcomes over which the leader has control. A leader may discuss with followers the potential growth opportunities and earnings available to those who accomplish specific tasks.
2.   Leaders may effectively increase motivation by paying higher incentives to those members who actually attain work goals.
3.   The leader may make the paths to the attainment of desired goals easier to travel by coaching or counseling. The leader who assumes a mentor role, for example, can increase follower motivation by assisting followers, through sage advice and sharing experiences, in accomplishing personal and organizational goals.
4.   Leaders can increase motivation by helping followers clarify goals and expectations. Particularly in jobs where ambiguities exist concerning what is expected, the leader can assist in clarifying expectations and by emphasizing the most effective paths for goal attainment.
5.   Leaders can improve motivation by removing barriers to goal attainment. Nothing is more helpful to highly motivated followers at times than leaders who make it easier for them to do what is expected.

There are, of course, many other ways in which motivation can be increased by innovative leaders. This brief list, however, is useful in suggesting some practical recommendations from a somewhat abstract theory.

Managers like to talk about leadership and researchers like to study it because so much of the success and survival of an organization depends on the quality of its leaders. Leadership is an art and one that must develop and evolve. Managers should never deceive themselves by thinking that because they are promoted into an executive position they automatically become leaders.

Effective leadership is a unique mixture of placement and style. Great care should be taken to place managers into positions where they have the greatest chance to succeed. All managers should strive to be effective leaders. It is an achievement no organization can bestow. There are no honorary leaders. Leadership effectiveness must be earned through hard work, enthusiasm, and commitment.

Implications and Conclusions

Again, as with motivation, the discussion in this chapter has taken us through the writings of a number of researchers and theorists. One conclusion is clear: Leadership has proven to be a more complex issue than most imagined, and it has occupied the attention of some of the greatest minds in management for decades.

It is safe to say that few, if any, managers today believe the oversimplistic notion that leaders have specific traits or respond consistently to unique situations. To the contrary, most researchers today are engaged in an ongoing search for consistent predictors of leadership ability. In the meantime, managers of organizations continue to wonder and worry about their ability to attract and retain the supply of leaders needed for effective operations. And we must again witness the mysteries of how leadership emerges. Television evangelists attract millions of viewers and raise incredible amounts of money. Sports heroes and rock stars have followers who are no less fanatical.

How do we explain leadership? We keep trying. We learn what we can from those before us, and we add as best we can from our own experiences. The world demands a supply of leaders, and for that reason leadership research will thrive. Although much has been accomplished in a relatively short time, leadership will continue to occupy the attention of management researchers and practicing managers. It is too important and too fundamental to the success of organizations of all types to be left to chance.

PART FIVE

Managing
Coordination and Change

Coordination, as we have seen, is a recurring theme of management. It was a particular concern for the administrative organization writers like Mooney and Reiley, Fayol, and Barnard. There has been a recognition in management that coordination is not the normal state of affairs. Left to their own devices, people and groups will not automatically direct their efforts toward the efficient accomplishment of organizational goals. Coordination, therefore, is an important responsibility of managers.

To coordinate effectively, managers must have the authority to get things done. Although authority cannot ensure that a particular manager will have the ability to coordinate diverse human effort, it is an important necessary first step. Chapter Eleven addresses the issue of coordination and authority. In fact, in the words of Mooney and Reiley, authority is looked on as the "supreme coordinating power."

The fact that Mooney and Reiley use the term *power* to define authority reveals an interesting difference between the views of early classical writers and modern analysts of authority and power. Today, a great deal of energy is devoted to ensuring that everyone understands that authority relates to rights that come by means of a person occupying a certain position. Authority, in modern management terminology, is very impersonal. Power, on the other hand, is the ability to get things done and is, therefore, quite personal. It relates to the personality of the person who is attempting to influence others. The classical writers apparently saw no reason to make such a distinction. They freely interchanged the words with little confusion. The frequency of this interchange is pointed out in the chapter.

Chapter Twelve examines the evolution of organizational design theory. Classical organization theory was built on a few, rather straightforward concepts. These concepts created an impression of absolutism and preciseness. More modern developments in organization theory are situational or relative—a fact reflected in the use of the name *contingency theory* to refer to modern approaches.

The final chapter of the book takes a backward glance at where we have been and summarizes the lessons for managers that are contained within the book. Ten fundamental recurring themes and the lessons each teaches current and prospective managers are presented and briefly discussed.

CHAPTER 11

Authority and Influence

Exercising Managerial
Rights and Abilities

Mooney and Reiley (1931) praised coordination as the first principle of organization. Organizations could accomplish their full potential and avoid the inefficiencies of conflict only when each unit was properly coordinated so as to obtain a unity of effort. Without coordination organizations could not exist, and without authority coordination was not likely, so to Mooney and Reiley authority was "the supreme coordinating power." Authority thus became an essential ingredient of organizational success.

If you are interested in authority and influence in management, you do not have to look hard to find others with similar concerns. Beware, however, of the mysterious and confusing task facing you if you wish to avoid becoming sidetracked into the semantic controversies that surround the topic. Perhaps the most familiar relates to similarities and differences between the terms *authority* and *power*. In recent years there has been relatively widespread agreement that authority is a *right* one has by virtue of the position one occupies in an organization. Authority, when viewed in this manner, is impersonal and has nothing to do with the individual occupying the position. Power, by contrast, is more personal and concerns an individual's *ability* to get things done by influencing others. Power is personal and a

203

direct result of the personality of the individual exercising influence.

This controversy is interesting and potentially important. We have all seen cases where high-level managers who possess all the rights that accompany an office in the executive suite appear to have little power or ability to influence others. We have seen an equal number of people with no right to influence others who nevertheless become extremely powerful. Since this is an important topic, we will address it at the end of the chapter. For now, we will not minimize the importance of semantic controversies, nor will we allow ourselves to lose sight of more important issues by needlessly arguing about words.

Making careful distinctions between authority and power is a recent development. Such distinctions did not occupy much time in the early discussions of authority. The lack of concern about the subject is evident in Mooney and Reiley's definition of authority as the "supreme coordinating power."

We begin our analysis of authority with classical thought—writings from a time when authority was indeed the supreme coordinating power and a readily available option for managers attempting to build and maintain efficient operations. Early writers were not timid about advocating the use of authority as a coordinating and motivating tool. However, authority fell out of favor as time passed. It has been consistently less prescribed as the appropriate path to efficiency, and it has slowly but surely been regarded as something that should be exercised only when more preferable methods of influence prove futile. The image of the manager as gang boss has given way to the image of the manager as behavioral scientist and agent of change who skillfully uses all the techniques social science has to offer yet is forbidden to draw on the legitimate authority of the position. The prohibition against authority, however, gets us ahead of the story. The tale begins long before the days of the behavioral scientists.

Weber on Authority

So far in this book Max Weber has been mentioned many times. For someone with only a passing interest in the practical aspects of business, this sociologist has contributed much to classical organization theory. His contributions are particularly significant with regard to authority.

Weber was concerned about social order and the ways in which it can best be achieved. Social order, however, does not exist in the absence of a coordinating influence. Perhaps there is validity in David Ricardo's view of human beings as self-interest-oriented "rabble." Without social order the rabble become anarchists, and without authority social order is only a dream. Even though Mayo (1945) and others found this view objectionable, it remained a realistic concern of Weber's.

In discussing authority, Weber did not find it necessary to distinguish between authority and power. He defined *power* as the "probability" that one person will be able to carry out his will despite opposition or resistance from others. Similarly, Weber defined *domination* as the "probability" that a command with a specific content will be obeyed by others (Weber, 1947). Both of these concepts possess some properties of authority, and the successful use of either could add order to the organization. Weber appreciated the fact that organizations require order to regulate the behavior of individual members. Interestingly, members of organizations generally honor rules because they are "legally" required to or because it is the "convention" to do so. Employees frequently agree to accept various guidelines because it ensures harmony and aids productivity. It is, in other words, in their best interest to do so.

In dealing with domination or imperative control, Weber made an important and surprising point that is usually associated with Chester Barnard. He noted that for imperative control to work there must be a certain degree of "willingness to submit" or acceptance of the domination on the part of the follower. This sounds like Barnard's acceptance theory, which will be discussed later. Did Max Weber propose the acceptance theory attributed to Barnard all these years?

Actually, whether or not Weber proposed acceptance theory has only vague historical significance, since he was primarily concerned with *legitimate authority.* This right to influence others can arise from a variety of sources—perhaps the most common being the legal system itself. According to Weber, legitimate authority can be one of three types: rational, traditional, or charismatic.

Rational authority is based on both legal grounds and the ability of the people in positions of influence to give orders and require conformity. Chief executive officers, admirals in the navy, and provosts in universities all have rational legitimate authority.

One does not have to look hard to find examples of rational-legal authority in management. Consider the case of James Dutt, the "controversial boss of Beatrice" (Louis, 1985). Beatrice is a diversified company with such well-known products as La Choy Chinese foods, Tropicana orange juice, and Samsonite luggage. When Dutt was chairman and CEO, he supposedly wielded his authority with a vengeance. Former employees draw a picture of Dutt as an executive who could not tolerate dissent, who built fear among subordinates, and who demanded so much obedience and loyalty that some referred to him as "Chairman Dutt." Some say that even though Dutt owned relatively little Beatrice stock, he ran "the company like a private fiefdom and abused his power [authority]" (p. 111). As we would predict, he frequently made decisions, like the $30 million one to sponsor racing teams, that few could understand given the demographics of Beatrice's consumers. When he was CEO he decided where the advertising budget would be spent, and since he was a racing fan why not spend it sponsoring cars? After all, the word *Beatrice* would be plainly displayed on the cars in clear view of thousands of male racing fans—many of whom have never cooked a meal or bought the family's groceries in their entire life.

Traditional authority, unlike the rational-legal variety, is based on the sacredness of customs or established principles and concepts. Parents have authority in the family unit because this is the traditional approach that has served us well. The monarchs of Europe and the pope also enjoy traditional legitimate authority.

Finally, *charismatic authority* is based on the perceived holiness, bravery, or good conduct of a person. Unlike the other types, charismatic authority is extremely personal and relates to the personality of a particular individual. To understand charismatic authority we will do best to leave the realm of management and study the lives of people like Jim Jones, Jim and Tammy Bakker, Oral Roberts, and perhaps even Lee Iacocca. Although Weber recognized the reality of charisma, he believed it came into play because of a failure of other forms of authority to provide the desired level of order. Charisma is, in other words, a last-ditch grasp for order.

The sociological view of authority provided by Weber is valuable to managers even though it was not meant to have practical implications. However, the views of Mary Parker Follett, herself a political scientist, were often focused on applied aspects of management.

Mary Parker Follett on Giving Orders

Like Weber, Follett had much to say about many topics, and for that reason her name appears frequently in this book. Her most important ideas on authority are given in *Freedom and Coordination* (1949), a series of lectures edited by Lyndall Urwick.

Authority as Illusion. Even though Follett was knowledgeable about authority, particularly the formal theory that states authority always flows down in the hierarchy, she believed that all authority is "functional." It belongs to the position or job, and when people talk about the limits of authority they are really talking about the definition of the task. Because Follett believed authority to be derived from the function or task, she saw it as having little to do with the vertical dimension, or hierarchy, of the organization. Bosses, according to her, do not delegate authority. The extent and direction of delegation are instead inherent in the plan of organization. The philosophy of delegation is established when the organization is structured.

In developing this approach, Follett related areas such as delegation of authority and task management and illustrated the interrelationship between authority and organizational design. For example, organizations often face conflicting demands in their need to closely control critical factors or resources while ensuring flexibility in operational matters. American Can Company, as an illustration, has been praised for its ability to keep capital allocation decisions centralized while simultaneously delegating operational decision making to relatively low levels in the organization (Marshuetz, 1985).

Follett, however, was skeptical of authority, and like many of the human relations writers who followed, believed that overall authority should be minimized and that people in organizations should have just enough authority to accomplish their task—no more and no less.

Follett was convinced that orders and authority come from the work or the job to be done. Thus, her view was less personal and emphasized the need to be certain that commands are not directed toward individuals. The "law of the situation" should operate freely, since it is inherently arbitrary to direct orders and authority toward individuals. The important thing is for the manager to consider the total situation before issuing commands. Follett favored, to the extent possible, the replacement of authority with the careful instruction and education of people to ensure that they know and practice the best available business practices and understand the reasons that orders and directions are necessary. In this manner, obedience to legitimate orders is active rather than passive. People submit because it is in their best interest to do so, not because they fear the consequences of nonsubmission. This places a perspective of voluntariness on authority and again hints at the acceptance theory of Barnard.

"Power With" Rather Than "Power Over." Perhaps no other single writing gives us so much insight into Follett's views on authority as her opinions on the exercise of power. Again, she saw no need to precisely differentiate between power and authority. To exercise power means merely to make things happen—to be a causal agent for change. Control means to exercise the power as a means to a specific end. Traditionally in management we have thought of "power over" the various resources of production and have made little differentiation between human and nonhuman resources. Follett believed that "power with" is a more constructive way of exercising influence. She presumed

that power could be jointly developed and co-active rather than coercive.

Power-with concepts can be built through *circular behavior*, the process whereby it is possible for you as a manager to influence other managers while the other managers are simultaneously influencing you. Workers at the same time are given open communication channels and allowed to influence managers while managers are in the process of influencing workers. This, in Follett's view, is the iterative, integrative way organizations should operate. She stated that the functional unity of organizations is a high and worthy goal that occurs when all individuals and groups know their function and each function corresponds as closely as possible to the abilities of the individuals and groups who perform the tasks. Moreover, each individual should be given the authority necessary to get his or her job done and should be held accountable for accomplishing the tasks.

The ultimate outcome of this type of relationship is participation—not merely consent but genuine participation. Participation means, in Follett's view, everyone taking part in the success of the organization according to the capacities of each person. True participation results in a unified whole made up of many related parts and functions that culminate in the consolidated organization all managers dream of and desire. True participation is not *self-sacrifice* but *self-contribution.*

Consider, for example, the participative management programs at Motorola, Inc. Participative Management Program I (PMP I) was directed primarily toward manufacturing employees. PMP II was dedicated to the needs of nonmanufacturing workers. Although the specifics of each program are designed for different types of employees, the principles are the same. First, in line with Theory Y, the company assumes that the performance of employees is the consequence of the treatment they receive. If people are treated as mature, responsible adults, they will behave accordingly. The company also states that employees deserve to understand the logic behind decisions made by higher-level managers. Finally, interdependence between individual and organizational goals is considered essential for successful implementation of the Motorola style of participative management.

For our purposes, the important point to note is that under this program, formal authority is minimized. This does not mean that accountability is lost. Nor does it mean that production will automatically fall. In fact, high-level performance standards are established by the group, and individuals are expected to equal or exceed the goal. In all, the program has been successful. Participation has been encouraged, communication has improved, and trust levels between workers and managers have increased significantly. The results obtained by Motorola have been very impressive to date and are likely to continue.

Some More Precise Distinctions

In spite of the fact that we have minimized the importance of precise semantic distinctions, some did appear in the writings of Urwick (1944) and in his summaries of Fayol and other classical writers. Urwick talked of authority as a principle and stated that the supreme authority for making any type of decision has to reside somewhere in the organization. Not only should the supreme authority exist, but a "scalar process" should provide a clear line from the point of supreme authority to every person in the organization. Authority "moves through the scalar chain" assigning and coordinating activities.

Urwick's Interpretations and Views on Authority. In the process of discussing and integrating many of the ideas of other writers, Urwick (1944) eventually arrived at some definitions. According to him, *duties* are the activities individuals are required to perform in connection with their jobs. *Authority* is the right to require actions of others. This authority or right, as he saw it, derives from a formal statement of such rights by the organization, from the technical expertise a person possesses, or from personal characteristics such as popularity or seniority. *Power* is the ability to get things done; *responsibility* is accountability for the performance of one's duties. The definitions sound nice, but we can easily see that the potential semantic problems are numerous. Pfeffer (1981), for example, introduced an additional factor by suggesting that authority is merely legitimized power. When power becomes legitimate through custom or acceptance, it becomes authority and most people rarely question it.

A Summary of Classical Concepts of Authority. Regardless of how much time a particular writer devoted to the nature of authority and in spite of the relatively progressive insights each had into the importance of the employee's acceptance, the dominant view of authority in early management thought was consistent. Authority was related to the rights of the manager, and these rights came from higher levels in the organization. Ultimately, all rights originated with the right of private property, could properly be delegated from one manager to another, and eventually could even be delegated to rank-and-file employees. Some writers expressed a concern for employee participation, but this concern was strong in the writings of only a few.

The traditional view of authority required managers to make decisions concerning the exercise of influence and to share the rights of influence with others. This led directly to the question of delegation. When examined from the perspective of conventional wisdom, delegation expanded into one of the most sacred prescriptions of management.

In spite of useful time-management techniques, few managers have the time to do the many things required of them. For decades managers have been taught that the proper response to this work overload is to become an effective delegator of authority. The logic of effective delegation goes as follows:

1. To be successful, managers must expand their abilities through the effective delegation of authority. When promising followers are identified and given additional responsibilities, they can frequently accept increasing levels of authority. This provides two valuable outcomes for the organization: (a) the higher-level manager frees his or her time to "be in more than one place at a time" and (2) those employees to whom authority is delegated have an opportunity to develop and practice their management skills. If the lessons are learned well, delegation will ensure the company a long succession of qualified and promising managers.

2. Although delegated authority can always be rescinded by
    the higher-level manager, he or she must give up the author-
    ity necessary for the subordinate to do the job while the
    delegation is in effect. To do otherwise could easily result
    in a violation of the principle of "unity of command" (in
    Fayol's terms) or the "one master" principle. If the boss
    fails to genuinely delegate the necessary amount of author-
    ity, employees might easily end up with more than one
    boss, and that is always confusing and dysfunctional for
    subordinates.

3. Delegating authority is risky business for a manager. The
    manager temporarily gives up an amount of authority, yet
    he or she is still accountable for getting the job done. The
    failure of a subordinate is not a valid excuse, because a
    manager's accountability can never be removed. There are
    no excuses accepted when it comes to delegated authority.
    Watergate, the Iran-Contra affair, and other familiar scan-
    dals provide evidence of the iron law of accountability.

In the 1930s many of the prescriptions of classical management thought were challenged and changed. Writers with
more humanistic persuasions not only revised ideas relating to
authority in organizations but actually began to reject traditional concepts of authority and the need for this "supreme
coordinating power." The result was a seemingly revolutionary
new way of conceptualizing authority. This radical approach
also established the conditions necessary to ensure the controversies discussed today.

Barnard's Acceptance Theory

Chester Barnard introduced, under what he called the *elements of formal organization*, his now-famous theory of authority. As was his style, Barnard did not describe a simple theory,
and the way he explained his ideas was more than a little confusing. Yet his points are important and are worth the trouble
involved in understanding them.

Chester Barnard was not a professor but a businessman

and philosopher—an admittedly unusual combination. He was born in 1886 in Molden, Massachusetts, and died in 1961. Barnard attended Harvard but did not graduate. He said he got his degree the hard way—he "earned it" in business. Barnard went to work for AT&T in 1909 as a statistician and moved up quickly. His rapid rise in the corporation was not the result of his education, so it probably had something to do with his knowledge of foreign languages. He soon became an expert on international telephone rates. By 1927 he was president of the New Jersey Bell Telephone Company. His only book, *The Functions of the Executive* (1938), remains widely recognized as one of the true classics of management.

Subjective and Objective Aspects of Authority. Barnard saw authority as closely related to communication. In fact, he defined authority as the "character of the communication (order)" by virtue of which the communication is accepted by members of the organization as governing their actions. Usually authority is accepted when orders are considered legal, legitimate, and necessary. Barnard presented his famous *acceptance theory* by stating that authority is vested in the people who are willing to be controlled. Thus, the reality of authority, in Barnard's view, has less to do with managers and more to do with employees. Instead of the manager possessing formal rights granted by the organization and forcing imperative control on employees, the employees are really the holders of authority because it is their decision to accept or not accept orders and thereby determine whether influence will take place at all and if so, where it will be directed. The subjective element of authority is the acceptance by employees, while the objective aspect relates to the character of the order or communication itself.

Authority, according to Barnard and contrary to popular belief, flows from the bottom to the top of the organization. The degree to which this authority is accepted is related to the following conditions:

1. The extent to which the follower understands the communication from the manager. Frequently the manager needs to interpret the order to assist an employee's understanding.

2. The extent to which the order/communication is considered in line with the purpose of the organization.
3. The extent to which the communication is consistent with the personal needs of followers and in line with the interests of employees.
4. The extent to which the follower is able, mentally and physically, to comply with the order.

Although *zones of indifference* exist whereby orders are acceptable without conscious thought, directions are usually accepted because of the *authority of position* or the *authority of leadership*. The former results from position, while the latter derives from superior knowledge, ability, or understanding. Again, Barnard found no reason to make a careful distinction between power and authority. In fact, had he recognized or acknowledged a difference, his theory of authority would have really become a theory of power. This, it might be noted, would have made the theory much less novel than it is in its present form.

An Extension of Barnard. Herbert A. Simon ([1946] 1976) simply defined authority as the "power to make decisions which guide the actions of another" (p. 125). Unlike Follett, however, Simon clearly believed that authority creates a hierarchical relationship between two or more people—some are the superiors and some are subordinates. The unique distinction provided by Simon is the way in which he explained authority in purely behavioral terms. Authority takes place only when certain behaviors occur, regardless of the "paper theory of organization" (p. 125). The superior behaves by issuing a command and develops an expectation that the subordinate will accept the order. The subordinate behaves by following the command and accepting the behavioral option that "is selected for me by the boss."

Interestingly, Simon did make a distinction between authority and other forms of influence such as persuasion. The distinction is that with authority, the subordinate "holds in abeyance his own criteria" for choosing behavioral alternatives and uses the superior's command as the sole basis for choice. Simon accepted the notion of a zone of indifference discussed by Barnard even though he referred to it as the "area of acceptance" (p. 133). The most striking aspect of the subordinate role is that it establishes an area of acceptance within which the follower is willing to accept the decisions made by the superior. This zone varies in size, but its existence is determined by the legitimacy attached to the order by the employee.

Authority, according to Simon, is important in organizations for three primary reasons:

1. Authority enforces the follower's responsibility to those who exercise control. This is closely related to Weber's idea of legitimate or legal authority. When authority is used for this reason, sanctions play an important part in the process.
2. Authority secures expertise in decision making. The expert on a particular issue may be located in a strategic position in the hierarchy of authority, requiring the expert's decisional premises to be accepted by others in the organization.
3. Authority permits coordination of activities. Coordination is aimed at getting members of the group to accept the *same* decision, whereas expertise involves the adoption of *good* decisions.

This view of authority from Simon's decision-making perspective highlights the fact that influence is important behaviorally as well as structurally. It also helps explain why authority and influence have continued to be a recurring theme of management even after the advent of the human relations orientation. It is interesting to note, for example, that even in books like Elliot Jacques's *The Changing Culture of a Factory* (1951) almost half of the issues discussed relate to authority, power, and influence. The regulation of power, elucidation of policy, organization of authority, and extended chain of command at the Glacier Metal Company were major topics addressed by Jacques and his associates. Throughout the book they discussed how modern organizations attempted to balance the critical need to control operations against providing as much flexibility as possible for decision making. This issue remains an important challenge for management today.

Authority and Human Relations

McGregor (1960), even before he introduced Theory X and Theory Y, stated that control in organizations is a process of selective adaptation. That is, it involves selection of the appropriate means of influence over the people being managed. While all the human relations writers were aware of the fact that authority exists in organizations, and some even admitted to its necessity, most believed that the best thing to do with traditionally conceived authority in organizations is to remove it. McGregor argued that less emphasis should be placed on formal authority and the rights of position and that more emphasis should be placed on "integration," or the creation of conditions that allows members of an organization to achieve their own goals while working toward the success of the enterprise.

Using Authority to Improve Performance. It was McGregor's contention that all organizations require some system of influence and control. Historically, in scientific management and early organization theory, control was based, according to McGregor, on the simple assumption that authority is an indispensable aspect of effective management. Managers too often assume that the authority they possess over subordinates is all they need to motivate successfully and to ensure high levels of performance. In reality they should freely use other forms of influence as well. Some of the more important are persuasion and professional influence. McGregor believed that through authority managers can force individuals to perform at minimally acceptable levels but that authority cannot command maximum performance. Individuals are committed to work toward organizational goals only when their personal needs are simultaneously fulfilled. The key to motivation is to selectively adapt that type of influence process that will build an interdependence between individual and organizational goals.

Authority and the Linking Pin. Rensis Likert (1967) followed up on some of the views of authority and power presented by Barnard and added some insights of his own. Managerial power/authority, in Likert's view, depends on how much influence employees allow the manager to exercise over them.

He reasoned that employees would feel more a part of decisions, be more committed to accomplishing organizational goals, and allow themselves to be influenced more by managers if they had an opportunity to participate in goal formulation. However, in developing the idea of the linking pin, described in Chapter Ten, Likert introduced a novel idea. This was the view that the degree of power a manager has upward with bosses and laterally with peers will constitute a major influence on the amount of power he or she has downward on employees. If the manager can build credibility and influence with his or her boss and gain support for actions that will reinforce employees' goals, it would be reasonable to assume that he or she would have increased support from lower-level members of the organization.

Likert and Likert (1976) illustrated the importance of this view of authority and influence in the practical area of conflict resolution. They began by agreeing in principle with McGregor that most conflicts historically have been settled using "win-lose" strategies. That is, when one person or party wins, the other must lose. This is the case with the authority-oriented solutions to organizational problems advocated by much of classical management theory and practice. Confrontations and ultimatums are frequently thought of as the only way to deal with deep-seated differences that sometimes exist between departments such as production and sales or data processing and marketing. Departments expend their efforts on mustering all the forces they can to compel other departments to do their bidding. Often one or a few powerful individuals emerge to ensure the success of this "steamroller" technique. The result of this exercise of *negative power* is all too often strikes, lockouts, work stoppages, and maybe even worker sabotage.

More productive approaches, according to Likert and Likert, are those leading to the exercise of *positive power.* Sometimes such approaches even result in "win-win" strategies of conflict resolution. Such approaches involve disputing parties that are genuinely trying to understand the perspective and needs of each other. Sometimes they are even willing to go more than halfway in reaching solutions that will be to everyone's advantage. Again, in terms that remind us of McGregor, the point is made that conflicts are resolved on the basis of one party influencing another. When one disputing party begins negotiation through the use of negative power (such as attempting to compel a resolution), that party's influence may actually be reduced by the negative response such an approach receives. On the other hand, efforts to resolve conflict that are based on positive power often increase influence because they do not entail negative attitudes. Even conflict, with all its reduction of coordination, can be channeled toward constructive results.

Confronting the Controversy

Now that we have discussed authority and influence in detail, we can conclude with an examination of the controversy we have attempted to avoid throughout this chapter, which has to do with the distinction between authority and power. Both of these themes, authority and power, have been debated and examined for years. According to Tolstoy in *War and Peace*, "What is power?" is the essential question of history. It may be accurate to say that the more fundamental the question, the less certain we are about the answer.

We noted earlier that the basic controversy relating to the definition of power and authority revolves around two basic theories or views on how influence originates. The traditional, formal theory of authority often attributed to Weber views authority as rights and proposes that such rights always flow down an organization. Of course, we pointed out the fact that Weber did assign importance to the acceptance of these rights by followers. In spite of this, the formal theory dominates most discussions of Weber's ideas on the subject. By contrast, the acceptance theory, which supposedly originated with Barnard but clearly predates him, maintains that a manager's authority rests in the willingness of followers to accept the commands of the manager. Clearly, much of this dispute could be clarified by simply referring to a formal theory of authority (rights) and an acceptance theory of power (ability). Such agreement, however, is not likely.

To illustrate the magnitude of the controversy, consider

one of the most famous papers on the subject of social power. This paper by French and Raven (1959) illustrates how confusing distinctions can be. The authors state that power can originate from one or more of the following sources. Using the criteria above to distinguish between authority and power, we will consider in each case whether it is power or authority that is being discussed.

1. *Reward power.* A manager can have power over another person if the other person believes the manager can provide or withhold rewards. If we are talking about the rewards distributed by the manager as a representative of the organization (monetary incentives, promotions, etc.), this would be considered a source of authority rather than power. But if we are referring to informal rewards like acceptance into a group, this would be a type of power.

2. *Coercive power.* A person can influence the actions of others if he or she controls the amount and type of punishments that can be administered to them. Again, if coercion means official demotion or the withholding of pay for violations of organizational rules and regulations, it can represent the authority that goes with management positions. But if it represents social punishments, it is more accurately described as power.

3. *Legitimate power.* This "power" is based on the rights of one person to rule over another because of their respective positions in the organization. This appears to be a relatively clear case of authority.

4. *Referent power.* This type of influence accompanies one person's identification with another. This appears to be more clearly a case of power.

5. *Expert power.* This type of influence is exerted when one person is perceived to possess a unique and valuable type of knowledge or information. Expert power has become increasingly important in high-technology industries and in other industries that require large numbers of highly trained professional employees. Expertise is more closely related to power than authority.

A review of this list emphasizes the confusion associated with the terms *authority* and *power.* Such confusion is unfortunate because it diverts too much attention from the more important issues involved in the nature of influence in organizations. Moreover, arguments over mere words blind us to the changing reality around us. For example, whether by rights or abilities, expert power has greatly increased as a source of influence in many organizations. In new and innovative industries much of what we think of as traditional and legitimate authority is being replaced by influence based on the possession of knowledge. Managers must be aware of these changing realities so they can recognize and appreciate the implications for building effective organizations.

Managers influence people in many ways. Sometimes their influence results from the position they occupy, and sometimes it results from their personality. Both types of influence are important and are needed to assist in the accomplishment of organizational goals.

Much of this chapter has focused on classical views of authority. Authority is called the glue that holds organizations together. Perhaps the most important lesson managers should remember from the early writers is the necessity of effectively delegating authority. Effective delegation is one of the manager's primary aids in time management. Few managers have the time to do all they are expected to accomplish. The only practical way they have to expand their ability is to delegate some of their authority. Delegation expands the manager's time and provides valuable training and development opportunities for deserving followers.

Implications and Conclusions

This chapter has looked at the question of authority and influence in organizations. The early emphasis was on the use of legitimate authority as the most efficient way to ensure the coordination of diverse organizational units. This is best illustrated by Mooney and Reiley's reference to authority as "the supreme coordinating power."

It is safe to say that early management theory and practice viewed authority in terms of managerial rights inherent in the positions people occupy. In other words, authority was viewed in terms of the organizational hierarchy, with the flow of influence always downward. The entry of the human relations writers changed all this. In the view of people like McGregor and Likert, authority is the ultimate coordinating force but one that should be evoked only as a last resort. They believed that persuasion, professional pride, and positive reinforcement and feedback are preferable to the exercise of managerial rights.

Even sacred ideas like the downward flow of authority were not safe. People like Barnard, Simon, and others became convinced that the ultimate source of authority and influence does not rest in the positions people occupy but in the willingness of subordinate employees to be led. This gave rise to the acceptance theory of authority, which saw it as flowing upward in organizations, and created a desire to more clearly differentiate between the right and the ability to influence. Thus, there emerged an ongoing discussion about the nature of organizational authority and the reality of social power.

There now exists a general agreement that managers should understand and appreciate the relationship among four basic terms that describe the managerial task. First, there are *rights* that come with every position in an organization, and these rights should be clearly specified and communicated to all members of relevant work groups. Second, there are *abilities* that all people have that can prove to be important sources of influence. Third, the rights that reside in a given position create legitimate expectations of *accountability*. Finally, all mature employees feel a *responsibility* to effectively use the right they are granted to get things done. Effective staffing and job design occur when all these diverse terms and phenomena are in balance. A person's rights should equal his or her abilities to do the job. All managers should expect to be held accountable for their actions and should feel a responsibility to use wisely the authority that has been entrusted to them.

CHAPTER 12

Organizational
Design and Change

Managing When There Are No Absolutes

Early management started with a search for "absolute" principles and that is as it should be. The legitimacy of a field of research and ultimately practice is not built on "what ifs," "in most cases," and "under certain circumstances." Besides, the early contributors to the field were engineers trained to look for order in events and the "one best way" of doing everything from laying bricks to building large corporations. Even more important was the fact that, as we discussed in a previous chapter, legitimacy required the application of some type of respectable science, and that required, or at least implied in the minds of most, that precise, normative guidelines could be offered to improve management action. When we go to the doctor, we like for her to tell us precisely what is wrong. We hope to learn that we are in good health, but even if the news is bad, we can seek a cure for a definite and known ailment.

Corporate executives expect the same from management theory, and employees expect assurance from the boss that things are under control. If the CEO is not confident with the use of the best available knowledge, employees are justifiably nervous about their future and that of the organization. We respect those who know the answers, even if they are wrong on occasion. We want, and deserve, answers from high-paid consultants, doctors, and lawyers, although we know reality does not lend itself to precise responses.

Classical Principles and the One Best Way

George Lombard (1971) argued that a fundamental change began taking place in American society in the 1920s. Prior to this time people seemed content with absolute prescriptions. Reality appeared simpler then, and people were more willing to accept traditional explanations. Myths, like science, are designed to help people understand events and make sense out of their surroundings. If science could not explain things, then myths would suffice.

In recent times people have become less willing to accept simple, universal, and sometimes authoritarian values. In ethics, questions are more "situational." The fact that something is right for me in this situation does not imply, to situational proponents, that the same is right for you in another. Even in medicine, theology, and education absolute solutions to historical problems are no longer unanimously accepted. It is little wonder, as Lombard notes, that a situational view of the postindustrial society emerged in management. World War I, the Great Depression, and unprecedented technological progress demanded change. However, before we get to the changes, we should look at the prescriptions of classical organizational design theory. These prescriptions reflect a way of looking at things that provided security but was often wanting in its ability to explain reality.

Classical Concepts of Organizational Design. The classical concepts of organization as practiced in management today emerged during the scientific management era and have continued to evolve to modern times. Obviously, we need not review all the principles to understand what early writers were saying. However, we should examine a few of the more important.

Several of the writers introduced previously had much to say about the best ways to design efficient and effective organizations. Fayol (1949) popularized a number of organizational concepts, including unity of command, unity of direction, centralization, and the scalar chain, even though he never really felt comfortable calling them principles in the scientific sense. Mooney and Riley were less timid. The revised edition of *Onward Industry* (1931) was called *The Principles of Organization* (1932). In the latter, they discussed four basic principles: the coordinative, scalar, functional, and "staff phase of functionalism." The *coordinative principle*, as we noted previously, was the first principle and "contained all the others." This principle stated: "Coordination is the orderly arrangement of group effort, to provide unity of action in pursuit of a common purpose." Coordination "makes the organization" while the leader merely leads its members. Whereas Fayol thought of coordination as a different function, Mooney and Reiley viewed it as the essence of all the principles.

Coordination begins at the top and goes down through the entire organization. This results in the *scalar principle*, whereby managerial authority and responsibility are graduated down the entire organization. It is a grading of duties not according to the work but according to the authority and responsibility of different managers. The effect is a hierarchy, or the vertical specialization of labor.

The horizontal division of work, whereby tasks are divided into different duties, follows the *functional principle*. Specification of the duties of each individual aids members in understanding the function they are to perform and helps them appreciate how their job relates to other functions, individuals, and the final purpose of the organization.

The fourth principle is called the *staff phase of functionalism*. Classical organizational design directed a great deal of attention toward the idea of staff. Staff units in organizations are created to give advice or counsel to the line. The staff is expected to provide useful, creative ideas to line managers. However, staff members should exercise only the "authority of good ideas." The line should always command.

Progress Toward a Science of Administration. Other important contributions include those of Luther Gulick and Lyndall Urwick. Gulick was born in 1892 and served as the president of the Institute of Public Administration from 1923 to

1961. He was an international consultant to organizations such as the World Health Organization, the United Nations, and UNESCO. Gulick held many important government positions, including membership on the War Production Board; on the U.S. Reparations Staff in Moscow, Potsdam, Tokyo, and Manila; and on the President's Committee on Administrative Management. His best-known work, *Papers on the Science of Administration* (1947), was coedited with Lyndall Urwick and is a collection of papers written by well-known contributors to classical management.

This collection represents, in one volume, some of the most comprehensive statements of the beliefs of the classical organization theorists. As with Mooney and Reiley, the overriding principle was coordination, and organization was seen as one important way of achieving it. Because work is specialized, the organization must provide a mechanism for coordinating different organizational units. Coordination is most effectively attained when specific organizational principles are observed. The *one master* principle, for example, reinforces the idea of unity of command. No person should have more than one boss at a single time. Also, the *span of control*, or the number of people that one person can effectively supervise, must be regulated. Urwick (1944) believed the number should be no greater than five or six people whose work is interrelated. The span might, however, be increased through the use of an "assistant to" position.

In Gulick's view, a staff specialist could be used to improve the technical efficiency of a manager's performance even though it should be recognized that specialized staff, by their very nature, tend to be narrow and myopic. Therefore, it is important to recognize the limitations of staff and not allow them to assume inappropriate authority. For example, the role of the legal counsel in the corporation is to provide expert advice on legal matters, not to make decisions. At times, and in an increasingly large number of regulated industries, there is a danger that staff experts will become too powerful, since it is the line decision maker who is ultimately responsible for managerial actions.

One of the most interesting discussions presented in *Pa-*

pers relates to the vertical and horizontal organization of different departments. It is argued that the vertical division of departments relates to the *purpose* of the organization while the horizontal division of departments is designed according to the *process* necessary to accomplish the purpose. The purpose of IBM, for example, is to manufacture and market products and services relating to information management. The process of accomplishing this purpose or mission, however, requires a large array of units such as manufacturing, sales, systems design, personnel, and so on. The managerial challenge is to weave the "tangled fabric" and make the purpose and the process work together for the overall welfare of the organization.

   Summary of Classical Concepts. Out of the collective work of individuals like Taylor, Fayol, Mooney and Reiley, and others there gradually emerged several important cornerstone concepts of classical design theory. The more important include:

1. *Division of work or specialization of labor.* The importance of this concept has been previously discussed in detail, and it remains one of the most fundamental of the cornerstone concepts. When it is applied vertically in an organization, it relates to hierarchy. When it is applied horizontally, it involves functions or tasks. If concerns about authority and responsibility are introduced, the scalar principle comes into play.

2. *Departmentalization.* Organizations can be departmentalized in various ways, depending on their purpose and other factors. Functional departments such as production, marketing, and finance are established to allow each unit to concentrate on some aspect of the business and in so doing to efficiently accomplish the organizational mission. Departments may be established on the basis of the clients or customers served. The organization of Dow Chemical will reflect a concern for household users of Scrubbing Bubbles and industrial users of chlorine gas. Departments may also be established according to geographical regions within the United States and around the world (Gulick and Urwick, 1947). Geographical departmentalization is especially critical for multinational firms.

3. *Span of control.* A recurring theme in classical design the-
    ory is, how many people can a supervisor properly super-
    vise? Urwick, as we noted earlier, thought it was only five
    or six. Others have argued ten or twelve. Regardless of the
    exact number, this has been an important issue in the de-
    velopment of classical management thought.
4. *Unity of command.* Gulick called it *one master* whereas
    Fayol used *unity of command.* The idea in both cases is
    that a person should have only one boss at any given time.
    To design a system otherwise is to risk reductions in effec-
    tive coordination. More about this principle and institution-
    al violations of the concept will be discussed later in this
    chapter.

Other principles, such as unity of direction, were discussed under goal setting, and some, such as delegation of
authority and related issues in the centralization and decentralization of organizations, were previously examined in detail. Regardless of the exact number of concepts and principles, it is
important to note that the classical writers attempted to provide a view of organization that was precise, rational, and consistent. In doing so, however, problems were created.

Principles or Proverbs? Principles and normative concepts
specify guidelines for behavior and therefore suggest relatively
universal and inflexible ways of doing things. While such an approach gives us the feeling of certainty, it greatly restricts our
ability to reconcile problems of logic and consistency that develop within the framework of normative organization theory.

Simon (1946) took a critical look at the four cornerstone
concepts of classical theory, and none of them survived his analysis "in very good shape." Instead of unequivocal principles,
Simon found "a set of two or more mutually incompatible principles apparently equally applicable to the administrative situation" (p. 66). Anderson and Duncan (1977) provided a similar
analysis of paradoxes associated with various principles of administration. In many, if not most, of the cases there was a suggestion that situational factors operated in a unique way to
complicate the application of the principle under review. For
this reason, the absolute orientation and the search for the one

best way has given way to the relative (in Lombard's terms) or situational view of organization design.

Roots of a Situational Theory of Organization

Henry Sturgis Dennison was an unusual executive. He was born in 1877 and graduated from Harvard before joining the family business, the Dennison Manufacturing Company. He became president in 1917 and served in that capacity for thirty-five years. In *Organization Engineering* (1931), Dennison stated that organizations are composed of four interacting forces: (1) members (the strength of any organization), (2) operating measures (policies and procedures), (3) structural relationships, and (4) purposes or goals. Structural relationships are our concern at this point.

Dennison was a product of the "absolute" view of classical organization design theory. For this reason, no doubt, he believed organizations must have a definite structure. However, he also insisted that principles of organization are good only insofar as they assist in building organizations faster and better than would be the case using trial-and-error techniques. An organization's structure should reflect its purpose and scope of operations, but it must always be adaptable. Adaptability was not a key to understanding and using classical theory. In fact, inflexibility was the primary problem of classically designed structures.

In Dennison's view, departmentalization is a necessary and practical way of dealing with the inability of people to contend with increasingly complex tasks. One way to simplify the complexity is to organize activities functionally. Dennison recognized the need for different degrees of centralization. When production is regular and uniform, decision making can be centralized. When it is irregular and highly specialized, decisions should be decentralized, with choices being made by those nearest to the changing circumstances. Dennison understood and appreciated the need for staff advice and even advocated the use of committees as a means of coordination. However, it was his insights into situational factors that have been greatly neglected in retrospective evaluations of his work.

We get the first hint of "Dennison the contingency theorist" in his discussion of cross-contacts. This is similar to the idea proposed by Fayol referred to as Fayol's bridge, or the *gangplank principle*. It also relates to Follett's idea of *cross-functioning*, or the violation of the scalar principle in the interest of faster and better horizontal communication. The way Dennison presented the idea is intriguing. He maintained that since all contacts cannot be perfect, communication must be adapted to the physical and psychological difficulties of *each situation*. This almost defensive way of justifying cross-functioning as a response to imperfect communication reveals his devotion, in principle, to the scalar chain.

Dennison developed the situational theme in greater detail with the introduction of the need for *continuous reorganization*. Continuous reorganization demands that the firm constantly rebuild its structure to meet changing environmental realities. The structure suitable for today may not be suitable for tomorrow. Therefore, reorganization should be a continuous evolution, and all units must maintain a balance so that one does not become so strong at the expense of others that the purpose of the entire organization is defeated. Dennison believed that change or "situations in flux" is not the exception but the rule, not the abnormal but the normal state of affairs.

No One Best Way

It was bound to happen. The growing discontent with absolute principles of management forced many managers and researchers to look for other answers to organizational problems. Interestingly, researchers in England were busy working on the solution. Therefore, we must move again to English factories for answers to management's perplexing questions.

Research at South Essex. We began this book with an Englishman and a Scotsman, Babbage and Ure, examining the factory system created by the Industrial Revolution. In the 1950s the British were again taking the lead by critically examining the way dominant themes in management had progressed for fifty years. They did not like what they saw, so Joan Woodward, an industrial sociologist at the Imperial College of Science and Technology, decided to examine the efficacy of management theory. Specifically, Woodward established a research program to test the usefulness of such concepts as span of control, unity of command, hierarchy, and decentralization. When the studies began, she headed a research team at the South Essex College of Technology, so the research came to be known as the South Essex studies. The most comprehensive report of the results is given in *Industrial Organization* (Woodward, 1965).

Initially, the team focused on a narrow range of issues, such as the dichotomy between executive and advisory responsibilities and the relationship between line and staff managers at different organizational levels. First, the researchers surveyed over 200 firms that differed in size and product line. Later a decision was made to drop respondents with fewer than 100 employees, thereby reducing the sample to 110 and eventually to 100.

Success from Failure. To assess the degree of success of the firms in the sample, Woodward collected information from five years of annual reports and financial statements. Using a variety of indicators, she was able to classify participating organizations as (1) average performers, (2) below-average performers, and (3) above-average performers. The data were analyzed to see whether all the above-average performers were adhering to the classical principles of management. They were not. The results were disappointing. However, the South Essex researchers were not easily discouraged. They had a large data base and a sound hypothesis, so "almost automatically" they turned to technology.

It was discovered that the firms in the sample could be grouped according to the technologies they employed. First, there were unit or small-batch production firms that manufactured products to customer specifications, produced prototypes, and fabricated large equipment in stages. A second technological category consisted of large-batch and mass-production firms. Many of these companies used assembly-line technology to produce the large batches. A typical product manufactured by mass production was blocks for internal combustion engines.

The third technology was process or flow production. Examples were oil refining and chemical production. Some companies used a combination of all three technologies.

When the sample was subdivided according to technologies, meaningful relationships emerged. The median number of levels in the hierarchy, for example, increased as the technologies changed from customized small batches to mass production and eventually to continuous processing. The average span of control, as we would expect, responded in the opposite direction. Whereas the number of levels in the hierarchy increased along with technological complexity, the size of the span of control varied inversely. This suggested that the "small spans of control and long lines of communication" in process industries made the firms appear peaked and narrow (p. 53). In unit or small-batch production firms the pyramid, by contrast, was short and broadly based.

Interestingly, the span of control for the chief executive officers provided an exception. In small-batch firms the median span of control for the CEO was four, in large-batch firms it was seven, and in process production it was ten. According to Woodward, this resulted from a change in the role and function of the executives as technological complexity increased. Management by committees, for example, was more common in process than in less complex systems. The CEO in process firms seemed to function more as a chair of a decision-making group than as an autocratic decision maker.

The researchers also found a link between the complexity of a firm's technology and the relative size of the management group. As technology became more complex (from unit to process), the ratio of managers and supervisors to nonsupervisory personnel increased. This finding supported the view that as technology becomes more complex, so does the need for management and managers.

Technology, Structure, and Success. Woodward, after examining the relationships between organizational factors and technological complexity, introduced some important factors relating to business success. First, the firms that were successful in each technological category possessed organizational characteristics that clustered around the median of the group. Those firms that were below average exhibited extremes relative to these same factors. In other words, companies that were above average in success in the unit or small-batch category seemed to be average when it came to measures like the number of levels in the hierarchy, span of control, and administrative ratios. The same was true of successful firms where technological complexity was greater.

Second, the findings varied by technological category. In the most successful large-batch firms, the duties and responsibilities of managers were precisely defined and written on paper. In process firms, surprisingly, this type of formality was more often associated with lack of success. In fact, the successful firms in mass-production industries more often displayed findings that were consistent with the prescriptions of classical management. Perhaps the tendency of most people to think of mass production as the "typical system of modern industry" explains the link between success and conformity to traditional management theory in this industrial environment.

In spite of this one inconsistent finding with regard to mass production, the publication of Woodward's studies did much to encourage and legitimize questions and doubts about the classical management literature. Woodward clearly illustrated that there is no one best way to organize. Success in the various technological categories was obviously not determined by organizational practices or structure. If it were, all successful firms would look the same—at least on the organization chart.

Testing the Theory. Attempts have been made to replicate Woodward's studies in the United States and in other countries. One attempt involved fifty-five firms in Minneapolis in the late 1960s (Zwerman, 1970). In general, the Minneapolis study reinforced many of Woodward's findings. For example, there were no consistent correlates of organizational characteristics and business success. This study also confirmed that the prescriptions of classical theory are more specific to the environment of mass-production firms. Finally, and most important, the Minneapolis study reinforced the finding that organizational structures are greatly influenced by the technology of the firm.

Some findings were not reinforcing, however. Span of control displayed no relationship to technological complexity. This, in fact, was the only finding that clearly contradicted Woodward.

In addition to the Minneapolis study, historical and theoretical analyses have underscored the importance of environmental factors on internal operations. Alfred Chandler (1962) presented a historical critique of almost eighty corporations while focusing specifically on the organizational evolution of Du Pont, General Motors, Standard Oil of New Jersey, and Sears, Roebuck and Company. The documented historical evolution of these companies illustrated four important stages in the life cycle of organizations and the relationship between these stages and the larger environment.

First, firms expand and accumulate resources. Organization structure follows functional lines and leadership is autocratic. Second, resources are "rationalized" and growth becomes selective as efforts are made to improve the efficiency of operations. The third stage involves expansion into new markets to ensure the effective use of resources. Finally, new structures are developed to optimize operations and ensure effective planning. At this stage, firms become more decentralized.

Clearly, as the strategies of Du Pont, General Motors, Standard Oil, and Sears, Roebuck changed, their organization structure had to respond. The need for strategic change, as Chandler noted, is driven by environmental changes. Thus, when the environment changes, the organization's strategy must change, and this has a direct impact on organizational design.

Next, Chandler divided his sample of almost eighty firms into nine industry groups. Some, such as metals and materials, were essentially stable and did not change to the extent of the four focal firms. Other industries, such as rubber and petroleum, changed in the direction of decentralization but not as completely as Du Pont, General Motors, Standard Oil, and Sears, Roebuck, while firms in industries such as power machinery and chemicals displayed evolutionary patterns similar to that of the four companies. Therefore, Chandler's historical analysis supports the contention that environmental forces significantly influence decision making, both organizationally and strategically.

Whereas Chandler provided historical validation, James D. Thompson offered a theoretical framework for understanding the relationship between environment and organization. In *Organizations in Action* (1967), Thompson illustrated the difference between closed and open organizational systems. The *closed system* seeks certainty and incorporates only those factors that are associated with goal accomplishment, whereas the *open system* explicitly recognizes the interdependence between organizations and their environment. The open system attempts to establish homeostasis or self-stabilization in its relationship to external, environmental factors.

Thompson skillfully argued the managerial necessity of ensuring the accomplishment of rational, task-related goals in the short run while remaining flexible and adaptive to environmentally induced change over the long run. In accomplishing short-term goals, efficiency and certainty are emphasized, while pursuit of long-term goals involves coping with uncertainty. Often, in highly dynamic industries special units are needed for purposes of boundary spanning, or facilitating the firm's interaction with its environment. Ultimately, Thompson declared, organizations exist as agencies of their environments. They acquire resources in exchange for outputs and even base their technologies on environmental realities.

Historical and theoretical arguments provide important evidence, but a more direct kind confirmation is needed to validate management concepts. Fortunately, there is additional evidence to support Woodward's findings.

Harvard Business School to the Rescue—Again

Paul Lawrence was born in Illinois and received his graduate education at Harvard. He has been the Donham Professor of Organizational Behavior at the Harvard Business School since 1968. Jay Lorsch was born in Missouri and received his doctorate at Harvard. Since 1972 he has been the Kirstein Professor of Human Relations there. These two colleagues collaborated in writing *Organization and Environment* (1967), which greatly expanded the findings of Woodward by examining more environmental contingencies and added to the insights provided by both Chandler and Thompson. Their empirical approach was more like that of Woodward and less like the historical analysis of Chandler or the theoretical review of Thompson.

Environments and Organizations. The objective of *Organization and Environment* was to examine the question of how the internal structure of an organization is affected by its environment. The authors argued and presented data to support their contention that different organizational designs are needed to cope with different environmental realities. Lawrence and Lorsch attempted to determine how successful organizations in a particular industry differed from their less successful competitors. They also attempted to determine how effective firms in various industries differed from one another.

Information on internal organizational functioning was obtained by distributing 30–50 questionnaires to upper- and middle-level managers in ten focal organizations. Personal interviews were also conducted, and data regarding industrial environments were obtained through interviews with and questionnaires to top executives in each organization.

The sample that was used included six firms in the plastics industry, each of which was a major part of a larger chemical business. The organizations had four functional units: sales, production, applied research, and basic research. Two of the plastics firms were considered high-performing, two were low-performing, and two exhibited intermediate levels of performance. In addition, two firms each (one high-performing and one low-performing) were selected in the standardized container and packaged foods industries. These two industries were included because of the critical differences each demonstrated relative to plastics. The plastics industry is dynamic and changes fast, whereas changes in standardized containers are, by comparison, slow. The packaged foods industry changes more slowly than plastics but faster than containers.

Some Findings. Organization charts and manuals were reviewed and interviews regarding the *formality of structure* were conducted in all the various departments of the plastics firms. Production departments were, in general, more formally structured, had fewer levels in their hierarchy, and had larger ratios of supervisory to nonsupervisory employees than the other departments in this industry. Lawrence and Lorsch also looked at interpersonal relationships, time, and goal orientations in all the different departments. In departments such as production where tasks were more certain, managers tended to be task oriented. Employee orientation tended to increase in departments such as sales and research and development, where tasks were more uncertain. Because research-and-development personnel were involved in tasks with slower feedback, employees in this department were more tolerant of activities that contributed less to long-term profitability. In production departments, feedback was faster and employees tended to have short-term orientations.

When the attitudes of managers in the functional departments such as production, sales, and research were found to be significantly different with regard to time, goal, and interpersonal orientations as well as formality of structure, the organization was said to be *differentiated.* High-performing groups in plastics displayed differentiation patterns that were consistent with the demands of the various subenvironments, such as production, sales, and research and development.

Integration (not to be confused with Follett's technique of conflict resolution) is the state of collaboration necessary to coordinate the activities of departments. In general, the greater the degree of differentiation, the greater the need for integration. In plastics, for example, the fact that production departments were oriented toward the short run, tended to be task oriented, and were more formal in structure made it inherently more difficult for production employees to work with the long-term–oriented employees in fundamental or basic research. The magnitude of the differences made it necessary to devote more attention to ensuring that integration of efforts took place in the pursuit of common goals. In fact, integration was so necessary that all the plastics organizations had formally developed units charged with the responsibility of facilitating integration of the functional units.

After a detailed examination of the plastics firms, Lawrence and Lorsch turned their attention to the companies making standardized containers and packaged foods. As with plastics, all firms were major product segments of larger corporations. The firms in the container industry displayed the least amount of differentiation (differences among functional managers' orientations and units' formality of structure), while plastics had the greatest degree of differentiation and packaged foods was in between. The extent of integration, however, did not show such significant differences. As in the case of plastics, firms in the container industry had "achieved states of differentiation that met the demands of their particular environments" (p. 105). Integration was uniformly better in high-performing firms than in lower-performing ones.

The research reinforced the necessity, in the plastics industry, of developing formal integrative measures between units such as marketing and research in order to test newly developed or modified products. It was also necessary to develop close integration between production and research to ensure successful product development.

Lawrence and Lorsch investigated the need for integration in other industrial settings. In the food industry there was less formal integration than in plastics. Managers in various departments were assigned integrative roles rather than developing integrative units. In the container industry integration was achieved by the managerial hierarchy with some use of direct contact among functional managers. This technique resembled Fayol's bridge of direct horizontal contacts.

Lawrence and Lorsch noted that, because of different environmental settings and variations in integrative techniques, conflict was resolved in different ways in the plastics, foods, and container industries. In plastics, with its high degree of differentiation among departments, the integrative department was highly influential in resolving interdepartmental conflicts. In packaged foods, where there was no formal integrative unit, managers in marketing and research became the most influential forces for resolving interdepartmental conflict. In containers, marketing and production managers were the most influential because of the importance of scheduling problems and customer service.

The researchers also found similarities relative to the resolution of interdepartmental conflicts. Of particular significance was the fact that in all three industries, the managers most centrally involved in achieving integration and resolving conflict had reputations of being especially competent and knowledgeable. Their influence was based primarily on expertise.

Disregarding the One Best Way

The theories discussed in this chapter represent a radical departure from one major aspect of classical organizational design theory. For lack of a better term we simply call it the "quest for the one best way." The holy grail of Taylor, Gilbreth, and even Mayo was the mystical best way of doing management activities. Gilbreth looked for the one best way with motion study, Taylor with time study, and Mayo through naive experiments and interviews.

The *contingency theorists* discussed in this chapter all agreed that there is no one best way to organize or manage. The best way in any particular time or situation is a function of the *contingencies* presented by the environment. The implications for management of this argument are nothing less than profound. The primary determinant of successful management is no longer finding the best way to do a task. Instead, it is the need for flexibility and the ability to diagnose and adapt to changing circumstances. Woodward started the tradition, and Lawrence, Lorsch, and others extended it. Yet to all it was a situational, contingency view. Woodward's contingency was limited to technology, while Lawrence and Lorsch included a broader range of influential environmental factors. Some of the important implications for management of this line of research are:

1. The clear-cut and formal differentiation of organizational units, when based on task and environmental differences, contributes to high performance (Lawrence and Lorsch, 1967). This suggests that specialization remains good economics and management and that it should be as "pure" as

possible. When distinctly different functional activities are combined, such as research and sales or research and production, problems develop. The low-performing packaged food company committed this error by combining applied and fundamental research in spite of indications that the two research tasks required different practices to deal successfully with different parts of the environment.

2. Lawrence and Lorsch also suggested that since specialization and the resulting differentiation are organizational realities, attempts should be made to ensure that the differentiation and integration approach has as much likelihood of success as possible. Production, sales, and research specialists naturally develop their own ways of looking at things in organizations. It is important to encourage these specialists, however, to tolerate the views of others and not to personalize disagreements that naturally arise. Building this type of tolerance requires conscious management action.

3. Most organizations can benefit from using a variety of conflict resolution techniques. When the degree of differentiation is not too great, simply appealing for decisions from the first supervisor with formal authority over the involved departments is often successful. This was the conflict resolution technique visualized most often by classical writers. However, many firms in the Lawrence and Lorsch sample used confrontation or problem-solving techniques to resolve conflicts.

The research of Woodward and of Lawrence and Lorsch has significant implications for the design of successful organizations in the future. Almost everyone agrees that technological changes will continue at accelerating rates. Organizations will face environments not unlike those faced by plastics firms today. Therefore, we can confidently speculate that differentiation will increase, and with this, concurrent increases in integrative skills and techniques will also be required. One of the important challenges for management theory and practice will be to provide better ways of achieving integration among highly differentiated functional units. This will require successful managers to develop conflict resolution skills. Yet many behavioral scientists insist that perceptive managers will beware of resolving conflict entirely, because conflict leads, under the proper conditions, to innovation. Thus, it is likely that managers will increasingly confront the dilemma currently felt in high-technology environments. Smooth, efficient operations require coordination of differentiated units, and efforts to achieve integration are essential. At the same time, a reasonable amount of conflict is functional in the sense that it stimulates innovation. Managers in organizational environments demanding innovation will find themselves managing rather than eliminating conflict. Some of the more traditional and current ways of looking at conflict resolution will be discussed in Chapter Thirteen.

Matrix Management: Organizations for Our Times

Organizations such as NASA, Monsanto, and the Chase Manhattan Bank have found the traditional functional pyramid type of organization unsatisfactory for various goals they have attempted to achieve. Sometimes the demands of the environment are such that resources must be mustered around a particular problem that will not likely recur, or a unique combination of resources is required to accomplish a particular plan. Sometimes a project structure or matrix organization is the answer.

The typical organization begins to evolve toward a matrix structure by establishing specialized projects outside the traditional hierarchy. In the case of NASA's Apollo Project, for example, a project director was named and allowed to draw needed resources from various functional departments in order to accomplish the project's mission. In this case, we see the first move toward a matrix structure with a second dimension of authority being created by the appointment of the project director. Authority flows vertically down the hierarchy, and now the director is given the right to exercise functional authority over the project. Thus, we have the two-dimensional flow of authority that provides the logic for the term *matrix organization.*

This two-dimensional flow of authority has the obvious potential of violating the principle of the scalar chain and unity of command.

Even though the danger is great for uncertainty and confusion created by the complex authority flow, the project structure provides advantages not found in the functional arrangement. The organization is problem oriented and can be dismantled when the project is complete. In this sense, a great deal of operational and strategic flexibility is created (Sayles and Chandler, 1971).

The evolution to a complete matrix organization takes place when temporary projects, for various reasons, become permanent and provide management with project flexibility over a longer period of time (Davis and Lawrence, 1977). The matrix structure is very useful in responding to environmental demands and is, therefore, quite applicable to high-technology settings. Unique developmental opportunities are provided for members of projects, and the leadership challenges for project directors are significant. The unique nature of many problems and the need for interdisciplinary approaches make the project/matrix organizational design a particularly valuable response to dynamic environmental demands.

Relativism in Management: Implications and Conclusions

"It all depends on . . . " is not a good way to begin offering a solution to a management problem. If you are a high-paid (or even low-paid) consultant, your client is likely to doubt he is receiving his money's worth if this is the best you can do. Seasoned executives do not like the uncertainty such an "explanation" entails. However, experience tells us that there is seldom an easy answer or a quick fix to complex problems of management and organization. We might like to offer pat answers for all management problems, but such responses would be equally unsatisfactory because they would seldom be correct.

Contingency theory is not likely to be the final answer, although for the present it allows us to understand some of the paradoxes and dilemmas created by "mutually contradictory" classical principles and prescriptions. If we are smart, and that is the purpose of reading and writing management books, we will not be satisfied with situational explanations for these paradoxes but will use them as they have been used in the physical sciences—as incentives for further study—so as to resolve in a more meaningful way the inconsistencies in contemporary management thought.

Management has moved quickly from the absolute to the relative and in doing so has achieved a better understanding of organizations, environments, and the relationship between the two. It must continue and offer managers even more assistance in applied decision making. In the process, management and organization theory must become flexible in its application to diverse environmental forces.

Sometimes responses require violations of classical theories. Such a violation, under some circumstances, is appropriate or even advisable. However, caution should be exercised in that the wholesale violation of sound, classical principles of organization always involves a cost in loss of coordination and efficiency. Only when the rewards of increased effectiveness are great enough to offset the uncertainty created should alternative organizational design be considered and used.

CHAPTER 13

Enduring Lessons from Classical Management Literature

Scientists of late have been talking about the Big Bang, of which we, according to Carl Sagan, are its most spectacular, although remote, descendants. Through the Big Bang, the theory goes, the cosmos was created from chaos. From nothing came something! Theologians have been telling us such things for years, but some find it more believable coming from astronomers.

There was also a big bang of sorts in management. Oh, something was happening in management before the beginning of the twentieth century, but not very much. People were "doing management" even if they had little basis for what they were doing. Pyramids were built, garbage was removed, and products eventually made it to market. If the system was not efficient, at least it was sufficient for a slower and less complicated time.

All that changed with the advent of factories, moving assembly lines, and standardized components. The world of work has not been the same since and never will be again. Somewhere around that time the "visible hand of managerial direction" replaced Adam Smith's "invisible hand" as the force responsible for coordinating the flow of goods from the suppliers of raw materials to the retailer and eventually to the consumer (Chandler, 1977). Management became an established institution, and the chaos that characterized the quest for management off and on throughout the course of human history evolved and took form. Since that time the management movement has gained momen-

tum, has increased its speed, and today seems almost in danger
of destroying itself as it spins wildly toward ever increasing
amounts of knowledge and technological improvements.

The purpose of this book has been to slow things down a
bit and try to make some sense out of what has been happening
for the past one hundred years in management. In doing so, we
have at times been overwhelmed by the complexity and opted
to focus on a few recurring themes. We did so to heed the advice the experienced pilot gave the apprentice steamboatman in
Mark Twain's *Life on the Mississippi.* After hearing of the
shapes the shadows of the shore cast on starlit, pitch-dark,
and gray mist nights, the apprentice asked how he could keep
all the thousands of variations of the river's shape in his head
without becoming stoop-shouldered. The pilot replied, "You
only learn the shape of the river; and you learn it with such absolute certainty that you can always steer by the shape that's in
your head, and never mind the one that's before your eyes."

We have not argued that the recurring themes of management are absolute truths or that they are never deserving of
variation. However, once learned and in the absence of compelling reasons to do otherwise, adhering to the prescriptions pro-
claimed by the recurring themes is not bad advice. The wisdom
of the ages (even though the ages are short in the case of management) demands a certain respect—certainly more than dis-
carding it to chase after fads and quick fixes.

We have examined the ideas of engineers, philosophers,
psychologists, and executives in our search for wisdom, values,
and instruction. What we have found is a collage of prescription, enigma, and paradox. At first glance it is tempting to accept the Durants' (1968, p. 12) jest that "most of history is
guessing and the rest is prejudice." A deeper look convinces us
instead that we have witnessed and traced the genesis and evolution of an exciting and increasingly important field of study as
well as an essential vocation. To a great extent the very fate of
humanity depends on people's ability to effectively manage resources, time, and energy—all of which seem in too short supply.

This chapter concludes the book with a look at ten bi-
polar terms that summarize some of the important lessons taught

by classical and modern writers. The lessons are recurring and remain relevant for successive generations of managers. Each of these lessons will be discussed, and the nature of the prescription, enigma, or paradox they present will be examined all too briefly.

Lesson One: Coordination and Conflict

Classical writers uniformly emphasized the importance of coordination. Mooney and Reiley called it the first principle of organization and suggested that the need for coordination was the single most important factor leading to the emergence of management as a recognized occupation. Specialized jobs and divisionalized organizations demanded that someone be responsible for putting everything together in a grand unified design. Management emerged to assume the coordinative responsibility.

The lesson taught by the classics, however, is that coordination is not the normal state of affairs. Coordination requires purposeful intervention, and intervention requires a plan, a goal, a purpose. While it is true that conflict can lead to innovation and new ideas, it also leads to inefficiency, loss of direction, and less fun at work.

In recent times, the lure of competition and the hint that conflict can bring about functional outcomes in organizations has led some managers and members of the public to go so far as to advocate a form of *cowboy management.* Cowboy management, we might note, is diametrically opposed to what classical concepts tell us. According to Kanter (1987), cowboy management "makes heroes out of hipshooters who fire before they aim" (p. 19). Cowboy managers are the rugged individualists who like to build competition among departments to keep everyone honest, to manage by the "seat of their pants," and to avoid goal statements because missions restrict their freedom to pursue new opportunities. Like all cowboys, managerial cowboys create excitement, and if we are not careful their yearning for adventure and rough and rowdy ways can carry us away in the excitement.

But cowboy management, with its emphasis on building

competition and "managing constructive conflict," is not the lesson we derive from the classics. Instead we are told that competition is for our competitors while cooperation is for our friends. One interesting point emphasized by Deming (1982), the hero of all who wish we could do a better job competing with Japan, is that cooperation created much of the Japanese economic miracle. Conflict between employers and employees, purchasers and suppliers, and so on builds only resentment, short-run orientations, and ultimately inefficiency.

The first lesson, then, is the importance of cooperation. When we compete, we should do so with those who challenge us in the marketplace. Internally, it is important to work as a team. Teamwork, whether in athletics, war, or business, is a sound principle of success. After all, as Durant and Durant (1968) noted, "We cooperate in our group in order to strengthen our group in its competition with other groups" (p. 19). Perhaps the reason we as a nation have lost our ability to compete is that we have lost our will to cooperate. The enigma is that, in the process of not cooperating, we have effectively become our own worst enemy.

Lesson Two: Dignity and Duty

Every person, when hired by an organization, should accept it as his or her duty to deliver a fair day's work for the agreed on pay. At the same time, workers should expect to retain their dignity. Although we are shocked to see the way many of the early writers described and treated human beings, there was, even in scientific management, a recognition of some need for human dignity. This was most evident in the concern for selecting the "right person for the right job." The futility and tragedy of putting people in jobs for which they are "constitutionally unqualified" was a recognition of human dignity on the part of management writers.

A good example of the importance of preserving human dignity at work is given by Irwin (1987) in a report on two American Motors study teams that visited eleven Japanese automobile manufacturing plants. The team members reported a number of impressions, some surprising and some not. They found that there were relatively few computer applications to manufacturing processes, that workers were allowed to share in the prosperity of the firm, and that participation was most often indirect, through representatives rather than directly from worker to manager. Most important, however, were the basic facts that quality was an obsession with workers (it was their duty), that all employees appeared engaged in the pursuit of common goals, and that workers were well trained to do the jobs they were responsible for completing. In line with Theory Y, workers were treated like intelligent adults—they were *never*, under any circumstance, placed in positions that would compromise their human dignity, and all were treated with respect and honor.

Early in U.S. history the work values built on the family farm were the type all of us would hope to inspire in others. Honesty, justice, hard work, frugality, dignity, and humility were developed and reinforced. People worked for themselves, were close to the land, lived with and near their kin, and took a little time to enjoy life through simple pursuits. The factory was a different place. It was not inherently evil, but it was alienating. The dignity naturally gained by being in touch with nature had to be worked for in the sweatshop, steamy factory, and pitch-dark mine. Yet human dignity and duty were no less important than before. The primary reason for the failure of welfare capitalism, well intended as it was, can be easily summarized: welfare capitalism was paternalistic and robbed workers of their dignity. As a consequence, duty turned to dependency and dependency to distrust.

Whether we are referring to job enrichment or positive reinforcement, the second lesson is clear. People work better, work harder, and take greater pride in what they do when their dignity is preserved. If workers are to faithfully fulfill their duty to perform a fair day's work, the minimum cost of such achievement is the preservation of dignity.

Lesson Three: Efficiency and Change

Most of what we have discussed in this book took place during what Haber (1964) called the Progressive Era. In this era, efficiency became a secular "Great Awakening" and "efficient and good came closer to meaning the same thing during these years than in any other period" (p. ix).

Efficiency was the gospel (good news) of scientific management. Through the improvement of efficiency, at least for Taylor, the Gilbreths, and Emerson, the solution to society's most troubling problems could be found. Efficiency made possible a win-win solution by simultaneously increasing the returns to workers and owners. Who could refuse such a deal? The catch, however, was that efficiency required order, specialization, standardization, and structure. Flexibility, adaptability, and perhaps even creativity had to take the backseat. Order and innovation rarely exist side by side. Yet to choose either to the exclusion of the other is clearly out of touch with contemporary reality (McFarland, 1976). Efficiency remains important, but we must also preserve the ability to adapt to changes quickly and decisively.

The continuous quest for efficiency regularly exposes one of the important lessons and serious paradoxes of management theory. In competitive economies firms must be efficient to survive. Yet the actions required to increase efficiency add structure, controls, and inflexibility when creativity demands the opposite. Thus, there appears to be, at least for the time being, a recognition that the ability to change is as important as efficiency in ensuring organizational survival.

To illustrate the potential conflict, consider the comments of the head of research and development at 3M Corporation, who says that managing creative people requires one to behave in a different way (Kiechel, 1985). Sometimes the manager must keep his or her mouth closed and eyes half shut. Often the most promising project begins with unauthorized actions. A manager has to trust the innovators and expect them to do their best. This is far from the close controls of early management.

Waterman (1987) captures the importance of change and the manager's ability to adjust to it in what he calls the *renewal factor.* According to him, successful businesses are those that understand and deal with uncertainty. Often we do not detect the changes taking place in highly successful organizations until we stop and analyze that they are constantly adapting and adjusting their structures, strategies, products, and services to new demands of consumers and markets. According to Waterman, these successful organizations have learned how to manage the "last frontier"—the challenge of renewal.

Taylor, the Gilbreths, and Emerson taught us about the importance of efficiency. Lawrence and Lorsch, Thompson, and Woodward illustrated the importance of innovation and change. The renewal factor is real, and firms that choose to deny or ignore it will put themselves in peril for the future.

Lesson Four: Purpose and Fate

When it comes to the future, managers have a choice. They can do their best to shape it, or they can be victims of fate. Successful executives always choose the former. Eisenberg (1987) uses the term *strategic opportunism* to define a type of behavior whereby managers focus on long-term objectives while remaining flexible enough to deal with day-to-day operating problems. Strategic opportunism puts the manager in control of fate rather than at its mercy. Missions, strategic goals, and strategies are not looked on as straitjackets that make the organization less responsive to new ideas and challenges. Instead, they are looked upon as providing a general framework within which managers can concentrate their energies while always looking for new opportunities.

Consider the task confronting AT&T after divestiture. How could such a company direct more than 300,000 employees and $30 billion of assets toward any type of purposeful behavior? The first step was to formulate and communicate a mission statement that was easy for employees to understand. In the words of the CEO, AT&T's mission is:

> global information services; the measure is customer satisfaction. And, we are one great enterprise . . .
> a single great river to which all essential tributaries add their particular strength to one determined course [Moran, 1984, p. 5].

Throughout this book we have made frequent reference to how managers really behave and how this behavior differs from the theory of effective management. Almost always we have been forced to admit that managers often get caught up in the emergencies of day-to-day activities and miss looking, even on occasion, at the larger picture. To deal with the urgent is natural, but it is not good management. To think about, formulate, and communicate the purpose of the organization in the form of a mission statement or similar message remains sound advice from the annals of management history.

The dysfunctional obsession with the urgent is evident in the erosion of quality in products and services. Many managers believe that quality improvements increase costs and reduce productivity, that cost cutting produces faster positive results on profits than quality improvements do, and that opportunities to improve productivity through quality improvements are limited (Shetty, 1986). In other words, short-term, bottom-line issues are perceived to be more important than long-term commitment to quality and productivity.

Improvement in quality requires a long-term commitment on the part of the organization and consequently its management team. Executives at firms such as Ford, Pitney Bowes, Northrup, Westinghouse, Monsanto, and Honeywell who have made quality improvements a part of their agenda agree on a number of points. Two of the more important are (1) top management has to be devoted to improvements in productivity and quality and *incorporate this commitment into company goals and policies;* and (2) quality-improvement standards must be carefully woven into strategic planning, budgeting, control, communication, and training activities of the firm.

Quality cannot be left to the whims of fate. If events are not planned, they are not likely to happen. Granted, some things happen in spite of a plan, but managers should never depend on fate. Fate is fickle and cannot be depended on to produce results. The prevoyance of Fayol is still good advice. Not only should we forecast the future, we should prepare for it as well. The epic *Beowulf* tells us that "fate often saves an undoomed warrior when his courage endures." Managers today, doomed or undoomed, need more than fate to survive. They need plans, a purpose, a reason to be.

Lesson Five: Rationality and Human Frailty

The fifth lesson management classics teach us is that human beings are frail in the face of complex decisions. Even though we are efficient information processors and outperform even the most powerful computer pound for pound, the typical manager can know relatively little about anything other than the most simple decision problems. No informed manager would debate the limits of human understanding, yet managerial behavior testifies to the existence of a large range of responses to bounded rationality.

Some managers act as if their knowledge about the situation is complete, make decisions, and deal with the consequences with seemingly little cognitive dissonance. Others deny or excuse away information outside their limits of knowledge and suggest that the result of less-than-perfect knowledge is really better than what one would expect from the perfectly informed decision maker. Both responses are naive and dangerous.

Managers need to become as knowledgeable as possible about the decisions they make. Information search should be expanded until it is no longer economical or practical. Even then, choices should be recognized as something less than optimum.

If we define rationality along with Simon as goal oriented or purposeful, we should become more rational by setting goals and pursuing them. Enough was said of this previously. If, on the other hand, we look at rationality in terms of the degree of information we possess, we should attempt to become as informed as possible. Even though the ideal of perfect knowledge will never be realized, it is a worthy goal. If decision making is the "heart of executive activity," it should be as informed as possible.

A few companies are beginning to examine the feasibility of a "back to basics" move to assist in focusing more directly on the few things they do best (Wilkins and Bristow, 1987). Theoretically, this should make them more informed decision makers. In the 1960s many companies began to conglomerate and stray into a number of unfamiliar businesses. R. J. Reynolds is a good example. Beginning in 1969, RJR acquired such diverse operations as Sea-Land Industries (transportation), Aminoil International and Burmah Oil, Del Monte Foods, Heublein, Kentucky Fried Chicken, and Canada Dry. In 1983, less than half of the firm's sales were accounted for by tobacco products. Reynolds, however, recognized that it had ventured into areas of the unknown. In the early 1980s it started going back to the basics it understood. It sold off Aminoil and Burmah and spun off Sea-Land to shareholders. The plan was to focus on consumer products: tobacco products, Canada Dry, Del Monte, and so on. By 1984 tobacco had moved back up, accounting for almost 80 percent of RJR's earnings. The company was clearly putting its eggs in the basket it knew best. Even at the risk of not being sufficiently diversified, Reynolds was determined to become as informed as possible about the relatively restricted industry segment of consumer goods.

Lesson Six: Responsibility and Compromise

If you believe the social responsibility controversy is something new, you are in for a surprise. In spite of Watergate, the Iran-Contra affair, insider-trading scandals, and tax evasion in high places, organizational societies—and democracies, for that matter—are built on trust. When people, especially managers, break the rules, the entire system is in peril. At least a few have always recognized the peril, written about it, and offered better ways to do business.

When corporations become large and complex, individuals get lost, and sometimes it is difficult to appreciate the significance of a single employee, managerial or nonmanagerial, to the overall functioning of the organization. An individual, for example, can easily ruin the reputation of a firm with a few misguided actions. For that reason, Vernon Loucks, Jr. (1987), chief executive officer of Baxter Travenol Laboratories, Inc., offers four specific guidelines to protect the corporation against socially irresponsible behavior. First, the right people should be hired. People with a history of dishonest or irresponsible behavior are greater ethical risks. Second, standards of responsible behavior should be set and communicated, and less attention should be placed on rules. Individual employees are mature human beings and should understand the need for responsible action. Third, managers should never allow themselves to be isolated from the everyday reality of the organization. Irresponsible actions are more likely when managers are out of touch with the employees, competitors, and other groups with whom they interact. Finally, managers must serve as role models. If responsibility is to be anything other than lip service, top management must provide the role models of how things are expected to be done.

In discussing "why good managers make bad ethical choices," Gellerman (1986) offers similar suggestions. Managers violate ethics, and sometimes the law, when organizations do not (1) establish a code of ethics for all employees, (2) stress formally and regularly that loyalty does not mean always doing what the organization says, and (3) teach managers guidelines, such as "when in doubt, don't."

What is important to recognize is that the question of the appropriate responsibility of management is as old as the field itself. There is nothing fundamentally different about today's managers, organizations, or society that makes us more concerned about the impact of managerial decisions on the larger society. The question is simply a continuing one that derives from the complex relationship between business and society.

The lesson for managers in classical writings is that management is an economic institution and responsible for building efficiency and ultimately profitability. However, management is part of a larger society and as such must be responsive to its demands. Business and management exist at the pleasure of society, and if they are not socially responsive they may cease to exist in their present form. Gantt, Barnard, Dennison, Tead, and others clearly recognized this reality, and today's managers can do no less.

Lesson Seven: Science and Art

Arguments about whether management is an art or a science are boring at best and certainly a waste of time. The fact is that management is neither—or perhaps it is both. Unfortunately, even though debates on this subject are, for the most part, meaningless, we cannot deny the fact that if managers and management researchers want a degree of respectability, there must be some scientific basis for the study and practice of management.

The classics provide an important lesson on the role of science in management. With the possible exception of Taylor and the Gilbreths, early writers thought of science as a worthy, although not completely obtainable, goal for management. Fayol even apologized for using the term *principle* and cautioned that it should not be thought of in a scientific sense. Much of management can and should be studied "scientifically." Certainly, a scientific attitude should characterize all our investigations. However, much of what the manager deals with—symbols, myths, and so on—defies scientific analysis in the traditional sense. This is why Deal and Kennedy (1983) found traditional scientific methods wanting in their application to organizations and management. These writers assert:

1. There is some reason to be skeptical about many of the "facts" in management research, especially the assumed relationships between elements such as goals and structure.
2. Many of the scientific theories of management simply have something wrong with them when it comes to implementation. Dealing with the human side of implementation requires an artist more than a scientist.
3. Some of the "outdated and situation specific paradigms" of management appear scientifically sophisticated but are less applicable today.
4. The new appreciation of magical, mystical, and metaphysical aspects of organization (the components of organizational culture) are not suited to study by "scientific" methods.

It is important to remain flexible on the issue of science and management. If we limit the boundaries of our knowledge to only those things that can be studied objectively and scientifically, we lose much of the richness of organizational phenomena.

Lesson Eight: Specialization and Meaning

We began this book with the proposition that specialization of labor made possible the factory system and the factory system led inevitably to the need for management. The logic was simple. When the family farm served as the economic unit, everyone was basically self-sufficient and had relatively less need to engage in exchange. At the level of work, farmers performed "logical modules," or reasonably complete tasks. As a result they took a great deal of pride in the field they planted or in the prize-winning animals, vegetables, and fruits they raised.

With the division of labor came the need to coordinate diverse and sometimes distant tasks into a unified whole culminating in a desired product or service. That was the role management was obliged to assume. This specialized approach to work has served us well. The accomplishments of the factory system allow all of us to enjoy unprecedented wealth and leisure. But, there is a problem. With specialization comes a loss of identity with what we do. The production worker whose job is to put hubcaps on the left side of cars moving down what seems to be an infinitely long assembly line has trouble relating to the quality of the finished product. The consequence is boredom, monotony, absenteeism, and probably job stress. The quality of work life and sometimes even productivity suffers.

The lesson management theory provides is that specialization leads to tremendous increases in productivity and for that reason it will continue to be an essential part of the ongoing drama of modern industrial life. At the same time, we are challenged to provide job and work designs that can preserve a degree of meaning in even highly specialized tasks.

The fact is that too much of a good thing, when it happens to be specialization, can be bad. As an example, consider the reorganization of McCormack and Dodge, a New England software company. The success of the company was attributed to its entrepreneurial spirit. However, with increased specialization came the temptation to be less and less innovative. The company intentionally reorganized because it "was becoming a monster company where jobs get too small" (Watts, 1987).

What a statement and what a challenge to management. Although the validity of theories of job enrichment remains in doubt, there is considerable evidence that American workers value more than high wages. The excitement of the job and its meaning to them personally are valued greater than a fat paycheck (Kovach, 1987).

Lesson Nine: Technique and Politics

Remarkably little is known about the nature of managerial work. To many, the myth of the manager as "reflective calculator" has been discarded forever. Others are not so sure. No one seriously doubts that managers have limited time for planning. The fact that time is limited may help us understand why managers plan so little, but it does not justify the fact that planning, in the best sense of the term, does not take place at all.

The importance of such traditional functions of management as planning, organizing, and controlling is illustrated by what some believe are signs that firms can no longer support futuristic exercises. For example, when *Business Week* published its article on "The New Breed of Strategic Planners" (1984) and pointed out how major corporations are trimming their planning staffs, many used this as evidence of the "death of strategic planning." A closer reading of the article, however, made it clear that only detached planning staffs (*planocrats* as they were called) are dying. This is happening because corporations are rediscovering that planning is part of the task of every line manager. To stick planning off in the air-conditioned executive suite was the mistake. The challenge is to "reenfranchise" line managers to plan more, not less.

This is not to deny that management also involves politics. The best-formulated plans will accomplish little unless there are managers capable of providing leadership in the implementation stage. Not only must managers know the techniques of management, they must understand political reality within the organization if they are to be successful (Bartolome and Laurent, 1986).

Managers are studies in paradox. They appear to approach

things systematically and to be in perfect control of situations, yet research tells us that most of the activities they perform take less than ten minutes. Almost never do they work on something for an hour. At the same time they are able to direct thousands of employees and distribute millions of dollars to uses that contribute to goal accomplishment. The fact is that managers are rarely in control. Their job demands that they build a strong network of supporting relationships. At work this is done by delegating authority, carefully selecting personnel, and communicating honestly. All these actions have the potential of making the manager look as if she or he is not in control of events. Actually, such actions are taken only by those managers who are self-reliant enough to give opportunities to others, let them make mistakes, and hold them accountable for achieving results (Quick, Nelson, and Quick, 1987).

Lesson Ten: Universal and Situational

The overall lesson of the classics of management is that management prescriptions are mostly relative. Only seldom are they absolute. That lesson does not satisfy our need to reduce uncertainty, but it keeps us skeptical of the quick fix. While there are fundamental themes of management, a number of which have been discussed throughout this book, managers must always remember that the situation is an important factor in all management decisions.

As the world enters a new era of internationalism, the situational or contingency questions are more important than ever. We are no longer talking of *situational* in terms of the managerial prescription today as compared to a year ago. What we are talking about is the very important issue of the relative nature of management theory. To illustrate, Hafsi, Kiggundu, and Jorgensen (1987) presented an analysis of how state-owned enterprises are governed given alternative assumptions about the nature of the degree of freedom, extent of political pressure, emphasis on accountability, and so on. The authors illustrated how organizational configurations varied with the extent of government involvement in the day-to-day operations of the state-owned corporation. The situation facing the decision maker clearly illustrated the importance of situational or contingency factors.

Perhaps one of the best illustrations of relativity in management is provided by management style. Dowd (1986) praised President Reagan with an article in *Fortune* titled "What Managers Can Learn from Manager Reagan." She stated that Reagan's style was simple: "Surround yourself with the best people you can find, delegate authority, and don't interfere as long as the policy you've decided upon is being carried out" (p. 33). The philosophy sounded good, and for more than one term it served President Reagan well. Unfortunately, less than a year after the article hit the press, top Reagan officials were sitting before a congressional hearing and the president himself was faced with one of the great crises of his administration. The management style that was praised a year before was being criticized with such terms as "bankrupt," "out of control," and "out of touch."

In the case of foreign policy, Mr. Reagan learned that another style of management was needed. Delegation could not be a trusted strategy when the stakes were as high as they were in "guns for hostages" and Contra aid situations. His style of "burning the midday oil" and letting his advisers and aides do their job appeared as inappropriate for his second term in office as it was appropriate for his first. The tragedy is that the president, like many managers, was not able to adapt his management style to changing situations.

Toward Professionalism in Management

Our survey of selected recurring themes in management thought is rapidly coming to an end. We can only hope that present and prospective managers have been made increasingly aware of the wealth they have available to them in the form of classic books in the field. These classics vary in length, sophistication, and content, but all have contributed significantly to what we know about management as a field of study and as an honorable occupation. It is hoped that management will soon realize the full potential of its legacy and arrive at the recognized and deserved status of a profession.

Follett maintained that there are two basic qualifications for a profession: It must be founded on science, and its knowledge must be used in the service of others. Both of these requirements are being met with the passage of time, and society is benefiting greatly from the increased professionalism of management and managers. Much remains to be accomplished, but no one associated with the field of management need bow his head in shame. The accomplishments of managers and management have been great. Because of better management, society's economic resources are being better allocated, and the influence of the field is rapidly becoming felt in less traditional areas such as health care and education. The future is bright indeed.

As for now, it is important that managers and management researchers/teachers continue the quest that others have so admirably started. The era of the classics did not end in 1968. There is a need for more and better works that will provide a deeper understanding of the economic and social institution of management. As we go into the future confident in our knowledge of the past, we must continue to build new ideas and concepts and ensure that society has the benefit of the best available management knowledge.

The legacy we have is greater than that of Taylor, Mayo, and even Maslow and Woodward. It is our heritage that makes continued progress possible. We should remember, as the Durants (1968) have shown us:

> If progress is real despite our whining, it is not because we are born any healthier, better, or wiser . . . but because we are born to a richer heritage. . . . The heritage rises, and man rises in proportion as he receives it [pp. 101–102].

References

Adams, B. "The Limitations of Muddling Through: Does Anyone in Washington Really Think Anymore?" *Public Administration Review*, 1979, *39*, 545–552.

Aharoni, Y. *The Evolution and Management of State-Owned Enterprises.* Cambridge, Mass.: Ballinger, 1986.

Alderfer, C. P. *Existence, Relatedness, and Growth: Human Needs in Organizational Settings.* New York: Free Press, 1972.

Alford, L. P. *Henry Laurence Gantt: Leader in Industry.* New York: American Society of Mechanical Engineers, 1934.

Anderson, J. P., and Duncan, W. J. "The Scientific Significance of the Paradox in Administrative Theory." *Management International Review*, 1977, *17*, 99–106.

Aranda, E. K. "Public Sector Productivity: A Focus on Phoenix." *National Productivity Review*, 1982, *1*, 336–347.

Arnold, W. J. "Extending the Scientific Gospel." In *Milestones of Management.* Vol. 2. New York: McGraw-Hill/Business Week Publication, 1966.

"At Emery Air Freight: Positive Reinforcement Boosts Performance." *Organizational Dynamics*, Winter 1973, *1*, 41–50.

Babbage, C. *On the Economy of Machinery and Manufactures.* London: Charles Knight, 1982. (Originally published 1832.)

Bailey, R. H. *The Home Front: U.S.A.* New York: Time-Life Books, 1977.

Barnard, C. I. *The Functions of the Executive.* Cambridge, Mass.: Harvard University Press, 1938.

Bartolome, F., and Laurent, A. "The Manager: Master and Servant of Power." *Harvard Business Review,* Nov./Dec. 1986, *64,* 77–81.

Bavelas, A. "Leadership: Man and Function." *Administrative Science Quarterly,* 1960, *5,* 448–455.

Behling, O. "The Case for the Natural Science Model for Research in Organizational Behavior and Organization Theory." *Academy of Management Review,* 1980, *6,* 483–490.

Biddle, W. "What Destroyed *Challenger?" Discover,* Apr. 1986, pp. 40–47.

Blake, R. R., and Mouton, J. S. *The Managerial Grid.* Houston, Tex.: Gulf Publications, 1964.

Bluedorn, A. C., Keon, T. L., and Carter, N. M. "Management History Research: Is Anyone Out There Listening?" *Proceedings of the Academy of Management,* Aug. 1985, pp. 130–133.

Boddewyn, J. "Frederick Winslow Taylor: An Evaluation." In P. Dauten (ed.), *Emerging Concepts in Management.* Boston: Houghton Mifflin, 1962.

Bolman, L. G., and Deal, T. E. *Modern Approaches to Understanding and Managing Organizations.* San Francisco: Jossey-Bass, 1984.

Bolte, K. A. "Productivity in the Engineering Discipline." *National Productivity Review,* 1986, *5,* 134–141.

Bolton, A. A., Toftoy, C., and Chipman, D. "Relay Assembly Productivity Factors." *Proceedings of the Southern Management Association,* 1987, pp. 214–216.

"Boosting Shop Floor Productivity by Breaking All the Rules." *Business Week,* Nov. 26, 1984, pp. 100–104.

Boynton, A. C., and Zmud, R. W. "An Assessment of Critical Success Factors." *Sloan Management Review,* Summer 1984, *25,* 17–27.

Breeze, J. D. "Harvest from the Archives: The Search for Fayol and Carlioz." *Journal of Management,* 1985, *11,* 43–54.

Bryant, K. L., and Dethloff, H. C. *A History of American Business.* Englewood Cliffs, N.J.: Prentice-Hall, 1983.

Burke, J. *Connections.* Boston: Little, Brown, 1978.

Carroll, S. J., and Tosi, H. L., Jr. *Management-by-Objectives.* New York: Macmillan, 1973.

Carter, N. M. "Review of *General and Industrial Management.*" *Academy of Management Review,* 1986, *11,* 454–456.

Cass, E. L., and Zimmer, F. G. (eds.). *Man and Work in Society.* New York: Van Nostrand Reinhold, 1975.

Chandler, A. C. *Strategy and Structure.* Cambridge, Mass.: MIT Press, 1962.

Chandler, A. D., Jr. *The Visible Hand: The Managerial Revolution in American Business.* Cambridge, Mass.: Harvard University Press, 1977.

CIGNA Corporation. *Annual Report.* Philadelphia, 1985.

Clark, W. *The Gantt Chart: A Working Tool of Management.* New York: Ronald Press, 1922.

Cochran, D. S., David, F. R., and Gibson, C. K. "A Framework for Developing an Effective Mission Statement." *Journal of Business Strategies,* 1985, *2,* 4–17.

Cohen, M. D., and March, J. G. *Leadership and Ambiguity.* New York: McGraw-Hill, 1974.

Cohen, M. D., March, J. G., and Olsen, J. P. "A Garbage Can Model of Decision Making." *Administrative Science Quarterly,* 1972, *17,* 1–25.

Cooke, M. L. *Our Cities Awake.* New York: Doubleday, 1918.

Copley, F. B. *Frederick W. Taylor: Father of Scientific Management.* Vols. 1 and 2. New York: Harper & Row, 1923.

Cyert, R. "Herbert Simon." *Challenge,* Sept./Oct. 1979, *22,* 62–64.

Davis, S. M., and Lawrence, P. R. *Matrix.* Reading, Mass.: Addison-Wesley, 1977.

Deal, T. E., and Kennedy, A. A. "Culture: A New Look Through Old Lenses." *Journal of Applied Behavioral Science,* 1983, *19,* 498–505.

Deming, W. E. *Out of Crisis.* Cambridge, Mass.: MIT Center for Advanced Engineering Study, 1982.

DeMott, J. S. "Manufacturing Is in Flower." *Time,* Mar. 26, 1984, pp. 50–52.

Dennison, H. S. *Organization Engineering.* New York: McGraw-Hill, 1931.

Diebold, J. T. *Automation: The Advent of the Automatic Factory.* New York: D. Van Nostrand, 1952.

Dowd, A. R. "What Managers Can Learn from Manager Reagan." *Fortune*, Sept. 15, 1986, pp. 33–41.

Dror, Y. "Muddling Through—'Science or Inertia'?" *Public Administration Review*, 1964, *24*, 16–25.

Drucker, P. F. *The Practice of Management.* New York: Harper & Row, 1954.

Drucker, P. F. *Management: Tasks, Responsibilities, Practices.* New York: Harper & Row, 1973.

Drucker, P. F. *Innovation and Entrepreneurship.* New York: Harper & Row, 1985.

Drucker, P. F. *The Frontiers of Management.* New York: Talley Books, 1986.

Drury, H. B. *Scientific Management: A History and Criticism.* New York: Longmans, Green, 1922.

Duncan, W. J. "The History and Philosophy of Administrative Thought: A Societal Overview." *Business and Society*, Spring 1971, *11*, 24–30.

Duncan, W. J. "Ethical Issues in the Development and Use of Business and Management Knowledge." *Journal of Business Ethics*, 1986, *5*, 391–400.

Duncan, W. J. "When Necessity Becomes a Virtue: The Case for Taking Strategy Seriously." *Journal of General Management*, Winter 1987, *13*, 28–42.

Duncan, W. J., and Gullett, C. R. "Henry Sturgis Dennison: The Manager and the Social Critic." *Journal of Business Research*, 1974, *2*, 133–146.

Durant, W., and Durant, A. *The Lessons of History.* New York: Simon & Schuster, 1968.

Eisenberg, D. J. "The Tactics of Strategic Opportunism." *Harvard Business Review*, Mar./Apr. 1987, *65*, 92–97.

Emerson, H. *Efficiency as a Basis for Operations and Wages.* (4th ed.) Easton, Pa.: Hive Publishing Company Reprint No. 63, 1976. (Originally published 1908.)

Emerson, H. *The Twelve Principles of Efficiency.* New York: Engineering Magazine, 1913.

Fayol, H. *General and Industrial Management.* (C. Storrs, trans.) London: Pitman, 1949.

Feeney, E. J., Staelin, J. R., O'Brien, R. M., and Dickinson, A. M. "Increasing Sales Performance Among Airline Reservation Personnel." In R. M. O'Brien, A. M. Dickinson, and M. P. Rosow (eds.), *Industrial Behavior Modification: A Management Handbook.* Elmsford, N.Y.: Pergamon Press, 1982.

Fiedler, F. E. *A Theory of Leadership Effectiveness.* New York: McGraw-Hill, 1967.

Fiedler, F. E. "The Contingency Model—New Directions for Leadership Utilization." *Journal of Contemporary Business,* 1974, *3,* 65–80.

Follett, M. P. *Creative Experience.* New York: Longmans, Green, 1924.

Follett, M. P. *Freedom and Coordination: Lectures in Business Organization by Mary Parker Follett.* (L. Urwick, ed.) London: Pitman, 1949.

Ford, R. N. "Job Enrichment Lessons from AT&T." *Harvard Business Review,* Jan./Feb. 1973, *51,* 95–99.

French, J.R.P., and Raven, B. H. "The Bases of Social Power." In D. Cartwright (ed.), *Studies in Social Power.* Ann Arbor: University of Michigan Institute for Social Research, 1959.

Frey, L. W. "The Maligned F. W. Taylor: A Reply to His Many Critics." *Academy of Management Review,* 1976, *1,* 124–139.

Friedman, G. *The Anatomy of Work.* Glencoe, Ill.: Free Press, 1961.

Friedman, M. "The Social Responsibility of Business Is to Increase Its Profits." *New York Times Magazine,* Sept. 13, 1970, pp. 32–33, 122–126.

Froehlich, L. "Babbage Observed." *Datamation,* 1985, *31* (6), 119–124.

Frost, P. J. "Special Issue on Organizational Symbolism: Introduction." *Journal of Management,* 1985, *11,* 5–12.

Gantt, H. L. *Work, Wages, and Profits.* New York: Engineering Magazine, 1910.

Gantt, H. L. *Organizing for Work.* San Diego, Calif.: Harcourt Brace Jovanovich, 1919.

Gellerman, S. "Why 'Good' Managers Make Bad Ethical Choices." *Harvard Business Review,* July/Aug. 1986, *64,* 85–90.

General Motors Public Interest Report. Detroit: General Motors, May 15, 1985.

George, C. S., Jr. *The History of Management Thought.* (2nd ed.) Englewood Cliffs, N.J.: Prentice-Hall, 1972.

Georgiou, P. "The Goal Paradigm and Notes Toward a Counter Point." *Administrative Science Quarterly,* 1973, *18,* 291–310.

Gilbreth, F. B. *Motion Study.* Easton, Pa.: Hive Publishing Company Reprint No. 77, 1980. (Originally published 1912.)

Gilbreth, F. B., and Gilbreth, L. M. *Applied Motion Study.* Easton, Pa.: Hive Publishing Company Reprint No. 28, 1973. (Originally published 1917.)

Gilbreth, L. M. *The Psychology of Management.* Easton, Pa.: Hive Publishing Company, 1973. (Originally published 1914.)

Gilbreth, L. M. *The Quest for the One Best Way: A Sketch of the Life of Frank Bunker Gilbreth.* Easton, Pa.: Hive Publishing Company, 1973.

Ginter, P. M., Rucks, A. C., and Duncan, W. J. "Planners' Perceptions of the Strategic Management Process." *Journal of Management Studies,* 1985, *22,* 581–596.

Greenwood, R. G., Bolton, A. A., and Greenwood, R. A. "Hawthorne a Half Century Later." *Journal of Management,* 1983, *9,* 217–231.

Greenwood, R. G., and Wrege, C. D. "The Hawthorne Studies." In D. A. Wren and J. A. Pearch II (eds.), *Papers Dedicated to the Development of Modern Management.* Chicago: Academy of Management, 1986.

Grove, A. S. *High Output Management.* New York: Vintage Books, 1985.

Grundstein, N. D. *The Managerial Kant.* Cleveland: Weatherhead School of Management, Case Western Reserve University, 1981.

Guest, R. H. "On Time and the Foreman." *Personnel,* May 1956, pp. 478–480.

Gulick, L., and Urwick, L. (eds.). *Papers on the Science of Administration.* (2nd ed.) New York: Institute of Public Administration, 1947.

Haber, S. *Efficiency and Uplift: Scientific Management in the Progressive Era 1890–1930.* Chicago: University of Chicago Press, 1964.

Hafsi, T., Kiggundu, M. N., and Jorgensen, J. J. "Strategic Apex

Configurations in State-Owned Enterprises." *Academy of Management Review,* 1987, *12,* 714–730.

Halberstam, D. "Robots Enter Our Lives." *Parade,* Apr. 10, 1983, p. 19.

Hales, C. P. "What Managers Do: A Critical Review of the Evidence." *Journal of Management Studies,* 1986, *23,* 88–115.

Hamel, R. "Robots Steer Automaking into the Future." *USA Today,* July 2, 1984, p. 1B.

Hart, D. K., and Scott, W. G. "The Optimal Image of Man for Systems Theory." *Academy of Management Journal,* 1972, *15,* 530–537.

Hartley, R. F. *Management Mistakes.* (2nd ed.) Columbus, Ohio: Grid Publishing, 1986.

"Having It All, Then Throwing It All Away." *Time,* May 25, 1987, pp. 22–23.

Heilbroner, R. L. *The Worldly Philosophers.* New York: Simon & Schuster, 1953.

Herzberg, F. *Work and the Nature of Man.* Cleveland: World Publishing, 1966.

Herzberg, F., Mausner, B., Peterson, R. O., and Capwell, D. F. *Job Attitudes: Review of Research and Opinion.* Pittsburgh, Pa.: Psychological Services of Pittsburgh, 1957.

Herzberg, F., Mausner, B., and Snyderman, B. *The Motivation to Work.* New York: Wiley, 1959.

Higgins, K. "Computerized Slot Machines Motivating Employees to Improve Their Productivity." *Marketing News,* 1983, *17,* 1.

Hoagland, J. H. "Management Before Taylor." In P. M. Dauten (ed.), *Emerging Concepts in Management.* Boston: Houghton Mifflin, 1957.

House, R. J., and Mitchell, T. R. "Path-Goal Theory of Leadership." *Journal of Contemporary Business,* 1974, *3,* 81–97.

Irwin, O. "Observations of the Japanese Automotive Industry: A Lesson for American Managers." *Industrial Management,* May/June 1987, *29,* 5–8.

Ivancevich, J. M. "A Longitudinal Assessment of Management-by-Objectives." *Administrative Science Quarterly,* 1972, *17,* 119–127.

Ivancevich, J. M., and McMahon, T. "The Effects of Goal Setting, External Feedback, and Self-Generated Feedback on Outcome Variables." *Academy of Management Journal,* 1982, *25,* 359–372.

Jacques, E. *The Changing Culture of a Factory.* London: Tavistock, 1951.

Kakar, S. *Frederick Taylor: A Study in Personality and Innovation.* Cambridge, Mass.: MIT Press, 1970.

Kanter, R. M. "The Case Against 'Cowboy Management.' " *Management Review,* Feb. 1987, *76,* 19–21.

Kantrow, A. M. "Why History Matters to Managers." *Harvard Business Review,* Jan./Feb. 1986, *64,* 81–88.

Katz, R. L. "Skills of an Effective Administrator." *Harvard Business Review,* Jan./Feb. 1955, *33,* 33–42.

Kerr, S. "Some Modifications in MBO as an OD Strategy." *Academy of Management Proceedings,* 1973, pp. 39–42.

Kiechel, W., III. "Managing Innovators." *Fortune,* Mar. 4, 1985, pp. 181–182.

Kilmann, R. H. *Beyond the Quick Fix: Managing Five Tracks to Organizational Success.* San Francisco: Jossey-Bass, 1984.

Komaki, J., Waddell, W. M., and Pearce, M. G. "The Applied Behavioral Analysis Approach and Individual Employees: Improving Performance in Two Small Businesses." *Organizational Behavior and Human Performance,* 1977, *25,* 337–352.

Kotter, J. P. *The General Managers.* New York: Free Press, 1982.

Kovach, K. A. "What Motivates Employees? Workers and Supervisors Give Different Answers." *Business Horizons,* Sept./Oct. 1987, *30,* 58–65.

Kronman, A. T. *Max Weber.* Stanford, Calif.: Stanford University Press, 1983.

Krupp, S. *Pattern in Organizational Analysis: A Critical Examination.* New York: Holt, Rinehart & Winston, 1961.

Lacey, R. *Ford: The Men and the Machine.* Boston: Little, Brown, 1986.

Lawrence, P., and Lorsch, J. *Organization and Environment.* Boston: Graduate School of Business Administration, Division of Research, Harvard University, 1967.

Lee, J. A. *The Gold and the Garbage in Management Theories and Prescriptions.* Athens: Ohio University Press, 1980.

Levitt, T. "The Dangers of Social Responsibility." *Harvard Business Review,* Sept./Oct. 1958, *36,* 42–50.

Likert, R. *New Patterns of Management.* New York: McGraw-Hill, 1961.

Likert, R. *The Human Organization.* New York: McGraw-Hill, 1967.

Likert, R., and Likert, J. G. *New Way of Managing Conflict.* New York: McGraw-Hill, 1976.

Lindblom, C. E. "The Science of 'Muddling Through.'" *Public Administration Review,* 1959, *19,* 79–88.

Lindblom, C. E. "Still Muddling, Not Yet Through." *Public Administration Review,* 1979, *39,* 517–526.

Locke, E. A. "The Ideas of Frederick W. Taylor: An Evaluation." *Academy of Management Review,* 1982, *7,* 14–24.

Locke, E. A., and Latham, G. P. *Goal Setting for Individuals, Groups, and Organizations.* Chicago: Science Research Associates, 1984.

Locke, E. A., Shaw, K. N., Saari, L. M., and Latham, G. P. "Goal Setting and Task Performance: 1969–1980." *Psychological Bulletin,* 1981, *90,* 125–152.

Lombard, G.F.F. "Relativism in Organizations." *Harvard Business Review,* Mar./Apr. 1971, *49,* 55–56.

Loucks, V., Jr. "A CEO Looks at Ethics." *Business Horizons,* Mar./Apr. 1987, *30,* 2–6.

Louis, A. M. "The Controversial Boss of Beatrice." *Fortune,* July 22, 1985, pp. 110–116.

Luthans, F., and Kreitner, R. *Organizational Behavior Modification.* Glenview, Ill.: Scott, Foresman, 1975.

Luthans, F., Rosenkrantz, S. A., and Hennessey, H. W. "What Do Successful Managers Really Do? An Observation Study of Managerial Activities." *Journal of Applied Behavioral Science,* 1985, *21,* 255–270.

McClelland, D. C. *The Achieving Society.* New York: Free Press, 1961.

McClelland, D. C. "Managing Motivation to Expand Human Freedom." *American Psychologist,* 1978, *33,* 201–210.

McClelland, D. C., and Winter, D. G. *Motivating Economic Achievement.* New York: Free Press, 1969.

Maccoby, M. *The Leader.* New York: Ballantine, 1981.

McConkey, D. D. *How to Manage by Results.* New York: AMA-COM, 1983.

McFarland, D. E. "Whatever Happened to the Efficiency Movement?" *Conference Board Record,* June 1976, *13,* 50–55.

McGregor, D. M. *The Human Side of Enterprise.* New York: McGraw-Hill, 1960.

McKean, K. "Decisions, Decisions." *Discover,* June 1985, *6,* 22–27.

McKean, K. "They Fly in the Face of Danger." *Discover,* Apr. 1986, *7,* 48–58.

March, J. G. "The 1978 Nobel Prize in Economics." *Science,* 1978, *202,* 851–861.

March, J. G., and Simon, H. A. *Organizations.* New York: Wiley, 1958.

"Marriott: Crusader for a Moral America." *Business Week,* Jan. 21, 1985, p. 75.

Marshuetz, R. J. "How American Can Allocates Capital." *Harvard Business Review,* Jan./Feb. 1985, *63,* 84–91.

Maslow, A. *Motivation and Personality.* New York: Harper & Row, 1954.

Maslow, A. *Motivation and Personality.* (2nd ed.) New York: Harper & Row, 1970.

Matsui, T., Okada, A., and Inoshita, O. "Mechanism of Feedback Affecting Task Performance." *Organizational Behavior and Human Performance,* 1983, *31,* 114–122.

Mayo, G. E. *The Human Problems of an Industrial Society.* (2nd ed.) New York: Macmillan, 1933.

Mayo, G. E. *The Social Problems of an Industrial Society.* Boston: Graduate School of Business Administration, Harvard University, 1945.

Mayo, G. E. *The Political Problems of an Industrial Society.* Boston: Graduate School of Business Administration, Harvard University, 1947.

Meyer, H. H., Kay, E., and French, J.R.P. "Split Roles in Performance Appraisal." *Harvard Business Review,* Jan./Feb. 1965, *43,* 123–129.

Mintzberg, H. *The Nature of Managerial Work.* New York: Harper & Row, 1973.

Mintzberg, H. "The Manager's Job: Folklore and Fact." *Harvard Business Review,* July/Aug. 1975, *53,* 49–61.

Mitchell, T. R. *Motivation and Performance.* Chicago: Science Research Associates, 1984.

Mooney, J. D., and Reiley, A. C. *Onward Industry.* New York: Harper & Row, 1931.

Mooney, J. D., and Reiley, A. C. *The Principles of Organization.* New York: Harper & Row, 1932.

Moran, L. "Setting Sail with One Enterprise, One Mission, One Measure." *AT&T Magazine,* 1984, *1* (1), 2–7.

Morita, A., with Reingold, E. M., and Shimomura, M. *Made in Japan: Akio Morita and Sony.* New York: Dutton, 1986.

Moseley, M. *Irascible Genius: A Life of Charles Babbage, Inventor.* London: Hutchinson, 1964.

Munsterberg, H. *Psychology and Industrial Efficiency.* Boston: Houghton Mifflin, 1913.

Murrin, T. T. "Productivity Needs a Game Plan." *Enterprise,* Oct. 1984, *7,* 14.

Naisbitt, J. *Megatrends: Ten New Directions Transforming Our Lives.* New York: Warner Books, 1984.

Nelson, D., and Campbell, S. "Taylorism Versus Welfare Work in American Industry: H. L. Gantt and the Bancrofts." *Business History Review,* 1972, *46* (1), 1–16.

Neuhaus, C. "A Simon Who Is Not So Simple." *Discover,* June 1981, *2,* 42ff.

"The New Breed of Strategic Planners." *Business Week,* Sept. 17, 1984, pp. 63–65.

Owen, R. *A New View of Society.* New York: E. Bliss and White, 1825.

Pearce, J. A., II, and David, F. "Corporate Mission Statements: The Bottom Line." *Academy of Management Executive,* 1987, *1,* 109–116.

Pecotich, A., and Churchill, G. A., Jr. "An Examination of the Anticipated Satisfaction Importance Valence Controversy." *Organizational Behavior and Human Performance,* 1981, *27,* 210–215.

Perrow, C. *Normal Accidents: Living with High Risk Technology.* New York: Basic Books, 1984.

Peters, T., and Austin, N. *A Passion for Excellence.* New York: Random House, 1985.

Peterson, P. B. "Correspondence from Henry L. Gantt to an Old Friend Reveals New Information About Gantt." *Journal of Management,* 1986, *12,* 339–350.

Pfeffer, J. *Power in Organizations.* Marshfield, Mass.: Pitman, 1981.

"Philippe Villers, The Social Conscience of Route 128." *Business Week,* Feb. 25, 1985, p. 65.

Pitt, B. *The Battle of the Atlantic.* Alexandria, Va.: Time-Life Books, 1977.

Poindexter, J. "Voices of Authority." *Psychology Today,* Aug. 1983, pp. 53–61.

"The Push for Quality." *Business Week* Special Report, June 8, 1987, p. 133.

Quick, J. D., Nelson, D. L., and Quick, J. C. "Successful Executives: How Independent?" *Academy of Management Executive,* 1987, *1,* 139–145.

Quinn, J. B. "Strategic Change: Logical Incrementalism." *Sloan Management Review,* 1978, *20* (1), 7–22.

Quinn, J. B. "Managing Strategic Change." *Sloan Management Review,* 1980a, *21* (4), 3–20.

Quinn, J. B. *Strategies for Change: Logical Incrementalism.* Homewood, Ill.: Irwin, 1980b.

Raia, A. P. *Management-by-Objectives.* Glenview, Ill.: Scott, Foresman, 1974.

Rathe, A. W. (ed.). *Gantt on Management.* New York: American Management Association, 1961.

Roach, J. "Simon Says: Decision Making Is a 'Satisficing' Experience." *Management Review,* Jan. 1979, *68,* 8–17.

Rockart, J. F. "The Changing Role of the Information Systems Executive: A Critical Success Factors Perspective." *Sloan Management Review,* Fall 1982, *24,* 3–13.

Rockart, J. F., and Crescenzi, A. D. "Engaging Top Management in Information Technology." *Sloan Management Review,* Summer 1984, *25,* 3–16.

Roethlisberger, F. J. *Management and Morale.* Cambridge, Mass.: Harvard University Press, 1941.

Roethlisberger, F. J. *Man-in-Organizations.* Cambridge, Mass.: Harvard University Press, 1968.

Roethlisberger, F. J. *The Elusive Phenomena.* Boston, Mass.: Division of Research, Harvard Business School, 1977.

Roethlisberger, F. J., and Dickson, W. J. *Management and the Worker.* Cambridge, Mass.: Harvard University Press, 1939.

Rosenberg, N. *The American System of Manufacturers, 1854–5.* Edinburgh, Scotland: University of Edinburgh Press, 1969.

"Saturn Makes Its Debut at GM." *Time,* Jan. 21, 1985, p. 50.

Sayles, L. R., and Chandler, M. K. *Managing Large Systems.* New York: Harper & Row, 1971.

Schriesheim, C. A., and Bird, B. J. "Contributions of the Ohio State Studies to the Field of Leadership." *Journal of Management,* 1979, 5, 135–145.

Scott, W. E., Jr. "The Development of Knowledge in Organizational Behavior and Human Performance." *Decision Sciences,* 1975, 6, 142–165.

Scott, W. E., Jr., and Podsakoff, P. M. *Behavioral Principles in the Practice of Management.* New York: Wiley, 1985.

Shartle, C. L. "Early Years of the Ohio State University Leadership Studies." *Journal of Management,* 1979, 5, 127–134.

Sheriff, D. R. *Administrative Behavior: A Quantitative Case Study of Six Organizations.* Monograph No. 12. Iowa City: Center for Labor and Management, University of Iowa, Jan. 1969.

Shetty, Y. K. "Quality, Productivity, and Profit Performance: Learning from Research and Practice." *National Productivity Review,* Spring 1986, 5, 166–174.

Simon, H. A. *Administrative Behavior.* (3rd ed.) New York: Free Press, 1976. (Originally published 1946.)

Simon, H. A. "The Proverbs of Administration." *Public Administration Review,* 1946, 6, 53–67.

Simon, H. A. *The New Science of Management Decision.* New York: Harper & Row, 1960.

Simon, H. A. "Making Management Decisions: The Role of Intuition and Emotion." *Academy of Management Executive,* Feb. 1987, 1, 57–64.

Skinner, B. F. *Science and Behavior.* New York: Free Press, 1953.

Skinner, B. F. *Beyond Freedom and Dignity.* New York: Knopf, 1971.

Skinner, B. F. *About Behaviorism.* New York: Knopf, 1974.

"Small Is Beautiful Now in Manufacturing." *Business Week,* Oct. 22, 1984, pp. 152–156.

Smiddy, H. "Wallace Clark's Contribution to International Management." *Society for the Advancement of Management Advanced Management Journal,* Mar. 1958, *23,* 17–26.

Smith, A. *An Inquiry into the Nature and Causes of the Wealth of Nations.* New York: Modern Library, 1937. (Originally published 1776.)

Smith, L. "Cracks in the Japanese Work Ethic." *Fortune,* May 14, 1984, pp. 162–168.

Spriegel, W. R., and Myers, C. E. (eds.). *The Writings of the Gilbreths.* Homewood, Ill.: Irwin, 1953.

Stewart, R. "The Nature of Management: A Problem for Management Education." *Journal of Management Studies,* 1984, *21,* 323–330.

Stogdill, R. M. "Historical Trends in Leadership Theory and Research." *Journal of Contemporary Business,* Autumn 1974, *3,* 1–17.

Taylor, F. W. "A Piece-Rate System, Being a Step Toward Partial Solution of the Labor Problem." *Transactions of the American Society of Mechanical Engineers,* 1895, *16,* 856–883.

Taylor, F. W. *Shop Management.* New York: Harper & Row, 1903.

Taylor, F. W. *The Principles of Scientific Management.* New York: Harper & Row, 1914.

Tead, O. *Instincts in Industry: A Study of Working Class Psychology.* Boston: Houghton Mifflin, 1918.

Tead, O. *Human Nature and Management.* New York: McGraw-Hill, 1929.

Tead, O. *The Art of Leadership.* New York: McGraw-Hill, 1935.

Tead, O. *The Art of Administration.* New York: McGraw-Hill, 1951.

Thompson, J. D. *Organizations in Action.* New York: McGraw-Hill, 1967.

Trombley, K. E. *The Life and Times of a Happy Liberal: Morris Llewellyn Cooke.* New York: Harper & Row, 1954.

Ure, A. *The Philosophy of Manufactures: On an Exposition of the Scientific, Moral, and Commercial Economy of the Factory System of Great Britain.* London: Charles Knight, 1835.

Urwick, L. F. "The Functions of Administration: With Special Reference to the Work of Henri Fayol." In L. Gulick and L. Urwick (eds.), *Papers on the Science of Administration.* New York: Institute of Public Administration, 1937.

Urwick, L. F. *Elements of Administration.* London: Harper, 1944.

Urwick, L. F. *Notes on the Theory of Organization.* New York: American Management Association, 1952.

Urwick, L. F. (ed.). *The Golden Book of Management.* London: Newman Neame, 1956.

Urwick, L. F. "Papers on the Science of Administration." *Academy of Management Journal,* 1972, *8,* 362–364.

Van Fleet, D. D. "The Ralph M. Stogdill Memorial Symposium." *Journal of Management,* 1979, *5,* 125–126.

Vroom, V. H. *Work and Motivation.* New York: Wiley, 1964.

Vroom, V. H., and Jago, A. G. "Decision Making as a Social Process: Normative and Descriptive Models of Leader Behavior." *Decision Sciences,* 1974, *5,* 743–769.

Vroom, V. H., and Yetton, P. W. *Leadership and Decision Making.* Pittsburgh, Pa.: University of Pittsburgh Press, 1973.

Waterman, R. H. *The Renewal Factor.* New York: Bantam, 1987.

Watts, P. "Streamlining to Get Closer to the Customer." *Management Review,* Nov. 1987, *76,* 94–99.

Weber, M. *The Theory of Social and Economic Organization.* (A. M. Henderson and T. Parsons, eds. and trans.) New York: Free Press, 1947.

Weick, K. E. *The Social Psychology of Organizing.* (2nd ed.) Reading, Mass.: Addison-Wesley, 1979.

Weiss, R. M. "Weber on Bureaucracy: Management Consultant

or Political Theorist." *Academy of Management Review,* 1983, *8,* 242–248.

Wheelwright, S. C., and Hayes, R. H. "Competing Through Manufacturing." *Harvard Business Review,* Jan./Feb. 1985, *63,* 99–109.

Whitsett, D. A., and Yorks, L. *From Management Theory to Business Sense: The Myths and Realities of People at Work.* New York: AMACOM, American Management Association, 1983.

"Why Image Counts: A Tale of Two Industries." *Business Week,* June 8, 1987, pp. 138–140.

Wilkins, A. L., and Bristow, N. J. "For Successful Organizational Culture: Honor Your Past." *Academy of Management Executive,* 1987, *1,* 221–229.

Wilson, C. *New Pathways in Psychology: Maslow and the Post-Freudian Revolution.* New York: New American Library, 1972.

Woodward, J. *Industrial Organization: Theory and Practice.* London: Oxford University Press, 1965.

Work, J. M., and Hamilton, L. "The Public Policy Process: Shaping Future Agendas." In *Perspective on National Issues.* Washington, D.C.: National Association of Manufacturers, June 1983.

Wrege, C. D., and Perroni, A. G. "Taylor's Pig Tale: A Historical Analysis of Frederick W. Taylor's Pig Iron Experiment." *Academy of Management Journal,* 1974, *17,* 6–27.

Wrege, C. D., and Stotka, A. M. "Cooke Creates a Classic: The Story Behind F. W. Taylor's Principles of Scientific Management." *Academy of Management Review,* 1978, *3,* 736–750.

Wren, D. A. "Scientific Management in the U.S.S.R. with Particular Reference to the Contribution of Walter N. Polakov." *Academy of Management Review,* 1980, *5,* 1–11.

Wren, D. A. *The Evolution of Management Thought.* (3rd ed.) New York: Wiley, 1987.

Zwerman, W. L. *New Perspectives on Organization Theory.* Westport, Conn.: Greenwood, 1970.

Index